2nd Grade Technology Curriculum: Teacher Manual

SECOND GRADE TECHNOLOGY

A COMPREHENSIVE CURRICULUM

Part Three of Nine in the SL Technology Curriculum

Version 6.4 2023

Part of Structured Learning's nine-volume Technology Curriculum

ALL MATERIAL IN THIS BOOK IS PROTECTED BY THE INTELLECTUAL PROPERTY LAWS OF THE USA.

No part of this work can be reproduced or used in any form or by any means—graphic, electronic, or mechanical, including photocopying, recording, taping, Web distribution or information storage and retrieval systems—without the prior written permission of the publisher

For permission to use material from this text or product, contact us by email at:
info@structuredlearning.net

ISBN 978-1-942101-24-6

Printed in the United States of America by Structured Learning LLC

Structured Learning LLC©. All Rights Reserved

Introduction

The educational paradigm has changed—again. Technology has become granular to learning, included in educational standards from Kindergarten onward, like these from Common Core:

- Expect students to demonstrate sufficient command of **keyboarding** to type a minimum of one page [three by sixth grade] in a single sitting
- Expect students to **evaluate different media**
- Expect students to **gather relevant information** from print and digital sources
- Expect students to integrate and evaluate **information presented in diverse media** and formats
- Expect students to **interpret information** presented visually, orally, or quantitatively [such as an interactive Web pages]
- Expect students to make **strategic use of digital media**
- Expect students to use print/digital **resources**...
- Expect students to use information from **illustrations and words in print or digital** text
- Expect students to communicate with a **variety of media**
- Expect students to **use text features and search tools** (e.g., key words, sidebars, **hyperlinks**) to locate information

But how is this taught? With the **Structured Learning Technology Curriculum**. Aligned with Common Core State Standards* and National Educational Technology Standards, and using a time-proven method honed in classrooms, students learn the technology that promotes literacy, critical thinking, problem-solving, and decision-making. It's project-based. The purpose is not to teach step-by-step tech skills (like adding borders, formatting a document, and creating a blog). There are many fine books for that. What this curriculum does is guide you in providing the **right information at the right time**.

Just as most children can't learn to read at two, or write at four, they shouldn't place hands on home row in kindergarten or use the internet before they understand digital risks and responsibilities. The Structured Learning curriculum gives students what they need at the right age with proper scaffolding. The end result is a phenomenal amount of learning in a short period of time.

If there are skills you don't know, visit our Help blog (AskATechTeacher) or visit the online companion resources at Structured Learning LLC.

* * *

"New technologies have broadened and expanded the role that speaking and listening play in acquiring and sharing knowledge and have tightened their link to other forms of communication. Digital texts confront students with the potential for continually updated content and dynamically changing combinations of words, graphics, images, hyperlinks, and embedded video and audio."
—*CCSS*

* * *

"Use of technology differentiates for student learning styles by providing an alternative method of achieving conceptual understanding, procedural skill and fluency, and applying this knowledge to authentic circumstances."
—*CCSS*

* * *

What's in the SL Technology Curriculum?

The SL Curriculum is project-based and collaborative, with wide-ranging opportunities for students to show their knowledge in the manner that fits their communication and learning style. Each grade level in the curriculum includes five topics that should be woven into 'most' 21st-century lesson plans:

- *keyboarding—more than typing*
- *digital citizenship—critical with the influx of Chromebooks and iPads*
- *problem-solving—to encourage independence, critical thinking*
- *vocabulary—decode unknown words in any subject quickly with technology*
- *publishing-sharing—to promote collaborative learning*

In most curricula, you find full lessons devoted to keyboarding, digital citizenship, and problem solving. Here's a quick overview of what is included:

- *list of assessments, images, articles*
- *articles that address tech pedagogy*
- *Certificate of Completion for students*
- *curriculum map of skills taught*
- *monthly homework (3rd-8th only)*
- *posters to visually represent topics*
- *Scope and Sequence of skills taught*
- *step-by-step weekly lessons*

Each weekly lesson includes:

- *assessment strategies*
- *big idea*
- *warm-up and exit ticket*
- *differentiation strategies*
- *educational applications*
- *essential question*
- *examples, rubrics, images, printables*
- *CCSS and ISTE Standards*
- *materials required*
- *pedagogic articles (if any)*
- *problem solving for lesson*
- *skills—new and scaffolded*
- *steps to accomplish goals*
- *supporting links*
- *teacher preparation required*
- *time required to complete*
- *vocabulary used*
- *weekly how-to video (online)*

Throughout the text are links to extend lessons, add enrichment, and/or provide flexibility in your teaching. No PDF? Usually the website is spelled out. If not, Google the name or contact our help site.

Programs Used

Programs used in this curriculum focus on skills that serve the fullness of a student's educational career. Free alternatives are noted where available:

General		2-8
Email	Drawing program	Word processing tools
Google Earth	Image editor	Spreadsheet tools
Web tools	Keyboarding tool	Desktop publisher
		Presentation tools

What's New in the Sixth Edition?

A good curriculum is aligned with best practices in technology and education. That means it must be updated every few years. Consider the changes to technology in education in less than a decade:

- *Windows updated its platform—twice.*
- *IPads have been joined by Chromebooks as a common classroom digital device.*
- *There is greater reliance in the classroom on internet-based tools than software. This underscores the importance of teaching digital citizenship to even the youngest learners.*
- *Student work is often collaborative and shared.*
- *Student work is done anywhere, not just the classroom and home, meaning it must be synced and available across multiple platforms, multiple devices.*
- *Keyboarding skills are often critical, especially to summative year-end testing.*
- *Technology in the classroom is the norm, but teacher training isn't.*
- *Education is focused on college and career with tech an organic, transformative tool.*
- *Teachers have moved from 'sage on the stage' to 'guide on the side'.*
- *Students have been raised on digital devices. They want to use them as learning tools.*
- *Using technology is no longer what 'geeky' students do. It's what all students want to do.*
- *Printing is being replaced with sharing and publishing.*
- *More teachers are willing to try technology when used authentically.*

In response, here are changes you'll find:

- *The lesson audience is now as likely to be the **grade-level teacher as the tech teacher**.*
- *Ideas deliver lessons on all **popular digital devices**.*
- *The importance of **higher order thinking**— analysis, evaluation and synthesis—is called out.*
- *The importance of **'habits of mind'**—critical to college and career goals—is included.*
- *It's easy to recognize which **skills are scaffolded** from earlier lessons and which are new.*
- *Each lesson points out **academic applications** of technology.*
- *Students learn to **understand the process**, not just replicate a skill.*
- ***Collaboration and sharing** is often required.*
- ***Differentiation** is encouraged. Teachers learn strategies to meet students where they learn.*
- *Each lesson includes a **warm-up and exit ticket**, to assess and reinforce student learning.*
- *A **Table of Images** and a **Table of Assessments** are included for easy reference.*
- *Updated **Scope and Sequence** includes more references to Common Core.*
- ***Curriculum Maps** shows which month topics are covered as well as which grade.*
- *Each grade-level curriculum includes **student workbooks** (sold separately).*
- *Each grade level has a **lesson on coding**.*

Who Needs This Book

You are the Tech Specialist, Coordinator for Instructional Technology, IT Coordinator, Technology Facilitator or Director, Curriculum Specialist, or tech teacher—tasked with finding the right project for a classroom. You have a limited budget, less software, and the drive to do it right no matter roadblocks.

Figure 1—Tomorrow's student

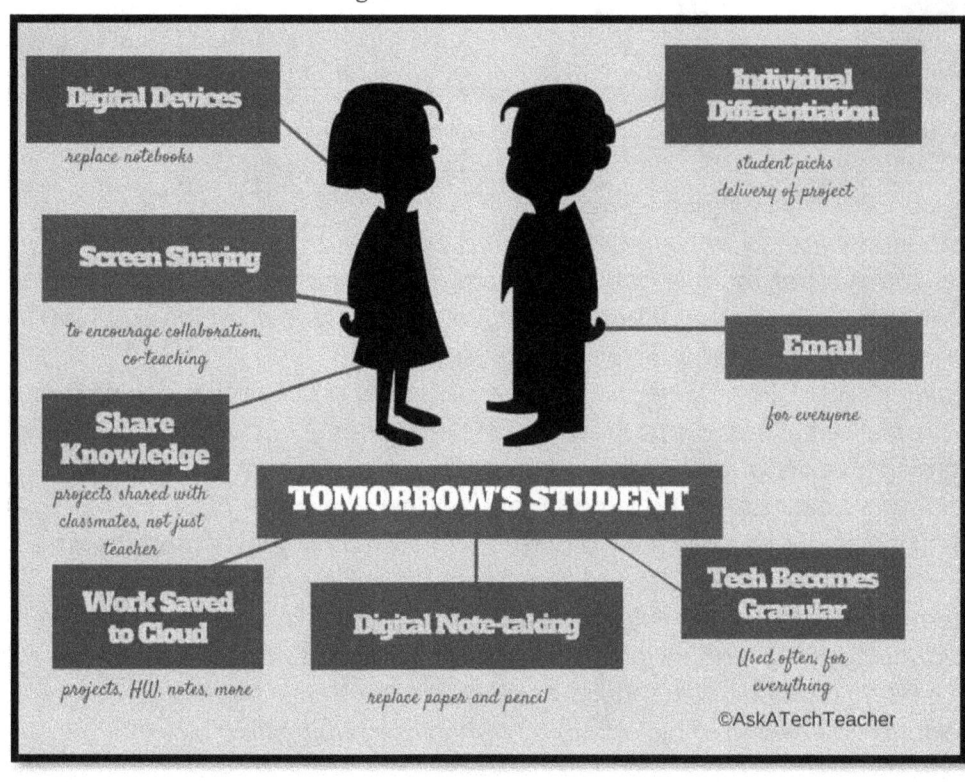

Or you are the class teacher, a tech enthusiast with a goal this year—and this time you mean it—to integrate the wonders of technology into lessons. You've seen it work. Others in your PLN are doing it. And significantly, you want to comply with Common Core State Standards, ISTE, your state requirements, and/or IB guidelines that weave technology into the fabric of inquiry.

You are a homeschooler. Even though you're not comfortable with technology, you know your children must be. You are committed to providing the tools s/he needs to succeed. Just as important: Your child WANTS to learn with these tools!

How do you reach your goal? With this curriculum. Teaching children to strategically and safely use technology is a vital part of society and should be part of every school's curriculum. If not you (the teacher), who will do this? To build Tomorrow's Student (*Figure 1*) requires integration of technology and learning. We show you how.

How to Use This Book

Figure 2a shows what's at the beginning of each lesson. *Figure 2b* shows what you'll find at the end:

- Academic Applications
- Assessment Strategies
- Big Idea
- Class Warm-up
- Essential Question

- Material Required
- Problem solving
- Skills
- Standards
- Steps

- Teacher Prep
- Time Required
- Vocabulary

Figure 2a—Beginning of each lesson; Figure 2b—end of each lesson

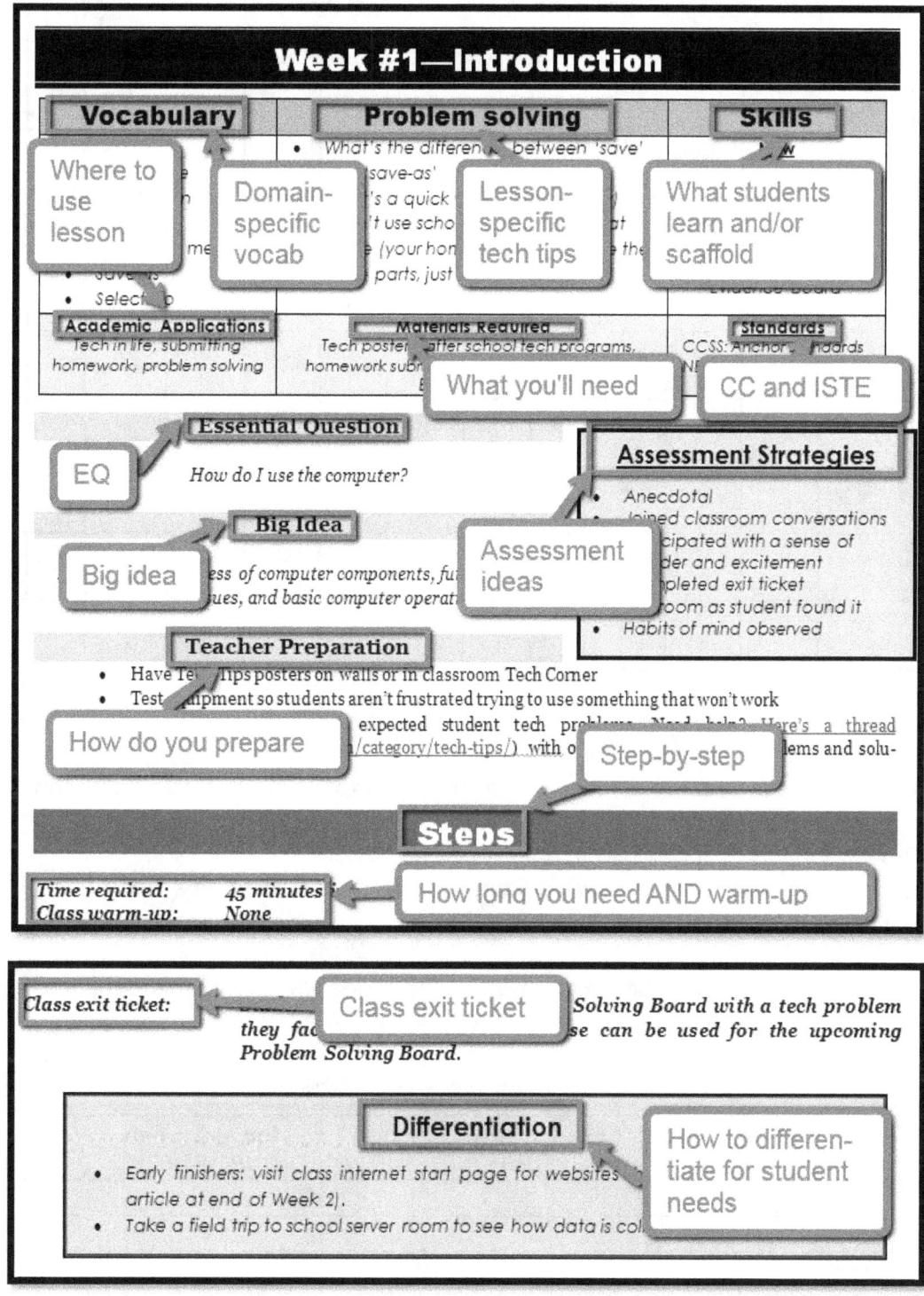

- *Class differentiation strategies*
- *Class exit ticket*

The curriculum map in *Figure 3* shows what's covered in which grade. Where units are taught multiple years, teaching reflects increasingly less scaffolding and more student direction.

2nd Grade Technology Curriculum: Teacher Manual

Figure 3—Curriculum Map—K-8

	Mouse Skills	Vocabulary - Hardware	Problem-solving	Platform	Keyboard	WP	Slide-shows	DTP	Spread-sheet	Google Earth	Search/ Research	Graphics/	Co-ding	WWW	Games	Dig Cit
K	☺	☺	☺	☺	☺					☺		☺	☺	☺		☺
1	☺	☺	☺	☺	☺			☺	☺	☺		☺	☺	☺		☺
2		☺	☺	☺	☺	☺	☺	☺	☺	☺		☺	☺	☺		☺
3		☺	☺	☺	☺	☺	☺	☺	☺	☺	☺	☺	☺	☺		☺
4		☺	☺		☺	☺	☺	☺	☺	☺	☺	☺	☺	☺		☺
5		☺	☺		☺	☺		☺	☺	☺	☺	☺	☺	☺		☺
6		☺	☺	☺	☺	☺	☺	☺	☺	☺	☺	☺	☺	☺		☺
7		☺	☺	☺	☺	☺			☺	☺	☺	☺	☺	☺	☺	☺
8		☺	☺	☺	☺	☺			☺	☺	☺	☺	☺	☺	☺	☺

If you're the grade-level teacher, here's how to use the map:

- Determine what skills were covered earlier years. Expect students to transfer that knowledge to this new school year.
- Review the topics and skills, but don't expect to teach.
- If there are skills listed as covered prior years, confirm that was done. If they weren't (for whatever reason), when you reach lessons that require the skills, plan extra time.

Figure 4 is a month-by-month curriculum map for this grade level. In the student workbook, students complete this themselves or as a group when they finish each lesson.

Figure 4—Curriculum Map—2nd grade, month-to-month

	Sept Wk1-4	Oct Wk5-8	Nov Wk9-12	Dec Wk13-16	Jan Wk17-20	Feb Wk21-24	March Wk25-28	April Wk29-32
Blogs								
Class mgmt tools	X							
Coding/Programming		X						
Communication		X	X	X	X	X		X
Computer etiquette	X							
Critical thinking	X		X					
DTP				X				
Digital Citizenship	X					X	X	

2nd Grade Technology Curriculum: Teacher Manual

Google Earth		X						
Graphics			X	X	X	X		
Hardware	X	X						
Internet	X		X	X	X	X	X	
Internet privacy	X						X	
Keyboarding	X	X	X	X	X	X	X	X
Problem solving	X	X	X	X	X	X	X	X
Publishing/sharing			X				X	X
Research		X					X	X
Slideshows					X	X	X	X
Speaking and Listening								X
Spreadsheets								
Visual learning		X		X	X	X	X	X
Vocabulary	X	X	X	X	X	X	X	X
Webtools			X	X	X	X	X	X
Word Processing			X		X		X	

Some topics are covered every month. The strategy: spiral and scaffold learning until it's habit.

Here are hints to assist using this curriculum:

- Get free curriculum-aligned resources at our online resource website (shown earlier). If you have difficulty, email askatechteacher@gmail.com with questions. Here, you get weekly videos on how to teach the upcoming lesson, how-to videos on skills, and more.
- Invest in student digital workbooks (sold separately through Structured Learning), perfect student-centric companions to your teacher guide. Here is how to use them:

    o Full-color projects complete (licensing may vary depending upon the plan your school selected).
    o With nominal direction, students learn tech. This is perfect to teach technology across classes and to develop good digital citizens.
    o Workbooks can be shared and students add their own notes, how-tos and more.
    o Students can work at their own pace.

- If you want to use student workbooks in your class, here's how:

    o buy a multi-user license to install workbooks on multiple devices (even at home with some licenses)
    o provide a weekly preview by reviewing the lesson on the class screen

Figure 1--Student workbook

- Teach lessons in the order presented in the book (grades K-5). Lessons introduce, reinforce, and circle back on skills and concepts. Certain skills scaffold others so you want them solid before moving on. Resist the urge to mix up lessons, even if it seems your perfect time for a particular project comes earlier/later than placement in the book. **One exception: Coding/Programming**. Unpack this lesson when it works best for you.
- Personalize the skills taught in each lesson to your needs with 'Academic Applications'. These are suggestions for blending learning into your existing curriculum.
- Each lesson starts with a warm-up to get students back into tech and give you time to finish up a previous class. This is especially useful to the tech teacher and the LMS.
- Each class includes an Exit Ticket to wrap up learning.
- 'Teacher Preparation' often includes chatting with the grade-level team. Why?

    o *tie tech into their inquiry*
    o *offer websites for early-finishers to address topics*

- Check off completed items on the line preceding the activity so you know what to get back to when you have time. If you have the ebook, use iAnnotate, Notable (Google for websites), or another annotation tool that works for your devices.
- We understand when kids and technology collide, sometimes the class is too excited about the learning to move on. Two solutions:

    o *Leave line in front of uncompleted activity blank and return to it when you have time. You'll notice after using this curriculum a few years that students finish material faster.*
    o *Take an extra week. Most school years run 35-40 weeks. This book includes 32 lessons. This provides flexibility also for missed time due to holidays, snow days, or field trips.*

- Don't skip the 'Problem Solving' section, even if the problems don't come up in your class. Bring them up! These are important scaffolding for student ability to think critically and troubleshoot issues when you won't be there to help.
- Some lessons provide options. For example, Lesson 7 has multiple choices to teach coding. Review the entire lesson prior to teaching and choose the option most suited to your students. All will accomplish the tech goals.
- Is class shorter than 45 minutes? Highlight items most important to goals and leave the rest for 'later'.
- Always use lesson vocabulary. Students gain authentic understanding of word use by your example. A complete glossary of lesson vocabulary can be found in the resource website (link

mentioned earlier). Here, you'll find several hundred easy-to-understand definitions of domain-specific tech words.

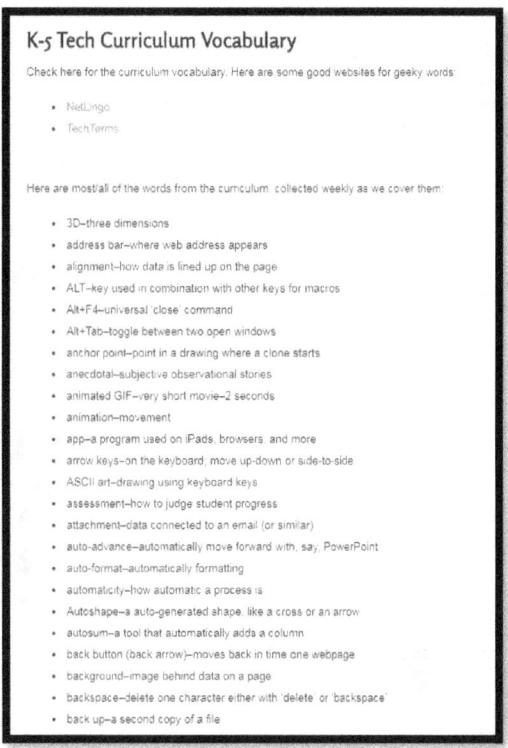

Figure 6—Glossary of tech ed vocabulary

- Expect students to be risk takers. Don't rush to solve their problems. Ask them to think how it was done in the past. Focus on problems listed in the lesson, but embrace all that come your way.
- Expect students to direct their own learning. You are a 'guide on the side'. You are a facilitator, not lecturer. Learning is accomplished by both success and failure.
- Encourage student-directed differentiation, opportunities for them to present their knowledge in ways suited to their abilities. If the Big Idea and Essential Question can be accommodated in other ways, embrace those.
- If you have the digital book, zoom in on posters, rubrics, lessons to enlarge as needed.
- Use as much technology as possible in your classroom—authentically and agilely. Make it adaptive and native. Encourage students to do the same whether it's a smartphone timing a quiz, a video of activities posted to the class website, or an audio file with student input. If you treat tech as a tool in daily activities, so will students.

- Remind students they've learned and understand skills. Check them off in the Scope and Sequence additional times as you circle back on them.

- Lessons expect students to develop 'habits of mind' (*Figure 7* and the article at the end of Lesson #1). In a sentence: Habits of Mind ask students to engage in their learning, not simply recite or memorize.

Figure 7—Habits of Mind

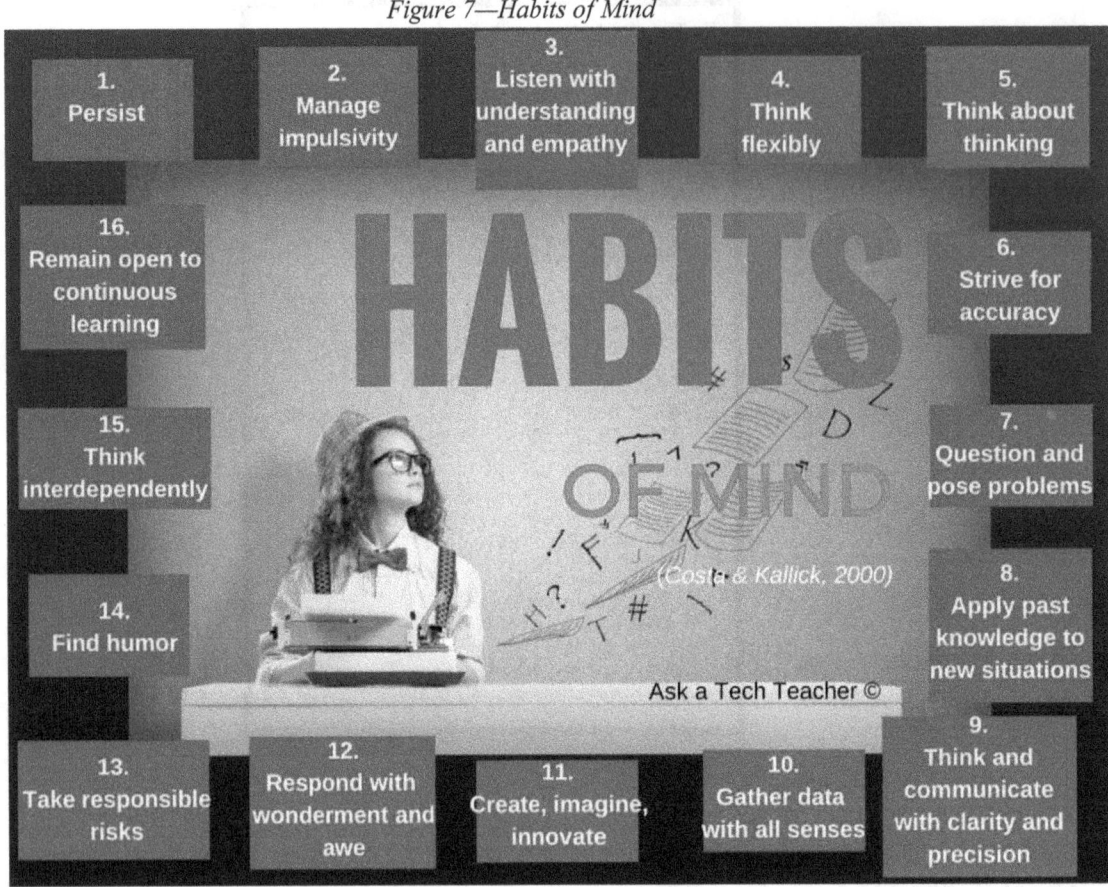

- If you need resources on specific topics, visit Ask a Tech Teacher resource pages.
- Look for the following icons in the book:

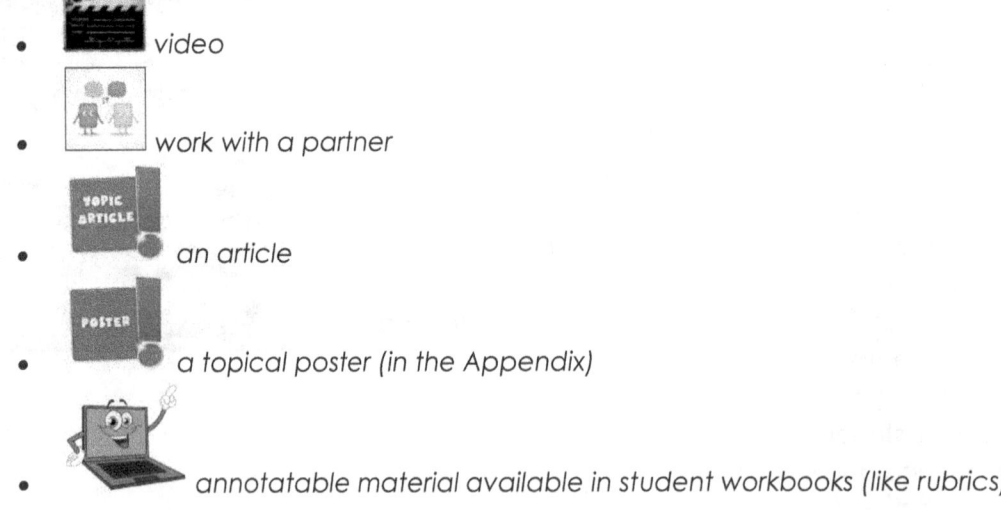

- Every effort has been made to accommodate Chromebooks, PCs, Macs, iPads, and other digital devices. You will often see examples in multiple platforms. If the activity is impossible in a particular digital device (i.e., iPads don't have mouses; software doesn't run in Chromebooks), focus on the **Big Idea and Essential Question**—the skill taught and its application to inquiry. Adapt instructions to the tool you use as you work through the steps.

Figure 8—Compatible digital devices

A desktop PC, iMac, laptop, MacBook, Chromebook, iPad, or smartphone

 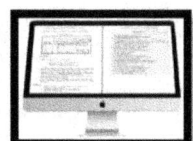     

- Throughout the year, circle back on lessons. It takes five times seeing a skill to get it—

    - *First:*   *They barely hear you*
    - *Second:*   *They try it*
    - *Third:*   *They remember it*
    - *Fourth:*   *They use it outside of class*
    - *Fifth:*   *They tell a friend*

- **Need more help?** Go to Ask a Tech Teacher©, run by teachers using the curriculum or the companion resource website (mentioned earlier). Leave a comment or question. You can also email admin@structuredlearning.net or askatechteacher@gmail.com.

Typical Lesson

Each lesson requires about 45 minutes a week, either in one sitting or spread throughout the week, and can be unpacked:

- *In the grade-level classroom*
- *In the school's tech lab*

Both are covered in each lesson. In general terms, here's how to run a lesson in **the tech lab**:

- Post a **simple written schedule** on class screen:

    - *Warm up*
    - *Main activity*
    - *Exit ticket*

This gives students a visual guideline to get started. Add it to your class blog for students not present. Expect students to start the warm-up when they arrive to class.

- **Warm up about 10 minutes,** often with typing practice. Youngers can work on alphabet sites such as Fischer Price's Learning Letters Puppy app.
- Three students complete **Board presentations** (grades 3-8).
- If it's the end of a grading period, use **Scope and Sequence to review** skills accomplished.
- If starting a **new project, review it** and take questions. If you're in the middle of one, students use the balance of class to work towards completion. Monitor activities, answer questions, help as needed.
- As often as possible, give **younger students two weeks** to finish a project—one to practice, one to save/export/share/print. This redundancy reinforces new skills and mitigates stress. If it's week two, start with the project and finish with typing so students have ample time to work.
- List age-appropriate websites that **tie into inquiry** for students who complete the current project on class internet start page. Students know websites on this page can be used during free time.
- **Class exit ticket** might include lining up in arrays, answering a poll posted on the class screen, or simply leaving stations as students found them.
- Always **use tech wherever possible.** Model what you ask of them.

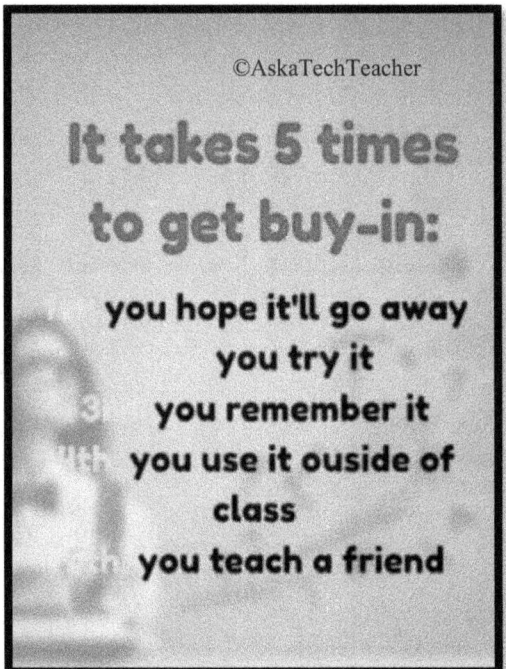

Figure 2--Five times for buy-in

Here's how to run the lesson in **the grade-level classroom**:

- Take the lesson pieces mentioned above and scatter them throughout the week. For example:
    - *3-10 minutes for the class warm-up*—at the start the week
    - *10-15 minutes keyboarding practice*—any day
    - *10-15 minutes Board presentations*—any day
    - *15-35 minutes for the project*—any day
    - *2-3 minutes for the class exit ticket*—to reinforce learning

- Check off accomplished activities so you know what remains each week.
- In every class, **use tech wherever possible.** Be the model for what you're asking of them.

Here are useful pieces to extend this curriculum (most found through Structured Learning):

- *Teacher manual—the roadmap. That's this book.*
- *Student workbooks—allow students to be self-paced*
- *Digital Citizenship curriculum— if this is a focus of your school*
- *Keyboarding Curriculum— if this is a focus of your school*

- *Class internet start page—provides a class agenda, themed links, and more. Created by you, the teacher, in Protopage (Figure 10a), Diigo, LiveBinders (Figure 10b), Symbaloo (Figure 10c) or another option.*

Figure 10a—Start page using Protopage; 10b—LiveBinders; 10c—Symbaloo

Copyrights

You have a single-user license of this book. That means you may reproduce copies of material in this textbook for classroom use only. Reproduction of the entire book (or an entire lesson) is strictly prohibited. No part of this publication may be transmitted, stored, or recorded in any form without written permission from the publisher.

About the Authors

Ask a Tech Teacher *is a group of technology teachers who run an award-winning resource blog. Here they provide free materials, advice, lesson plans, pedagogical conversation, website reviews, and more to all who drop by. The free newsletters and articles help thousands of teachers, homeschoolers, and those serious about finding the best way to maneuver the minefields of technology in education.*

*Throughout this text, we refer to Common Core State Standards, and a license granted for "…a limited, non-exclusive, royalty-free license to copy, publish, distribute, and display the Common Core State Standards for purposes that support the CCSS Initiative. These uses may involve the Common Core State Standards as a whole or selected excerpts or portions. **CCSS:** *© Copyright 2010. National Governors Association Center for Best Practices and Council of Chief State School Officers. All rights reserved.*

2nd Grade Technology Curriculum: Teacher Manual

Table of Contents

Introduction

Curriculum Maps

Technology Scope and Sequence K-6

Table of Images

Table of Assessments

Lessons
- 1   Introduction
- 2   Digital Tools in the Classroom
- 3   Internet and Digital Citizenship
- 4   Keyboarding
- 5   Problem Solving
- 6   Tools and Toolbars
- 7   Coding
- 8   Google Earth
- 9   Intro to Word Processing
- 10 Holiday Story
- 11 Holiday Letter I
- 12 Holiday Letter II
- 13 Reading on the Internet
- 14 Graphic Organizers
- 15 3 Ways to Send Greetings
- 16 Around the World I
- 17 Around the World II
- 18 Valentine Greeting
- 19 About Me: A Summative Project
- 20 Develop Details
- 21 Where I Live
- 22 My Body
- 23 Stories with Words and Pictures
- 24 The End (of the Slideshow)
- 25 Internet Pictures
- 26 Report in Word Processing I
- 27 Report in Word Processing II
- 28 Slideshows I
- 29 Slideshow II
- 30 Slideshow III
- 31 Slideshow IV
- 32 Presentations

Appendices
1. Certificate of Completion
2. Posters

Articles

"21st Century Lesson Plan" 34
"Habits of Mind vs. CC vs. IB" 36
"Which Class Start Page is Best" 38
"6 Tech Best Practices" 40
"10 Ways to be Inquiry-based" 42
"Do you make these 9 mistakes?" 56
"How to Teach Digital Citizenship" 64
"11 Ways Twitter Improves Ed" 66
"Is Keyboarding Dead?" 74
"5 Ways to Make Keyboarding Fun" 76
"18 Techie Problems" 84
"How to Teach Students to Solve" 86
"The Secret to Teaching Tech" 88
"Power of Symbols" 92
"Want to Code on an iPad?" 98
"How Do I Teach a Program I Don't Know?" 100
"3 Digital Tools for Close Reading" 127
"Write a Novel with 140 Characters" 154
"Where Can I Find Kid-safe Images?" 181
"PS" 199

16

Table of Images

Figure 1—Tomorrow's student 7
Figure 2a—Beginning of each lesson; Figure 2b—end of each lesson 8
Figure 3—Curriculum Map—K-8 9
Figure 4—Curriculum Map—2nd grade, month-to-month 10
Figure 5—Student workbook 11
Figure 6—Glossary of tech ed vocabulary 12
Figure 7—Habits of Mind 13
Figure 8—Compatible digital devices 14
Figure 9—Five times for buy-in 15
Figure 10a—Start page using Protopage; 10b—LiveBinders; 10c—Symbaloo 16
Figure 11a-d Wall posters 31
Figure 12a-c—More wall posters 31
Figure 13a—Tech rules; 13b—Digital student 32
Figure 14a—Keyboard posture; 14b—position 32
Figure 15a—Parts of computer; 15b—Parts of iPad 45
Figure 16—Mouse hand position 45
Figure 17a—Menu bar; 17b and c—Toolbar; 17b—Ribbon; 17d—Taskbar 46
Figure 18—Curation of log-ins 47
Figure 19—Desktop 48
Figure 20—Chromebook desktop 48
Figure 21a—PDF annotation with iAnnotate; 21b—Notability; 21c—Acrobat 49
Figure 22a—Class calendar; 22b—Padlet; 22c—DTP 50
Figure 23—Internet start page 50
Figure 24a—Avatar; 24b—DTP badge; 24c—digital storytelling; 24d—RAZ Kids 51
Figure 25a-b—What is the Internet? 59
Figure 26—Internet basics 59
Figure 27—Digital neighborhood 60
Figure 28—Internet safety 60
Figure 29—2nd grade Digcit topics 61
Figure 30—Privacy on the internet 62
Figure 31a—Netiquette rules; 31b—Digcit topics wall chart 63
Figure 32—Padlet wall on digital citizenship 63
Figure 33a—Why learn to keyboard? 33b—Keyboard curriculum map 69
Figure 34—Hand position 70
Figure 35a—Keyboard posture; 35b—Keyboarding hints 70
Figure 36—Important non-letter keys 72
Figure 37—Keyboard shortkeys 73
Figure 38—How to Solve a Problem 79
Figure 39—Hardware and solutions 80
Figure 40—Troubleshooting computer problems 81
Figure 41-Common shortkeys 82
Figure 42a—Problem-solving Board; 42b—FREE sample 83
Figure 43a-b: Pictures as symbols 90
Figure 44a-d: Common symbols 90
Figure 45a-b: Mathematical symbols 91
Figure 46a—Toolbar symbols; 46b—desktop icon symbols 91

2nd Grade Technology Curriculum: Teacher Manual

Figure 47a—Symbols poll; 47b—result of poll 92
Figure 48a-b: Which is programming? 94
Figure 49a—Kodable; 49b—Hopscotch; 49c—Tynker 95
Figure 50a-c: Correct sequence 96
Figure 51a-c—Stick figure animation 96
Figure 52a-b: Google Earth projects in K/1 104
Figure 53a-c: Mashup using Google Earth and drawing program 104
Figure 54—Number Square 107
Figure 55—Number Square in a spreadsheet 108
Figure 56—Word processing start-up page 111
Figure 57a-c—Word processing projects in K, 1 111
Figure 58a-b—Story in Google Doc; 58c—in Word 112
Figure 59—Proper keyboarding posture 112
Figure 60a-b—Story in word processing program 113
Figure 61a-c—Letters from Kindergarten and 1st grade 117
Figure 62a-c—Three levels of letter writing complexity 117
Figure 63—I can't find my file 120
Figure 64a-c—Student letters 121
Figure 65—Safe online reading 124
Figure 66—Why read digital books 125
Figure 67a-b—Graphic organizers from kindergarten, 1st grade 130
Figure 68a—Graphic organizer in 2nd grade; 68b—3rd grade; 68c—4th grade; 68d—5th grade 130
Figure 69a-c—Online graphic organizers 131
Figure 70a—Graphic organizer with MS Word; 70b—with Google Draw 131
Figure 71a-b—How I'm Connected (with and without images 132
Figure 72—Compare-contrast software vs. online tool 134
Figure 73a-c—Holiday drawings in K-1 134
Figure 74a-c: Holiday card on iPads and Chromebooks 135
Figure 75a-b—Holiday cards 135
Figure 76a—Greeting card in Publisher; 76b—Word; 76c—Open Office; 76d—Avery 136
Figure 77—IPad greeting cards (online) 136
Figure 78—Fold a printed card 137
Figure 79a-c—QR code cards 138
Figure 80a—Annotatable template on laptop; 80b—iPad 140
Figure 81—Using templates 143
Figure 82a-c—Letters written in 2nd grade 146
Figure 83a-c—Valentine letters in 2nd grade 146
Figure 84—Slide 1 in story 150
Figure 85—Slide 2 in story 150
Figure 86—Slide 3 in story 151
Figure 87—Slide 4 in story 151
Figure 88a-b—Scene on in slideshow story 152
Figure 89—1st grade story example 157
Figure 90—Story with insufficient detail 158
Figure 91—Slide two with writing suggestions 161
Figure 92a-b—Slide 2 examples 162
Figure 93—Slide 2 using image 162
Figure 94a-b: Fill in the blank templates of human body 164
Figure 95—Completed human body template 165
Figure 96a-b—Label student picture 166
Figure 97—Mashup of Google Draw and PicMonkey 166

Figure 98a-b—Label avatar bodies 167
Figure 99a-c—Third slide: Plot 170
Figure 100a-c—Closure of digital story 172
Figure 101a—Want to use this image? 101b—Using online images legally 174
Figure 102—Google safe search 174
Figure 103a—Google search; 103b—Select one 175
Figure 104—Image use settings on Google 175
Figure 105—Image use permissions 176
Figure 106a-c—Animals created with drawing tool 179
Figure 107a-b—Report cover 179
Figure 108a-b—Report interior pages 180
Figure 109a-b—Report with Canva; 109c—PicCollage 180
Figure 110a-b—Compare-contrast slideshows vs word processing 185
Figure 111—K/1st grade slideshows 186
Figure 112a—2nd grade slideshow cover; 112b—interior slide; 112c—ending slide ... 186
Figure 113a—PowerPoint canvas; 113b—Haiku Deck canvas 187
Figure 114a-c—Slideshow slides 190
Figure 115a-b—The End slide 192
Figure 116a-b—About the Author 192
Figure 117—Slideshow rubric 195
Figure 118—Presentation rubric 198
Figure 119—Certificate 198

Table of Assessments

1—Hardware Quiz 53
2—Parts of an iPad 54
3—Parts of a Smartphone 55
4—Keyboarding technique 71
5—Number Square 109
6—Story rubric 115
7—Letter writing rubric 122
8a-b—Around the World Template 141
9—Around the World rubric 144
10 Valentine letter rubric 148
11—Parts of human body template 168
12—Slideshow rubric 196

2nd Grade Technology Curriculum: Teacher Manual

K-5 TECHNOLOGY SCOPE AND SEQUENCE©

Aligned with ISTE (International Society for Technology in Education) and Common Core State Standards
Check each skill off with I (Introduced), W (Working on), or M (Mastered)
Organized by ISTE Standards 1-7

	Empowered Learner	K	1	2	3	4	5
	Students leverage technology to take an active role in choosing, achieving and demonstrating competency in their learning goals, informed by the learning sciences.						
	Use technology strategically and capably (CCSS C&CR profile)	I	W	M	M	M	M
	Are familiar with the strengths and limitations of various technological tools and mediums and can select and use those best suited to communication goals (CCSS C&CR Profile)	I	W	M	M	M	M
	Strategize personal learning						
	Understand how inquiry contributes to creative and empowered learning	I	W	M	M	M	M
	Understand how technology contributes to class and personal learning	I	W	M	M	M	M
	Understand how higher order thinking skills are buttressed by technology	I	W	M	M	M	M
	Select between available options, choosing one best suited to learning	I	W	M	M	M	M
	Compare-contrast available tools, determining which is best suited to need	I	W	M	M	M	M
	Know what digital tools are available and how to use them for class and home (i.e., digital calendars, blogs, websites, and annotation tools)	I	W	M	M	M	M
	Know how to read digital books both online and through readers	I	W	M	M	M	M
	Be responsive to varied needs of task-audience-purpose	I	W	M	M	M	M
	Interact, collaborate, publish with peers employing a variety of digital media			I	W	M	M
	Develop cultural understanding by engaging with learners of other cultures			I	W	M	M
	Share work in a way that suits communication style	I	W	M	M	M	M
	Seek feedback to demonstrate learning				I		
	Add comments to class blogs, forums, discussion boards, webtools	I	W	M	M	M	M
	Work in groups collaboratively and productively	I	W	M	M	M	M
	Transfer knowledge						
	Scaffold learning year-to-year and lesson-to-lesson	I	W	M	M	M	M
	Transfer understanding of one digital tool or device to others	I	W	M	M	M	M
	Understand tools, toolbars, and how they relate to many digital tools	I	W	M	M	M	M
	Use tech tools (like Google Earth's ruler) to solve real-world problems	I	W	M	M	M	M
	Hardware						
	Know digital devices used at school and home and how to connect them	I	W	M	M	M	M
	Know parts of keyboard	I	W	M	M	M	M
	Understand difference between power buttons on monitor and tower	I	W	M	M	M	M
	Can troubleshoot hardware	I	W	M	M	M	M
	Operating Systems (PC, Mac, Chromebook, iPads)						
	Understand concept of Desktop or Home	I	W	M	M	M	M
	Know how to run a slideshow using the native tool in a particular platform	I	W	M	M	M	M
	Know how to log-on	I	W	M	M	M	M
	Know how to Open/Close programs	I	W	M	M	M	M

©AskaTechTeacher

2nd Grade Technology Curriculum: Teacher Manual

	Understand concepts of taskbar, start button, icons, drop-down menus	I	W	M	M	M	M
	Know how to find files, add more, save to network file folder and/or cloud	I	W	M	M	M	M
	Know how to drag-drop (or copy-paste) within a doc and between folders					I	W
	Know how to use tool tips (hover over icon) and right-click menus				I	W	M
	Know how to access different drives					I	W
	Can troubleshoot operating systems	I	W	M	M	M	M
	Know how to use software installed on PCs and/or Macs	I	W	M	M	M	M
	Online Tech for Classroom Management						
	Understand school technology				I	W	M	M
	Understand dropbox for homework				I	W	M
	Understand online tools like blogs, digital portfolios						I
	Understand Cloud for transferring school work to home						I
	Understand how to use class digital tools (digital devices, annotation, blogs, internet start page)	I	W	M	M	M	M
	Know how to use a website--back button, links, scroll bars, home, address	I	W	M	M	M	M
	Understand layout of a website and where to click and where you shouldn't	I	W	M	M	M	M
	Know how to annotate a PDF or online document			I	W	M	M
	Know how to share out classwork (including homework)				I	W	M
	Know how to use online vocabulary decoding tools quickly and efficiently	I	W	M	M	M	M
	Understand the basics of using the Internet (toolbar, tabbed browsing, home button)	I	W	M	M	M	M
	Know how to safely play online videos from a variety of sources	I	W	M	M	M	M
	Know how to legally copy-paste from internet for a project				I	W	M
	Know how to log onto webtool accounts			I	W	M	M
	Mouse Skills						
	Know how to click, hold, drag, double-click	I	W	M	M	M	M
	Know how to hover	I	W	M	M	M	M
	Introduce right mouse button			I	W	M	M
	Keyboarding						
	Know how to practice keyboarding on internet sites and software	I	W	M	M	M	M
	Strive to achieve grade-appropriate keyboarding speed and accuracy goal			I	W	M
	Type with hands on keyboard, curved, fingers on home row			I	W	M	M
	Practice touch typing				I	W	M
	Compose at keyboard by creating classroom-based projects				I	W	M
	Understand speed difference between handwriting and keyboarding				I	W
	Select shortkeys instead of toolbar tools when appropriate	I	W	M	M	M	M
	Use correct posture, elbows at sides	I	W	M	M	M	M
	Know parts of keyboard--keys, numbers, F keys, arrows, Esc			I	W	M	M
	Know escape, period key, shift key, spacebar, tab	I	I	I	W	M	M
	Word Processing						
	Know when to use a word processing program, software and online tools			I	W	M	M
	Use grammar, spelling when word processing on computer	I	W	M	M	M	M

©AskaTechTeacher

2nd Grade Technology Curriculum: Teacher Manual

				I	W	M	M
		Know basic page layout--heading, title, body, footer			I	W	M	M
		Know how word-wrap works			I	W	M	M
		Know how to highlight a word, sentence, line, select/deselect, doublespace			I	W	M	M
		Know how to add a watermark, bullet list, table, pictures, graphic organizer					I	W
		Know correct spacing after sentences, paragraphs		I	W	M	M	M
		Know how to use grade-appropriate heading on all Word docs				I	W	M
		Know how to use the thesaurus					I	W
		Know how to format a document—i.e., add header, footer, border, cover page, embedded link			I	W	M	M
		Know to put cursor in specific location, i.e., for graphic			I	W	M	M
		Know how to Print Preview before printing			I	W	M	M
		Know how to select and then do--two-step process in editing, formatting			I	W	M	M
		Know how to compose at Keyboard			I	W	M	M
		Can use Ctrl+Enter to force a new page			I	W	M	M
		Know how to write a letter using digital tools	I	W	M	M	M	M
		Can troubleshoot word processing			I	W	M	M
	Google Earth							
		Display familiarity with tools for moving around world	I	W	M	M	M	M
		Know how to find a location, add a picture, placemark, save a picture				I	W	M
		Understand latitudes and longitudes				I	W	M
		Know how to use ruler to measure distances					I	W
		Run a tour of placemarks around the planet				I	W	M	M
2	**Digital Citizen**							
Students recognize the rights, responsibilities and opportunities of living, learning and working in an interconnected digital world, and they act and model in ways that are safe, legal and ethical.								
		Gather relevant information from print and digital sources, assess credibility of source, and integrate the information while avoiding plagiarism. (CCSS C&CR Writing Anchor Standards)				I	W	M
	Internet privacy and safety							
		Know how to configure privacy settings					I	W
		Understand cyberbullying, use of passwords	I	W	M	M	M	M
		Understand digital footprint and online presence				I	W	M
		Understand how online entities track student activity online				I	W	M
		Understand the appropriate use of the 'digital neighborhood'	I	W	M	M	M	M
	Legal use of online materials							
		Discuss copyright law			I	W	M	M
		Discuss plagiarism and how to cite sources			I	W	M	M
		Discuss 'fair use'			I	W	M	M
		Discuss 'intellectual property', rights and obligations of using and sharing			I	W	M	M
	Digital Netiquette							
		Understand etiquette in the digital neighborhood	I	W	M	M	M	M
		Know to stay out of other file folders	I	W	M	M	M	M
	Digital Citizenship							

©AskaTechTeacher

2nd Grade Technology Curriculum: Teacher Manual

		Understand what a 'digital citizen' is	I	W	M	M	M	M
		Exhibit a positive attitude toward technology that supports collaboration and learning	I	W	M	M	M	M
		Demonstrate personal responsibility for lifelong learning	I	W	M	M	M	M
		Exhibit leadership for digital citizenship--set the standard for classmates	I	W	M	M	M	M
	Interactions online							
		Address digital commerce						I
		Use safe, responsible and ethical behavior on the internet	I	W	M	M	M	M
		Discuss social media					I	W
		Discuss digital rights and responsibilities	I	W	M	M	M	M
		Recognize irresponsible and unsafe practices on the internet				I	W	M
		Know how to leave a useful comment for a classmate				I	W	M
		Know how online comments follow same rules as speaking and listening				I	W	M
3	**Knowledge Constructor**							
	Students critically curate a variety of resources using digital tools to construct knowledge, produce creative artifacts and make meaningful learning experiences for themselves and others.							
		Use the internet to build strong content knowledge (CCSS C&CR profile)	I	I	W	M	M	M
		Use technology to produce and publish writing and collaborate with others (CCRA.W.6)	I	I	W	M	M	M
		Use technology strategically and capably (CCSS C&CR profile)	I	I	W	M	M	M
		Comprehend as well as critique. (CCSS C&CR profile)			I	W	M	M
		Value evidence (CCSS C&CR profile)			I	W	M	M
		Compare-contrast documents across digital media (CCSS Anchor Standards)			I	W	M	M
		Gather relevant information from multiple digital sources (CCRA.W.8)			I	W	M	M
		Assess credibility of digital sources (CCSS Anchor Standards)			I	W	M	M
		Integrate and evaluate information from diverse media (CCRA.R.7)			I	W	M	M
		Make strategic use of digital media to express information (CCRA.SL.5)			I	W	M	M
		Use electronic menus and links to locate key facts (RI/)			I	W	M	M
	Effective online research strategies							
		Use screenshots to collect information			I	W	M	M
		Locate, organize, analyze, evaluate, and synthesize information from a variety of sources	I	W	M	M	M	M
		Evaluate and select information sources and digital tools based on task			I	W	M	M
		Read search results before clicking link and know how to identify reliable resources			I	W	M	M
		Guide inquiry by knowing how to choose links and menus	I	W	M	M	M	M
		Know how to search effectively and efficiently, limit search as needed, and use Ctrl+F				I	W	M
		Know how to effectively use LMS systems and the Cloud					I	W
	Technology as knowledge curator							
		Evaluate the accuracy, perspective, relevancy of information, media, data or other resources.				I	W	M
		Curate information from digital resources using a variety of tools and methods that demonstrate meaningful connections or conclusions (such as outlines, mindmaps).				I	W	M
		Understand the difference between software and webtools		I	W	M	M	M

2nd Grade Technology Curriculum: Teacher Manual

	Understand how parts make up a whole in, say, a puzzle or a divided picture	I	W	M			
	Know how to read digitally using both online websites and dedicated ereaders	I	W	M	M	M	M
	Know how to evaluate accuracy and relevance of websites					I	W
	Build knowledge by exploring real-world issues, developing ideas, and pursuing solutions.			I	W	M	M
	Online collaborative environments						
	Use blogs for journaling and tracking project progress						I
	Incorporate text, images, widgets to better communicate ideas						I
	Know how to use Discussion boards and forums					I	W	M
4	**Innovative Designer**						
	Students use technology to identify and solve problems by creating new, useful or imaginative solutions.						
	Respond to varying demands of audience, task, purpose, and discipline (CCSS C&CR profile)	I	W	M	M	M	M
	Use glossaries or dictionaries to clarify meaning of key words and phrases (CCSS.L.K.4)		I	W	M	M	M
	Gather, comprehend, evaluate, synthesize, and report on information in order to answer questions or solve problems, (CCSS Key Design Consideration)			I	W	M	M
	Draw on information from multiple print or digital sources, demonstrating the ability to locate an answer to a question quickly or to solve a problem efficiently (CCSS. RI.5)				I	W	M
	Reason abstractly and quantitatively (CCSS. Math.Practice.MP2)		I	W	M	M	M
	Use appropriate tools strategically (CCSS. Math.Practice.MP5)	I	W	M	M	M	M
	Attend to precision (CCSS. Math.Practice.MP6)	I	W	M	M	M	M
	Design Process						
	Use planning tools such as mindmaps and brainstorming to organize ideas and solve problems				I	W	M
	Use presentation tools like graphic organizers, Infographics, screencasts, and videos to share in-depth topical ideas and solve authentic problems in a variety of creative ways				I	W	M
	Use templates and patterns to create new designs (like shapes, letters)	I	W	M	M	M	M
	Select and use digital tools (such as comics) to plan and manage a design process that considers design constraints and calculated risk	I	W	M	M	M	M
	Develop, test and refine prototypes as part of a cyclical design process			I	W	M	M
	Able to tolerate ambiguity, persevere, with a capacity to work with open-ended problems.	I	W	M	M	M	M
	Use established patterns and design processes in solving common tech problems	I	W	M	M	M	M
	Recognize the part 'failure' plays in solving problems	I	W	M	M	M	M
	Know how to use tables, charts, and why			I	W	M	
	Decision Making						
	Identify and define authentic problems and questions for investigation					I	W
	Collect, analyze data to identify solutions and make informed decisions	I	W	M	M	M	M
	Able to debug programs using sequencing, if-then thinking, logic, or other strategies	I	W	W	W	W	W
	Able to evaluate which program is right for which task	I	W	M	M	M	M
	Students recognize digital designs in the world around them	I					

©AskaTechTeacher

2nd Grade Technology Curriculum: Teacher Manual

	Slideshows						
	Know when to use presentation tools			I	W	M	M
	Know how to add/rearrange slides, auto-advance			I	W	M	M
	Know how to add a variety of backgrounds, animations, movies, transitions			I	W	M	M
	Know how to insert pictures from file, internet, clip-art			I	W	M	M
	Know how to insert text, images, slides, multimedia			I	W	M	M
	Understand how to deliver a professional presentation			I	W	M	M
	Can troubleshoot presentation tools	I	W	M	M	M	M
	Familiar with slideshow tools including software and online tools	I	W	M	M	M	M
	Graphics						
	Use drawing software and web-based tools efficiently	I	W	M	M	M	M
	Know how to insert images, clipart			I	W	M	M
	Know how to import from a file			I	W	M	M
	Know how to resize/move/crop/wrap an image			I	W	M	M
	Know how to mix text and pictures to convey unique message	I	W	M	M	M	M
	Know how to create and annotate screenshots to share information	I	W	M	M	M	M
	Desktop publishing						
	Can identify parts of the desktop publishing screen			I	W	M	M
	Know when to use a desktop publishing program to share information			I	W	M	M
	Know how to make a card, flier, cover page, magazine, trifold, newsletter			I	W	M	M
	Know how to insert a picture, blank page, text box, footer, border			I	W	M	M
	Know how to work with color schemes			I	W	M	M
	Know how to plan a publication				I	W	M
	Can troubleshoot publishing tools				I	W	M
	Know how to use greeting cards to reinforce writing skills as well as tech skills	I	W	M	M	M	M
	Screencasts, Videos						
	Know how to create screencasts and videos to share information						I
	Know how to upload screencasts and videos to easily-accessible locations for peers						I
	Know how to use the design process to prepare screencasts						I
5	**Computational Thinker**						
	Students develop and employ strategies for understanding and solving problems in ways that leverage the power of technological methods to develop and test solutions.						
	Gather, comprehend, evaluate, synthesize, and report on information to conduct original research in order to answer questions or solve problems, (CCSS Key Design Consideration)	I	W	M	M	M	M
	Draw on information from multiple sources, demonstrating the ability to locate an answer to a question quickly or to solve a problem efficiently (CCSS. RI.5)	I	W	M	M	M	M
	Make sense of problems and persevere in solving them (CCSS.Math.Practice.MP1)	I	W	M	M	M	M
	Reason abstractly and quantitatively (CCSS. Math.Practice.MP2)	I	W	M	M	M	M
	Construct viable arguments and critique the reasoning of others (CCSS. Math.Practice.MP3)	I	W	M	M	M	M

©AskaTechTeacher

2nd Grade Technology Curriculum: Teacher Manual

		Model with mathematics (CCSS. Math.Practice.MP4)	I	W	M	M	M	M
		Use appropriate tools strategically (CCSS. Math.Practice.MP5)	I	W	M	M	M	M
		Attend to precision (CCSS. Math.Practice.MP6)	I	W	M	M	M	M
		Look for and make use of structure (CCSS. Math.Practice.MP7)	I	W	M	M	M	M
		Look for and express regularity in repeated reasoning (CCSS. Math.Practice.MP8)	I	W	M	M	M	M
	Critical Thinking							
		Understand how to identify, define authentic problems, questions	I	W	M	M	M	M
		Understand that class computer pod is just like the computer lab	I	W	M	M	M	M
		Know what digital tools are available and how to use them for class and home, including digital calendars, blogs, websites, and annotation tools	I	W	M	M	M	M
		Understand the part tools, toolbars, menus, taskbars, symbols play in unpacking digital tools	I	W	M	M	M	M
		Always attempt to solve a problem before asking for teacher assistance	I	W	M	M	M	M
		Know how to print to a physical or cloud-based location	I	W	M	M	M	M
		Know how to save work to a local drive and the cloud	I	W	M	M	M	M
		Know how to use programs not yet learned	I	W	M	M	M	M
		Know the difference between save and save-as				I	W	M
		Know the difference between backspace and delete				I	W	M
		Know how to use digital tools to compare-contrast		I	W	M	M	M
		Know why a particular digital tool is suited to a specific need		I	W	M	M	M
		Know how to analyze data digitally and represent data in various ways to facilitate problem-solving and decision-making.			I	I	W	M
	Problem solving							
		Identify, define, and solve authentic problems, questions for investigation	I	W	M	M	M	M
		Know user name and password	I	W	M	M	M	M
		Know how to determine the date, undo	I	W	M	M	M	M
		Learn to use keyboard shortkeys as alternative solutions				I	W	M
		Know what to do if double-click doesn't work	I	W	M	M	M	M
		Know what to do if document or program disappears, or screen freezes	I	W	M	M	M	M
		Can visually compare own screen with instructors	I	W	M	M	M	M
		Follow established procedure when asking for help	I	W	M	M	M	M
		Know what to do when part of computer doesn't work	I	W	M	M	M	M
		Can use Alt+F4 to shut down frozen program				I	W	M
		Can use Task Manager to shut down locked program				I	W	M
		Know how to access work from anywhere in the school	I	W	M	M	M	M
		Know how to solve common hardware problems	I	W	M	M	M	M
		Know what to do if computer doesn't work				I	W	M
		Can trouble shoot a non-working program				I	W	M
		Can recognize and use up to 13 different problem-solving strategies	I	W	W	W	M	M
		Can break problems into component parts, extract key information, and develop descriptive models to understand complex systems or facilitate problem-solving.				I	W	W
		Able to use graphic organizers to decode problems and automate solutions				I	W	W
	Programming							

2nd Grade Technology Curriculum: Teacher Manual

	Understand technology contributes to higher-order thinking in Habits of Mind, DoK, or another	I	W	W	W	M	M
	Understand the cause-effect relationship inherent in actions	I	W	W	W	M	M
	Understand If-then and conditionals in coding	I	W	M	M	M	M
	Understand sequencing, algorithms, loops, functions, and variables	I	W	M	M	M	M
	Eagerly experiment with programming tools	I	W	M	M	M	M
	Understand how automation works; use algorithmic thinking to develop a sequence of steps to create and test automated solutions. (i.e., timelines, brainstorming)			I	W	W	W
	Recognize that codes are simply another language			I	W	W	W
	Able to debug programs using sequencing, if-then thinking, logic, or other strategies	I	W	W	W	W	W
	Scratch						
	Create/add/edit/broadcast sprites						I
	Add sound, text bubbles, backgrounds, movement						I
	Complete program task cards for most common skills						I
	Use models created by others; remix to develop unique Scratch video						I
	Robotics						
	Contribute to project teams to produce original works or solve problems						I
	Build, program, debug a robot						I
	Trouble shoot simple problems						I
	Use sensors to monitor the environment						I
	Measure distances with robots						I
	Spreadsheets						
	Process and sort data, report results by collecting data into Excel and reporting it				I	W	M
	Know how to add text, graphics, data, color			I	W	M	M
	Know how to use paint bucket fill--coordinate drawing			I	W	M	M
	Know how to add, subtract, multiply, divide formulas, and label x/y axis				I	W	M
	Know how to name a chart				I	W	M
	Know how to recolor tabs; rename worksheets				I	W	M
	Explore a business using models/simulations to study complex systems and issues					I	W
	Know how to publish spreadsheet through a widget to blog and/or website					I	W
	Can troubleshoot spreadsheets				I	W	W
6	**Creative Communicator**						
	Students communicate clearly and express themselves creatively for a variety of purposes using the platforms, tools, styles, formats and digital media appropriate to their goals.						
	Use technology and digital media strategically and capably (CCSS C&CR profile)	I	W	W	W	M	M
	Use technology to produce and publish writing and interact/collaborate with others (CCSS.ELA-LITERACY.CCRA.W.6)	I	W	M	M	M	M
	Explore digital tools to produce and publish writing (CCSS.ELA-Literacy.W)	I	W	M	M	M	M
	Explore digital tools to collaborate with peers (CCSS.ELA-Literacy.W)	I	W	M	M	M	M
	Use multimedia to aid comprehension (CCSS.ELA-Literacy.W)					I	W
	Ask and answer questions from information presented (CCSS.ELA-Literacy.SL)		I	W	M	M	M

2nd Grade Technology Curriculum: Teacher Manual

		Include audio recordings and multimedia to enhance main ideas (CCSS.ELA-Literacy.SL)		I	W	M	M
		Integrate and evaluate information presented in diverse media and formats, including visually, quantitatively, and orally (CCSS.ELA-LITERACY.CCRA.SL.2)	I	W	M	M	M	M
		Use multimedia to organize ideas, concepts, info (CCSS.ELA-Literacy.WHST)	I	W	M	M	M	M
		Interact, collaborate, and publish with peers, experts, employing a variety of digital media			I	W	M	M
	Vocabulary						
		Understand domain-specific vocabulary	I	W	M	M	M	M
		Communicate ideas effectively using variety of media, formats (CCSS Anchor Standards)	I	W	M	M	M	M
		Use digital tools to decode academic and domain-specific vocab		I	W	M	C
	Blogs						
		Interact, collaborate, publish with peers employing a variety of digital media						I
		Develop cultural understanding and global awareness by engaging learners of other cultures						I
		Contribute to project teams to produce original works or solve problems						I
	Digital Tools						
		Communicate information, ideas effectively to multiple audiences using a variety of media and formats including visual organizers, infographics		I	W	M	M
		Use web-based communication tools to share unique and individual ideas		I	W	M	M
		Learn a variety of tools that address varied communication styles (from written to visual to video) by teaching them to classmates		I	W	M	M
		Know how to use models and simulations to explore complex systems and issues				I	W
		Simulate running a business to identify trends, forecast sales				I	W
		Interact, collaborate, and publish employing digital media including greeting cards for youngers	I	W	M	M	M	M
		Develop cultural understanding by engaging with learners of other cultures	I	W	M	M	M	M
	Digital Storytelling, Quick Writes						
		Compose short stories, quick writes, letters, comics using online tools	I	W	M	M	M	M
		Collaborate and share stories in an online tool		I	W	M	M	M
		Use select digital tools to collaborate and publish with peers employing a variety of digital environments and media	I	W	M	M	M	M
		Participate in a virtual field trip that tells the story of a student's experience	I	W	M	M	M
	Speaking and Listening						
		Engage in impromptu speaking such as the Evidence Board			I	W	W
		Present well-prepared presentations such as slideshows, knowing how to use multimedia props		I	W	M	M
		Engage in short presentations such as the Presentation Boards			I	W	M
7	**Global Collaborator**						
	Students use digital tools to broaden their perspectives and enrich their learning by collaborating with others and working effectively in teams locally and globally.						
		Understand other perspectives and cultures. (CCSS C&CR profile)	I	W	M	M	M	M
		Respond to the varying demands of audience, task, purpose, discipline. (CCSS C&CR Profile)	I	W	M	M	M	M
		Use digital tools to connect with learners from a variety of backgrounds and	I	W	M	M	M	M

©AskaTechTeacher

	cultures, engaging with them in ways that broaden mutual understanding and learning						
	Explore local and global issues and use collaborative technologies to investigate solutions	I	W	M	M	M	M
	Know what 'Cloud computing' is				I	W	M
	Collaborate with Others						
	Use digital tools like Padlet to collaborate with peers in projects				I	W	M
	Use collaborative technologies to work with others, including peers, experts or community members, to examine issues and problems from multiple viewpoints.	I	W	M	M	M	M
	Contribute to project teams, assuming responsibilities to work toward a common goal.	I	W	M	M	M	M
	Use blogs, forums, Discussion Boards to collaborate and share					I	W
	Use programs to collaborate					I	W

©AskaTechTeacher

Lesson #1 Introduction

Vocabulary	Problem solving	Skills
• CPU • Digital citizenship • Internet start page • Landscape • Mouse wheel • Portrait • Power buttons • Right-click • Save-as	• Double-click doesn't work (push enter) • Monitor doesn't work (check power) • Volume doesn't work (check plugs) • Headphones don't work (are they plugged in?) • Computer doesn't work • Holding the mouse this way feels weird (you'll get used to it) • I don't have to sit this way at home	**New** **Scaffolded** Mouse hold Hardware problems Digital citizenship Posture
Academic Applications Problem solving	**Materials Required** Last year's class rules, posters, sample keyboard/mouse if using those	**Standards** CCSS.ELA-Literacy.SL.2.1 NETS: 1a, 1b

Essential Question

How do I use the computer?

Big Idea

Students develop an awareness of computer components, fundamental hardware issues, and basic computer operations

Teacher Preparation

- Have all technology posters on walls.
- Have class digital tools ready to use.
- Integrate domain-specific tech vocabulary into lesson.
- Know if you need extra time to complete this lesson.
- Have a list of class rules that worked in past years. Have a marker to add student suggestions to list.

Assessment Strategies

- Anecdotal observation
- Joined class conversations
- Made decisions that followed class rules
- Completed exit ticket
- Left room as s/he found it
- Higher order thinking: analysis, evaluation, synthesis
- Habits of mind observed

Steps

Time required: 45 minutes in one sitting or spread throughout the week
Class warm-up: None

_____Start by explaining your expectations for student time with you. Discuss the *"21st-century Tech-infused Lesson Plan"* and *"Habits of Mind"* (articles at end of lesson) in 2nd grade terms—that you expect persistence, thoughtful work, independence and more.

_____Discuss student tech goals in terms of blended learning—how tech supports education and life. What are student goals? Help them phrase goals organically, as authentic tasks:

    Not: I want to learn PowerPoint.
    Rather: I want to communicate effectively.

_____Discuss student responsibility to make up missed classes.
_____Show students where you post lessons.

_____Tour classroom. Show students where everything is. Review important posters, i.e., the difference between 'save' and 'save-as' (*Figure 11a*), 'backspace' and 'delete' (*Figure 11b*), portrait and landscape orientation (*Figures 11c and 11d*). Full-size posters are in Appendix.

Figure 11a-d Wall posters

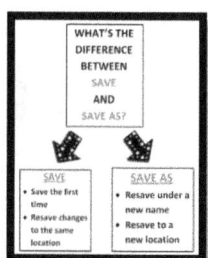

_____Point out the Undo shortkey (*Figure 12a*). More on that later.
_____Point out 'save early save often' (*Figure 12b*). What's this mean? Why is it a good idea?
_____Review 'Select-Do' (*Figure 12c*). What does that mean? (Hint: Select something before you do to it).

Figure 12a-c—More wall posters

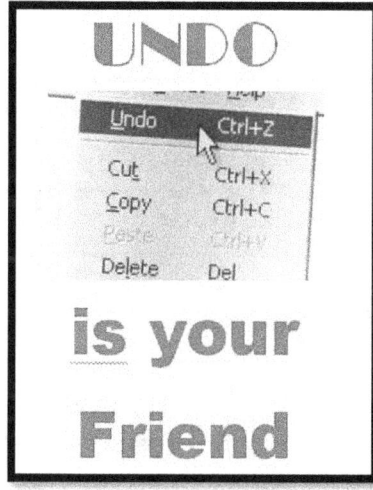

_____Collect rules from students to guide classroom actions, including:

- no excuses; don't blame others; don't blame digital device
- save early, save often—about every ten minutes
- no food or drink around digital devices
- respect the work of others and yourself
- keep hands to yourself. Feel free to help neighbors, but with words only.
- listen politely to classmates
- don't interrupt classmates
- arrive to class prepared for activities
- take turns while speaking

_____You may start with a list like *Figure 13a* from the prior year:

2nd Grade Technology Curriculum: Teacher Manual

Figure 13a—Tech rules; 13b—Digital student

_____Clarify technology in student lives by drawing a silhouette of a student on the class screen and ask students what they use technolgoy for in their lives. As they mention activities, add them to your drawing. It may look like *Figure 13b*.

_____Review posture and position (*Figure 14a* and *Figure 14b*):

Figure 14a—Keyboard posture; 14b—position

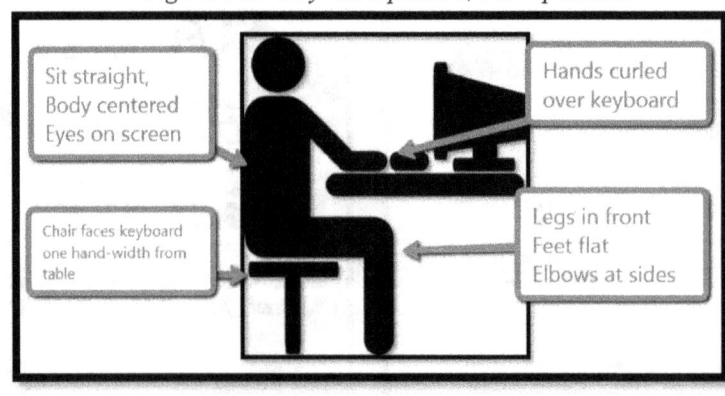

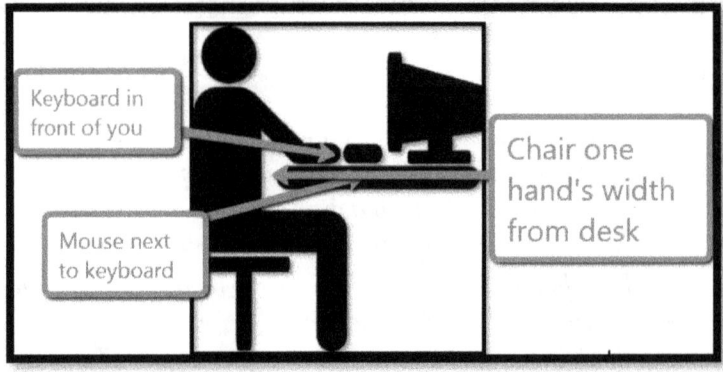

_____Have students check posture of their neighbor. Remind them to sit this way everywhere they use a computer—home, school, the library, everywhere.

32

2nd Grade Technology Curriculum: Teacher Manual

_____Discuss **digital citizenship**. You'll cover it in depth this year and discuss it every time students use the internet. If you want more, see K-8 Digital Citizenship curriculum (from Structured Learning). Remind students any time they visit the internet, do so safely and legally.
_____Open class internet start page on class screen (read *"Which Class Internet Start Page is Best"* article at end of lesson). This is where students find websites to be used during the current week, bundles of themed websites, and more. Do students remember it from last year?

_____With whatever time is left, have students visit these websites:

- *ABCYa's Computer basics*
- *JigZone's Computer puzzle*

_____For more on teaching tech, see article at end of lesson, *"6 Tech Best Practices for New Teachers"*.

Class exit ticket: **Load a poll on class screen where students click their answer to 'How I used tech this summer' as they leave class.**

Differentiation

- We often suggest discussing issues with students. This is part of an inquiry-based classroom. For more on that, check *"10 Ways to be an Inquiry-based Teacher"* at the end of this lesson.
- Embed a calendar of class events (created in Google Calendar or similar) into class website or blog with project due dates and more.
- If this lesson doesn't work for students, use one from *Inquiry-based Teaching with PBL* (from Structured Learning). It has 5 projects aligned with curriculum.

Computing—the art of calculating how much time you wasted and money you spent in a doomed attempt to master a machine with a mind of its own.

Article 1 "21st Century Lesson Plan"

21st Century Lesson Plan

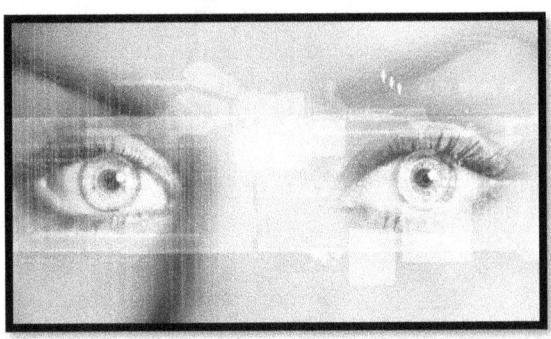

Technology and the connected world put a fork in the old model of teaching—teacher in front of the class, sage on the stage, students madly taking notes, textbooks opened to a particular chapter being reviewed, homework as worksheets based on the text, tests regurgitating important facts. Did I miss anything? This model is outdated **not because it didn't work** (many statistics show students ranked higher on global testing years ago than they do now), **but because the environment changed.** Our classrooms are more diverse. Students are digital natives, already in the habit of learning via technology. The 'college and career' students prepare for is different so education must be different.

Preparing for this new environment requires radical changes in teacher lesson plans. Here are seventeen concepts you'll want to include in your preparation:

1. Students are graduating from high school unable to work in the jobs that are available. It's the teacher's responsibility to insure students **learn over-arching concepts** such as how to speak to a group, how to listen effectively, how to think critically, and how to solve problems. The vehicle for teaching these ideas is history, science, literature, but they aren't the goal.
2. To focus on the over-arching concepts above, make earning **platform-neutral**. For example, when teaching spreadsheets, make the software or online tools a vehicle for practicing critical thinking, data analysis, and evidence-based learning, not for learning one brand of software or a particular spreadsheet tool. Besides, what you use at school may not be what students have at home. You don't want students to conflate your lessons with 'something done at school'. You want them to apply them to their life.
3. **Morph the purpose from 'knowing' to 'understanding'.** Teach the process, not a skill. Students should understand why they select a particular tool, not just how to use it. Why use a slideshow instead of a word processing program? Or a spreadsheet instead of a slideshow? Expect students to be critical thinkers, not passive learners.
4. **Transfer of knowledge is critical.** What students learn in one class is applied to all classes (where relevant). For example, *word study* is no longer about memorizing vocabulary, but knowing how to decode unknown academic and domain-specific words using affixes, roots, and context.
5. **Collaboration and sharing** is part of what students learn. They help each other by reviewing and commenting on projects before submittal to the teacher. The definition of 'project' itself has changed from 'shiny perfect student work' to *review-edit-rewrite-submit*. You grade them on all four steps, not just the last one. This makes a lot of sense—who gets it right the first time? I rewrote this article at least three times before submitting. Why expect differently from students? **Plus:** No longer do students submit a project that only the teacher sees (and then a few are posted on classroom bulletin boards). Now, it is shared with all classmates, so all benefit from every student's work.
6. **Self-help methods** are provided and you expect students to use them. This includes online dictionaries and thesauruses, how-to videos, and access to teacher assistance outside of class. These are available

24/7 for students, not just during classroom hours. This happens via online videos, taped class sessions, the class website, and downloadable materials so students don't worry that they 'left it in their desk'.

7. **Teachers are transparent** with parents. You let them know what's going on in the classroom, welcome their questions and visits, communicate often via email or blogs when it's convenient for them. That doesn't mean you're on duty around the clock. It means you differentiate for the needs of your parents. Your Admin understands that change by providing extended lunch hours, compensatory time off, or subs when you're fulfilling this responsibility.
8. **Failure is a learning tool.** Assessments aren't about 'getting everything right' but about making progress toward the goal of preparing for life
9. **Differentiation is the norm.** You allow different approaches as long as students achieve the Big Idea or answer the Essential Question. You aren't the only one to come up with these varied approaches—students know what works best for their learning and present it to you as an option.
10. The **textbook is a resource**, supplemented by a panoply of books, primary documents, online sites, experts, Skype chats, and anything else that supports the topic. This information doesn't always agree on a conclusion. Students use habits of mind like critical thinking, deep learning, and evidence-based decisions to decide on the right answers.
11. The **lesson plan changes from the first day to the last**—and that's OK. It is adapted to student needs, interests, and hurdles that arise as it unfolds, while staying true to its essential question and big idea.
12. **Assessment** includes a quiz or test, but it also judges the student's transfer of knowledge from other classes, their tenacity in digging into the topic, their participation in classroom discussions, and more.
13. **Vocabulary is integrated into lessons,** not a stand-alone topic. Students are expected to decode words in class materials that they don't understand by using quickly-accessed online vocabulary tools, or deriving meaning from affixes, roots, and context.
14. **Problem solving is integral** to learning, not a stressful event. It's viewed as a life skill. Who doesn't have problems every day that must be solved? Students are expected to attempt a solution using tools at their disposal (such as prior knowledge, classmates, and classroom resources) before asking for help.
15. **Digital citizenship is taught,** modeled and enforced in every lesson, every day, and every classroom. It's no longer something covered in the 'tech lab' because every class has as much potential for working online as offline. Every time the lesson plan calls for an online tool or research using a search engine or a YouTube video, teachers review/remind/teach how to visit the online neighborhood safely. It's frightening how students blithely follow weblinks to places most parents wouldn't allow their child to visit in their neighborhood. Just as students have learned how to survive in a physical community of strangers, they must learn to do the same in a digital neighborhood.
16. **Keyboarding skills are granular.** They aren't used only in the computer lab, but in every class students take. If students are using iPads, Chromebooks, laptops, or desktops for learning, they are using keyboarding—which means they must know how to do so efficiently, quickly, and stresslessly. Since keyboarding benefits all classes, all teachers–including the librarian–become partners in this effort. I go into classrooms and show students the broad strokes; the teacher reinforces it every time the student sits down at the computer.
17. **Play is the new teaching.** It is a well-accepted concept for preschoolers and has made a successful leap to the classroom, relabeled as 'gamification'. Use the power of games to draw students into learning and encourage them to build on their own interests. Popular games in the classroom include Minecraft, Mission US, Scratch, and others on this list. If your school is new to this concept, clear it with admin first and be prepared to support your case.

Article 2 "Habits of Mind vs. Common Core vs. IB"

Habits of Mind vs. Common Core vs. IB

Pedagogic experts have spent an enormous amount of time attempting to unravel the definition of 'educated'. It used to be the 3 R's—reading, writing, and 'rithmetic. The problem with that metric is in the fullness of time, those who excelled in the three areas weren't necessarily the ones who succeeded. As long ago as the early 1900's, Teddy Roosevelt warned:

"C students rule the world."

It's the kids without their nose in a book that notice the world around them, make connections, and learn natively. They excel at activities that aren't the result of a GPA and an Ivy League college. Their motivation is often failure, and taking the wrong path again and again. As Thomas Edison said:

"I have not failed. I've just found 10,000 ways that won't work."

Microsoft founder, Bill Gates, and Albert Einstein are poster children for that approach. Both became change agents in their fields despite following a non-traditional path.

In the face of mounting evidence, education experts accepted a prescriptive fact: student success is not measured by milestones like 'took a foreign language in fifth grade' or 'passed Algebra in high school' but by how s/he thinks. One curated list of cerebral skills that has become an education buzz word is Arthur L. Costa and Bena Kallick's list of sixteen what they call Habits of Mind (Copyright ©2000):

1. *Persisting*
2. *Managing impulsivity*
3. *Taking Responsible Risks*
4. *Thinking Flexibly*
5. *Thinking about Thinking*
6. *Striving for Accuracy*
7. *Questioning and Posing Problems*
8. *Finding Humor*
9. *Thinking Interdependently*
10. *Applying Past Knowledge to New Situations*
11. *Think and Communicate with Clarity, Precision*
12. *Listening with Understanding and Empathy*
13. *Gathering Data through All Senses*
14. *Creating, Imagining, Innovating*
15. *Responding with Wonderment and Awe*
16. *Remaining Open to Continuous Learning*

Together, these promote strategic reasoning, insightfulness, perseverance, creativity and craftsmanship.

But they're not new. They share the same goals with at least three other widely-used education systems: 1) Common Core (as close as America gets to national standards), 2) the International Baccalaureate (IB) program (a well-regarded international curriculum, much more popular outside the

US than within), and 3) good ol' common sense. Below, I've listed each Habit of Mind with a brief explanation of what that means (in italics). I then point out connections to Common Core, the IB Program, and the common sense your grandma shared with you. The result is a compelling argument that education is less a data download and more a fitness program for our brains.

Persisting

Stick with a problem, even when it seems hopeless.

Winston Churchill said, "Never, never, in nothing great or small, large or petty, never give in..." The same decade, Albert Einstein said:

"It's not that I'm so smart, it's just that I stay with problems longer."

The Common Core is not a curriculum, rather a collection of forty-one overarching Standards in reading, writing, language, math, and speaking/listening that shape a student's quest for college and career. Sprinkled throughout are fundamental traits that go beyond the 3R's and delve deeply into the ability of a student to think. The math standards require students learn to 'persevere in solving problems'.

The IB Program has twelve attitudes that are fundamental to every learner: *appreciation, empathy, commitment, enthusiasm, confidence, independence, cooperation, integrity, creativity, respect, curiosity, and tolerance.* Students exhibiting the attitude of commitment persist in their own learning, persevere no matter the difficulties.

Managing Impulsivity

Consider options. Think before speaking.

Among his endless words of wisdom, Benjamin Franklin said:

"It is easier to suppress the first desire than to satisfy all that follow it."

Common Core Standards tell us to 'Use appropriate tools strategically'.

Besides the twelve attitudes listed above, the IB Program names ten traits that profile a learner: *inquirer, knowledgeable, thinker, communicator, principle, open-minded, caring, a risk-taker, balanced, and reflective.* Students who are reflective give thoughtful consideration before acting.

For the rest of the article, visit Ask a Tech Teacher.

Article 3 "Which Class Internet Start Page is Best"

Which Class Internet Start Page is Best?

The internet is unavoidable in education. Students go there to research, access homework, check grades, and a whole lot more. As a teacher, you do your best to make it a friendly, intuitive, and safe place to visit, but it's challenging. Students arrive there by iPads, smartphones, links from classroom teachers, suggestions from friends—the routes are endless. The best way to keep the internet experience safe is to catch users right at the front door, on that first click.

How do you do that? By creating a **class internet start page**. Clicking the internet icon opens the World Wide Web to a default page. Never take your device's default because there's no guarantee it's G-rated enough for a typical classroom environment. Through the 'settings' function on your browser, enter the address of a page you've designed as a portal to all school internet activity, called an 'internet start page'. Sure, this takes some time to set-up and maintain, but it saves more than that in student frustration, lesson prep time, and the angst parents feel about their children entering the virtual world by themselves. They aren't. You're there, through this page. Parents can save the link to their home digital device and let students access any resources on it, with the confidence of knowing you've curated everything.

In searching for the perfect internet start page, I wanted one that:

- *quickly differentiates for different grades*
- *is intuitive for even the youngest to find their page*
- *is customizable across tabbed pages to satisfy changing needs*
- *presents a visual and playful interface to make students want to go there rather than find work-arounds (a favorite hobby of older students)*
- *includes an immediately visible calendar of events*
- *hosts videos of class events*
- *provides collaborative walls like Padlet*
- *includes other interactive widgets to excite students about technology*

Here are four I looked at:

Symbaloo

A logo-based website curation tool with surprising flexibility in how links are collected and displayed. It's hugely popular with educators because collections are highly-visual and easy to access and use. Plus, Symbaloo collections made by one teacher can be shared with the community, making link collections that much easier to curate.

The downside: Links are about all you can collect on Symbaloo.

Only2Clicks

Great for youngers with their big bold buttons, colorful interface.
The downside: Too often, I have technical glitches as I try to set up collections. Maybe it's just me. Another downside: Like Symbaloo, Only2Clicks is focused mostly on link curation. If I want to add widgets, I have to select from their list. With kids, no matter how comprehensive the list, it misses the one I really really need.

Ustart

Offers a good collection of useful webtools for students including links, news, calendar, notes, even weather. It provides tabs for arranging themed collections (like classes) and is intuitive to set up and use. It even includes options for embeddable widgets like Padlet. This is the closest to what I needed of all three.

Overall: This is a good alternative to the one I selected.

Protopage

Protopage did everything on my list. It's flexible, customizable, intuitive, and quick to use with a scalable interface that can be adjusted to my needs (2-5 columns, resize boxes, drag widgets between tabs—that sort). I set up a separate tab for each grade (or you can set up tabs for subjects). The amount of tabs is limited only by space on the top toolbar. Resources included on each tab can be curated exactly as you need. Mine includes:

- *oft-used websites*
- *themed collections of websites*
- *a To Do list*
- *an interactive map*
- *a calculator*
- *a calendar of events*
- *edit-in-place sticky notes*
- *pictures of interest*
- *rss feeds of interest*
- *weather*
- *news*
- *widget for polling the class (Padlet)*

In addition, the Protopage folks are helpful. Whenever I have a problem (which is rare), they fix it quickly.

Article 4 "6 Tech Best Practices for New Teachers"

6 Tech Best Practices for New Teachers

A study released last year by the National Council on Teacher Quality found that nearly half of the nation's teacher training programs failed to insure that their candidates were STEM-capable. That means new teachers must learn how to teach science, technology, engineering and math on-the-job. Knowing that, there are six Best Practices teachers in the trenches suggest for integrating technology into classroom instruction:

Digital Citizenship

Many schools now provide digital devices for students, often a Chromebook or an iPad. Both are great devices, but represent a sea change from the Macs and PCs that have traditionally been the device-of-choice in education. While I could spend this entire article on that topic, one seminal difference stands out: Where PCs and Macs could be used as a closed system via software, materials saved to the local drive, and native tools, Chromebooks and iPads access the internet for everything (with a few exceptions) be it learning, publishing, sharing, collaborating, or grading. There's no longer an option to hide students from the online world, what is considered by many parents a dangerous place their children should avoid. In cyberspace, students are confronted often—if not daily—with questions regarding cyberbullying, digital privacy, digital footprints, plagiarism, and more.

The question is: **Who's teaching students how to thrive in this brave new world?** Before you move on to the next paragraph, think about that in your circumstance. Can you point to the person responsible for turning your students into good digital citizens? When second grade students use the internet to research a topic, do they know how to do that safely and legally?

When asked, most educators shrug and point at someone else. But it turns out too often, no one is tasked with providing that knowledge.

The answer to *who's responsible*: Everyone's responsible, starting with you, the New Teacher. Adopt this topic as your own, blend it into your teaching. Don't assume students know until they provide evidence of that.

Problem Solving

Lots of new teachers are intimidated by technology in their classrooms. Besides so many digital tools—how does anyone stay up to date on them—there's a worse problem: What happens when something doesn't work? Waiting for the school's IT folks can quickly derail a tech-infused lesson.

New teachers need to learn rudimentary tech troubleshooting like these 25 common problems, and then teach them to students. It shouldn't be a stand-alone lesson, rather teach it organically as it arises in class. When a student's headphones don't work, figure out how to solve it as a class. When a website freezes, show how to unfreeze and then move on with the lesson. Once a problem is solved, ask students to retain that knowledge, transfer it to other classes, and teach their friends. Surprisingly quickly, students will no longer be slowed down by tech problems. Sure, they'll happen, but everyone will know the solution.

Keyboarding

PARCC and SBAC may have convinced many educators that keyboarding is a critical, granular skill, but it can't be taught by a once-a-week tech lab session of 10-15 minutes. Think how often keyboarding is part of student work—entering website addresses, adding comments to blogs, typing docs, and taking online assessments. All of these require keyboarding skills, yet no one is responsible for teaching them.

Students who can keyboard well blossom. Those who can't—well, you know. Teaching keyboarding requires two steps: 1) an overarching curriculum map of what to teach when, and 2) reinforcement every time students sit at the computer. No matter the class, that teacher—be s/he history, literacy, social studies, math, reading, writing, or tech—reminds students of the right way to keyboard. It adds minutes to her teaching and saves students hours as practice and skill eventually (by about 4th grade) allows their typing fingers to keep pace with their thinking brain.

As the New Teacher, set the example. Blend keyboarding training into your lesson plans.

Vocabulary

An important part of succeeding in core classes is understanding the language. Common Core has three levels of vocabulary:

- *basic*
- *academic*
- *domain-specific*

Current best practices embrace students **learning by using**. This isn't accomplished with memorized word lists. Instead, when students uncover unknown words, they decode them and then use them throughout the lesson. This is accomplished by addressing basic and academic vocabulary across all subjects, whether students are in history, science, math, or reading. Every digital device should be preloaded with instantly-available age-appropriate dictionaries that allow students to quickly research a word almost without leaving the academic topic.

Tenacity

Try, fail, try again. A lot of learning is accomplished by failure. Make this a strategy in the classroom. No longer have students submit a final project and get a grade. Instead, recognize Common Core's plan-revise-edit-rewrite as a flexible learning path that is both practical and transformative. This isn't just for writing, though. Use it for all projects—a science poster, a history magazine, and math homework. Always give students the opportunity to edit and resubmit work that's granular to their learning.

Student Choice

You teach the Big Idea; let students pick how they share their learning. You make an effort to teach using as many of the multiple intelligences as possible—audio, visual, tactile, kinesthetic, logical, or linguistic. Let students pick which approach best serves them in conveying what they've learned. They might write a report, share a movie, add music and color, draw a picture, or build an infographic. Introduce this wide variety of options early in the school year and make them available for as many assessments as possible.

These six topics integrate technology—a tool students want to use—into everything, making your teaching authentic, scalable, motivating, and rigorous.

Article 5 "10 Ways to be an Inquiry-based Teacher"

10 Ways to be an Inquiry-based Teacher

It's hard to run an inquiry-based classroom. Don't go into this teaching style thinking all you do is ask questions and observe answers. You have to listen with all of your senses, pause and respond to what you heard (not what you wanted to hear), keep your eye on the Big Ideas as you facilitate learning, value everyone's contribution, be aware of the energy of the class and step in when needed, step aside when required. You aren't a Teacher, rather a guide. You and the class move from question to knowledge together.

Because everyone learns differently.

Where your teacher credential classes taught you to use a textbook, now it's one of many resources. Sure, it nicely organizes knowledge week-by-week, but in an inquiry-based classroom, you may know where you're going, but not quite how you'll get there—and that's a good thing. You are no longer your mother's teacher who stood in front of rows of students and pointed to the blackboard. You operate well outside your teaching comfort zone as you try out a flipped classroom and the gamification of education and are thrilled with the results.

And then there's the issue of assessment. What students accomplish can no longer neatly be summed up by a multiple choice test. When you review what you thought would assess learning (back when you designed the unit), none measure the organic conversations the class had about deep subjects, the risk-taking they engaged in to arrive at answers, the authentic knowledge transfer that popped up independently of your class time. You realize you must open your mind to learning that occurred that you never taught—never saw coming in the weeks you stood amongst your students guiding their education.

Let me digress. I visited the Soviet Union (back when it was one nation) and dropped in on a classroom where students were inculcated with how things must be done. It was a polite, respectful, ordered experience, but without cerebral energy, replete of enthusiasm for the joy of learning, and lacking the wow factor of students independently figuring out how to do something. Seeing the end of that powerful nation, I arrived at different conclusions than the politicians and the economists. I saw a nation starved to death for creativity. Without that ethereal trait, learning didn't transfer. Without transfer, life required increasingly more scaffolding and prompting until it collapsed in on itself like a hollowed out orange.

So how do you create the inquiry-based classroom? Here's advice from a few of my efriend teachers:

1. *ask open-ended questions and be open-minded about conclusions*
2. *provide hands-on experiences*
3. *use groups to foster learning*
4. *encourage self-paced learning. Be open to the student who learns less but deeper as much as the student who learns a wider breadth*
5. *differentiate instruction. Everyone learns in their own way*
6. *look for evidence of learning in unusual places. It may be from the child with his/her hand up, but it may also be from the learner who teaches mom how to use email*
7. *understand 'assessment' comes in many shapes. It may be a summative quiz, a formative simulation, a rubric, or a game that requires knowledge to succeed. It may be anecdotal or peer-to-peer. Whatever approach shows students are transferring knowledge from your classroom to life is a legitimate assessment*
8. *be flexible. Class won't always (probably never) go as your mind's eye saw it. That's OK. Learn with students. Observe their progress and adapt to their path.*
9. *give up the idea that teaching requires control. Refer to #8—Be flexible*
10. *facilitate student learning in a way that works for them. Trust that they will come up with the questions required to reach the Big Ideas*

In the end, know that inquiry-based teaching is not about learning for the moment. You're creating life-long learners, the individuals who will solve the world's problems in ten years. Your job is to ensure they are ready.

Lesson #2 Digital Tools in the Classroom

Vocabulary	Problem solving	Skills
• Annotation • Decode • Desktop • Digital tool • Flying windows • Font • Icons • iPad • Menus • Network • Right click • Start button • Taskbar • Toolbar	• Monitor doesn't work (check power) • Shift doesn't work (Check caps lock) • Can't find drawing program (use 'search' on Start button) • What color do I use to annotate? • How do I print (Ctrl+P) • Taskbar's gone (push flying windows) • I use Caps Lock to capitalize a letter (for one letter: Use Shift) • Why can't I touch neighbor's mouse? (help—with your words) • Where's class internet start page (where was it last year?) • There are too many digital tools	**New** Log-ins Class website Annotation tools **Scaffolded** Digital citizenship Digital tools Digital portfolio Annotate workbooks (if using student workbooks)
Academic Applications General, digital citizenship, digital literacy	**Materials Required** Internet, digital devices, drawing program, keyboarding software, student workbooks (if using)	**Standards** CCSS Student Portrait NETS: 1b, 4b

Essential Question

How does technology make learning easier and more authentic?

Big Idea

Students develop an awareness of the digital tools that contribute to education

Teacher Preparation

- Have class digital tools ready to use.
- Know student log-ins for digital tools that require one.
- Talk with grade-level team so you tie into conversations.
- Integrate domain-specific tech vocabulary into lesson.
- Know which tasks weren't completed last week.
- Know whether you need extra time to complete this lesson with your student group.

Assessment Strategies

- Followed directions
- Anecdotal observation
- Able to annotate workbook (if using workbooks)
- Completed exit ticket
- Joined class conversations
- Made decisions that followed class rules
- Left room as s/he found it
- Higher order thinking: analysis, evaluation, synthesis
- Habits of mind observed

Steps

Time required: 45 minutes in one sitting or spread throughout the week
Class warm-up: None

_____Review hardware (adapt this to your particular digital device):

- *mouse buttons—left and right, double click, scroll; how to hold mouse*

- *CPU—power button, disk drives, connections*
- *monitor—power button, screen*
- *headphones—volume, port*
- *keyboard—separate or built-in*
- *peripherals—what are those?*

_____Find the parts listed in *Figure 15a* on your school's devices or *Figure 15b* for iPads (See *Assessment 1* and *2* at end of lesson). For example, where are 'headphones'? Or mouse? USB Port? The microphone? And the charging dock on a desktop computer? What are the smartphone parts (see *Assessment 3* at end of lesson)?

Figure 15a—Parts of computer; 15b—Parts of iPad

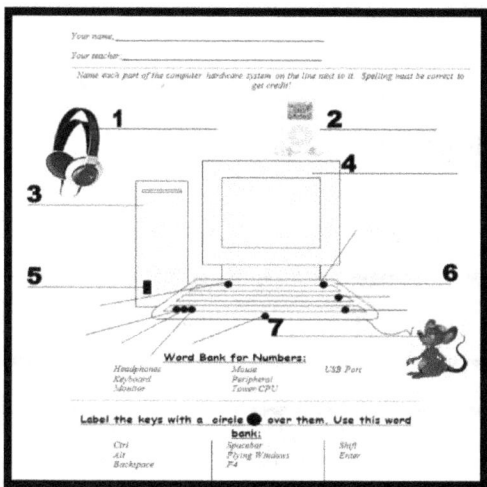 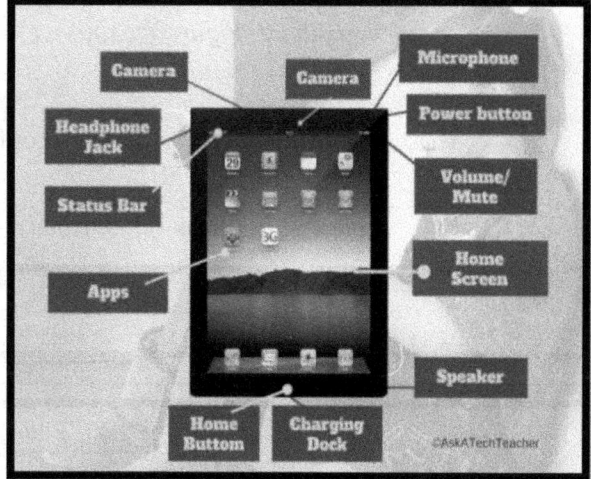

_____Have students review mouse hold with a neighbor (see *Figure 16*).

Figure 16—Mouse hand position

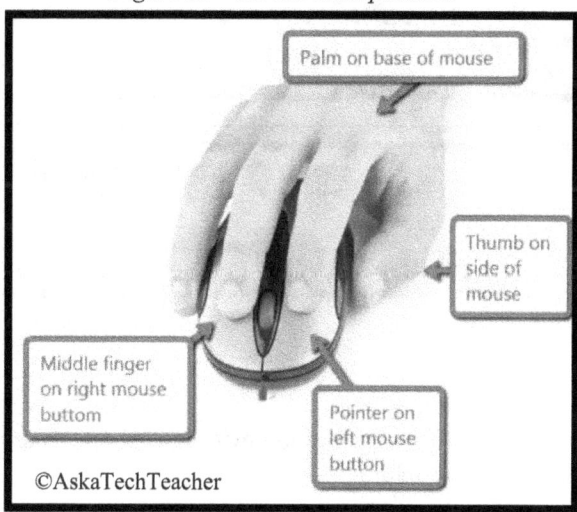

_____If using student workbooks, have students annotate their copy of the hardware parts (*Assessment 1, 2* or *3*) with a tool like Notability, iAnnotate, Notable, or Adobe Acrobat. More on this digital tool later in the lesson.

_____Review how parts connect—behind CPU, under table, in ports, or built in. Adapt to student digital device at school and home whether a laptop, Chromebook, iPad, or desktop.
_____Discuss the proper care of a digital device. What rules would students add to the following list?

- *no food or drink around computer—not even water*
- *no banging on keyboard, monitor or any other part of computer*
- *demonstrate how to help a neighbor: Use words, don't touch their computer parts*

_____Discuss the difference between:

- *menus (Figure 17a)*
- *ribbons (Figure 17b)*
- *toolbars (Figure 17b and 17c)*
- *taskbar (Figure 17d)*

_____These organizational techniques are confusing. Circle back on them often.

Figure 17a—Menu bar; 17b and c—Toolbar; 17b—Ribbon; 17d—Taskbar

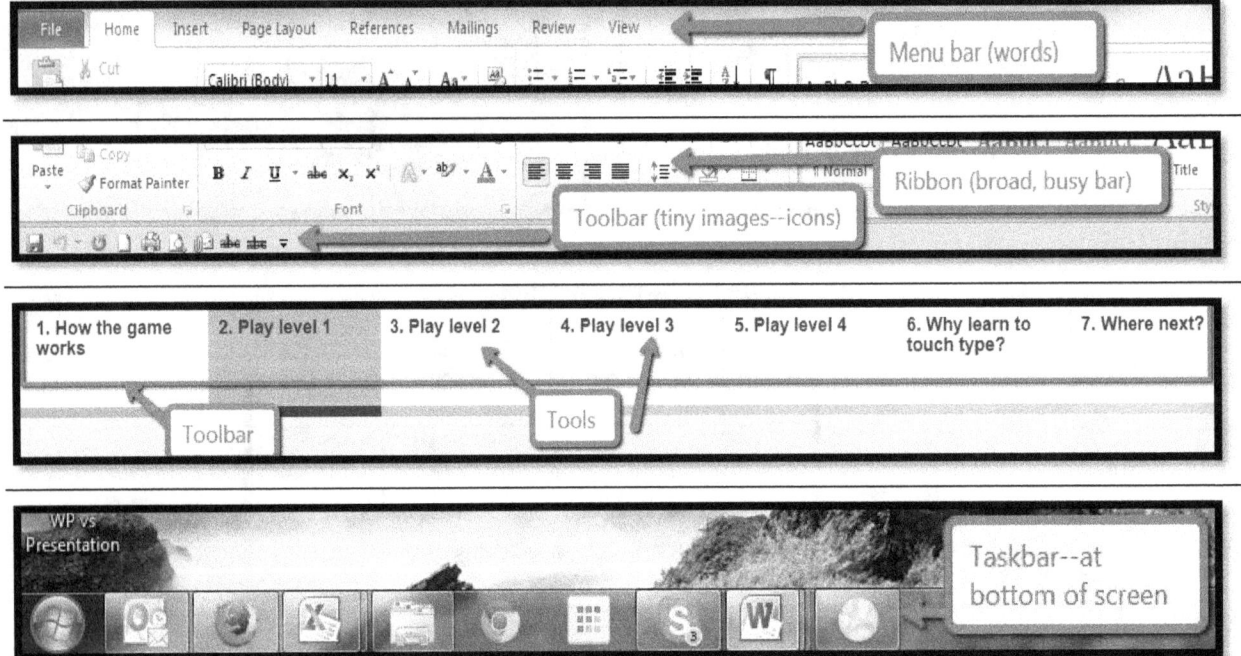

Log-ins

_____Review how students log into digital devices using user names and passwords.
_____Required log-ins may include:

- *class etextbooks*
- *keyboarding program*
- *class website (with grades)*
- *class math and/or reading program*
- *online webtools*

2nd Grade Technology Curriculum: Teacher Manual

_____Have a method for tracking log-ins. It might be as simple as a 3x5 card (*Figure 18*):

- *Keep a physical copy by the student's seat or in their personal binder.*
- *Keep a digital copy in the student's digital portfolio.*
- *Take a snapshot to keep on their digital device for quick reference.*

Figure 18—Curation of log-ins

User Name/Passwords		
PROGRAM	**UN**	**PASSWORD**
Keyboarding Program		
Math Program		
Computer		
Class wiki		
Add'l		

_____Have students log into school digital portfolios—website, class pages, other.

Desktop

_____Review the screen that greets students when they sign onto their digital device. For example, *Figure 19* is a Windows desktop and *Figure 20* is for a Chromebook:

- clock
- icons
- recycle bin
- screen
- start button
- taskbar
- tasks

48

Figure 19—Desktop

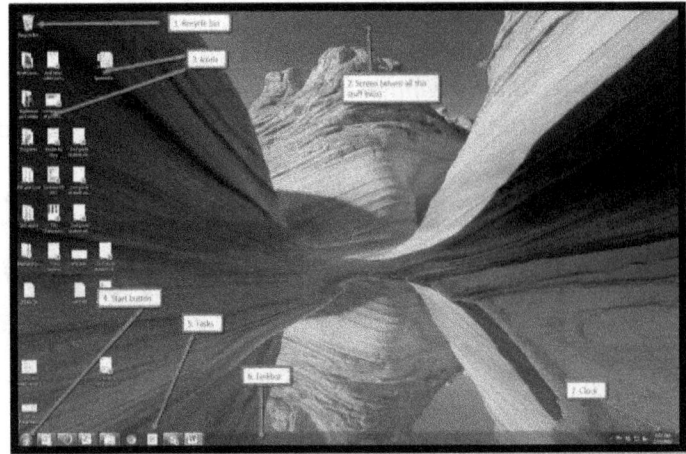

_____Where are these Windows desktop parts on a Chromebook screen (*Figure 20*):

Figure 20—Chromebook desktop

Class Digital Tools

Student workbooks

_____If using student workbooks that go along with this curriculum, introduce them now. Show how to open them, find rubrics and project samples, and take notes using the annotation tool. Students can circle back to review concepts or forward to preview upcoming lessons.

Annotation Tool

_____If you're using student workbooks, show how to annotate with a tool such as iAnnotate (*Figure 21a*), Notability (*Figure 21b*), Notable for Chromebooks, Adobe Acrobat (*Figure 21c*)) or another tool available in your school.
_____If students are sharing a PDF (for example, it's loaded on a computer that multiple classes visit), show how to select a personal color that's different from other students.

_____Review options available in the annotation tool you use, such as:

- *highlighting*
- *text*
- *note*
- *freeform*

Figure 21a—PDF annotation with iAnnotate; 21b—Notability; 21c—Acrobat

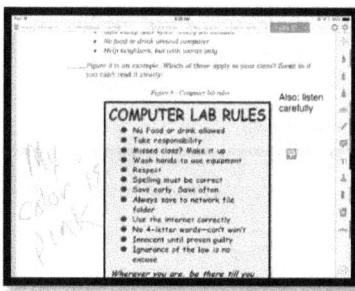 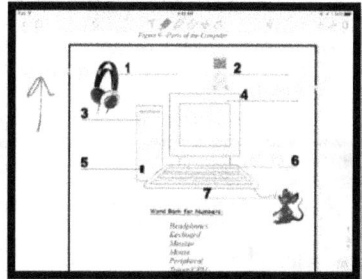 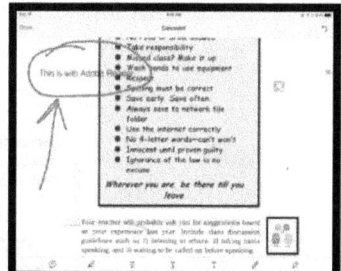

Student digital portfolios

_____Discuss how students use digital portfolios (also known as digital lockers or digital binders):

- *store work (in Cloud) required in other classes or at home*
- *interact, collaborate, and publish with peers, experts, or others*
- *contribute to project teams*
- *edit or review work in multiple locations*
- *submit class assignments*

_____There are a variety of digital portfolios that satisfy some or all of the above: 1) folders on school network, 2) fee-based programs, 3) cloud-based storage like Dropbox, 4) online collaborative sites like Google Classroom, or 5) an LMS like Otus (Google for addresses if interested).
_____Have students practice by uploading something to their digital portfolio.

Class Calendar

_____Demonstrate how to access and edit (if they are permitted to do this) class calendar that tracks due dates, class events, and other important information.

Figure 22a—Class calendar 22b—Padlet; 22c—DTP

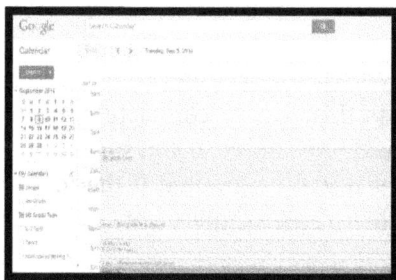  

2nd Grade Technology Curriculum: Teacher Manual

_____Try Google Calendar, Office 365, a Padlet calendar template (*Figure 22b*), or another option (i.e., Publisher shown in *Figure 22c*). If possible, embed it into class website.

_____Assign a student each month to be responsible for adding events to the class calendar.

Class Internet Start Page

_____An internet start page is a website that comes up when students open the internet. It organizes critical content into a single location and curates links students will use on a weekly basis.

_____Include what students visit daily (i.e., guidelines, calendar, 'to do' list, typing websites, research locations, sponge sites, calculator) as well as info specific to current project.

_____*Figure 23* is an example using Protopage.com.

Figure 23—Internet start page

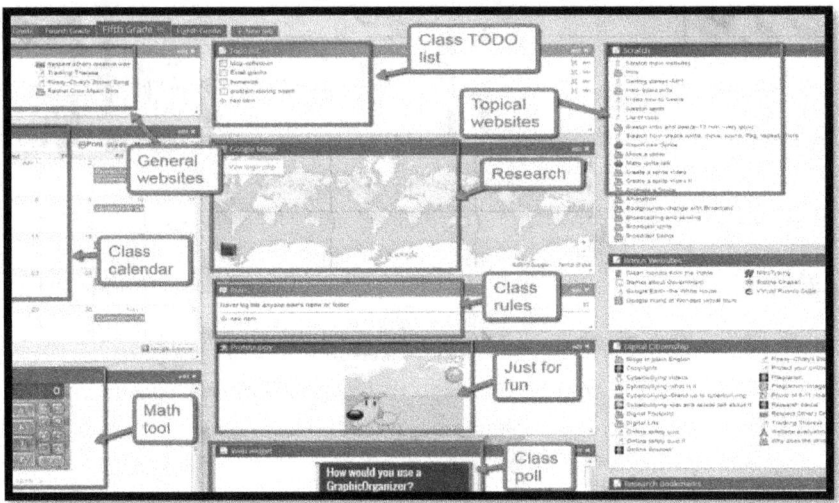

Class website

_____Available with Google Apps for Education, these websites encourage reflection, organization, logical thinking, and embedding of sharable projects i.e., Tagxedos and Animotos. If your school doesn't have Google Apps, free websites can be created at Weebly, Wix, or a blog account like WordPress (Google for addresses).

Google Apps (or Office 365)

_____Show students how to access their student account, use the storage drive, and share documents with others. Demonstrate similarity between Google Docs/Sheets/Presentation and Office.

Class Webtools

_____Discuss the wide variety of digital tools students will use this year to complete projects. Let students know that you are open to alternative suggestions. For example, if you suggest Wordle, a student can request Tagxedo. Approval is required, but it will be granted if the tool fulfills project needs. Expect students to use evidence to build their case, compare-contrast their tool to your suggestion, and draw logical conclusions.

_____*Figures 24a-d* are examples of webtools you might use with your students. These may include:

- online math program (i.e., Khan Academy)
- digital keyboarding program (i.e., Type to Learn, Typing Web)
- an avatar creator for digital citizenship
- a badge to assess progress
- RAZ Kids for close reading

Figure 24a—Avatar; 24b—DTP badge; 24c—digital storytelling; 24d—RAZ Kids

_____If any class requires a log in, have students test their log-in.

Vocabulary Decoding Tools

_____Show students how to access the native apps or webtools available on their digital devices used to decode vocabulary. Depending upon the device, these will be on the homepage, the browser toolbar, a shortkey, or a right click. Show students how to quickly look up words rather than skipping over content that includes the word. Let them practice with several words in this lesson's *Vocabulary* list.

_____Options for dictionary tools include:

- *Kids Wordsmyth*
- *Merriam-Webster for Kids*
- *right click on word in MS Word and select 'Look up'.*
- *right click in Google Apps (i.e., Google Docs) and select 'research'.*

_____Have students attempt to access all school digital tools.

Class exit ticket: **Have students vote in a poll for which tool they'll use the most this year.**

Differentiation

- Take a field trip to the server room--track cables from class to the switches and modem.
- Visit grade level classroom and explain how digital devices are the same there as in tech lab—on a smaller scale (see directions at end of lesson, "Take Tech to Classroom").
- Those who finish: Go to class internet start page and visit websites that tie into class conversations. If necessary, go over how to access this link with class.
- Replace with one from Inquiry-based Teaching with PBL (from Structured Learning).

Assessment 1—Hardware Quiz

HARDWARE—PARTS OF THE COMPUTER

Name each part of computer Draw your own lines for key names. Spelling must be correct to get credit

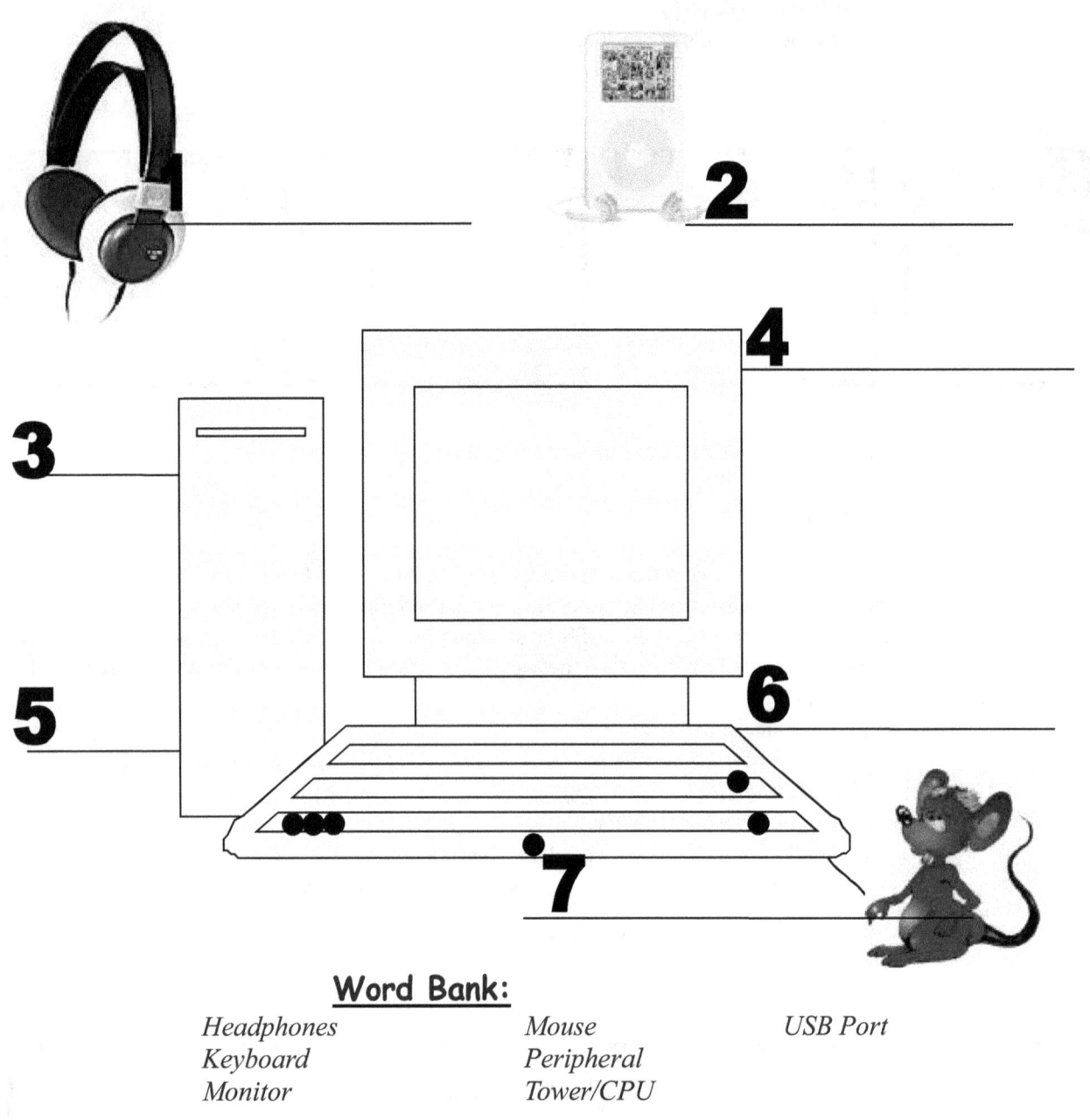

Word Bank:

Headphones	Mouse	USB Port
Keyboard	Peripheral	
Monitor	Tower/CPU	

Label the keys with a circle ● over them. Use this word bank:

Ctrl	Spacebar	Shift
Alt	Flying Windows	Enter
Backspace	F4	

53

2nd Grade Technology Curriculum: Teacher Manual

Assessment 2—Parts of an iPad

Parts of an iPad

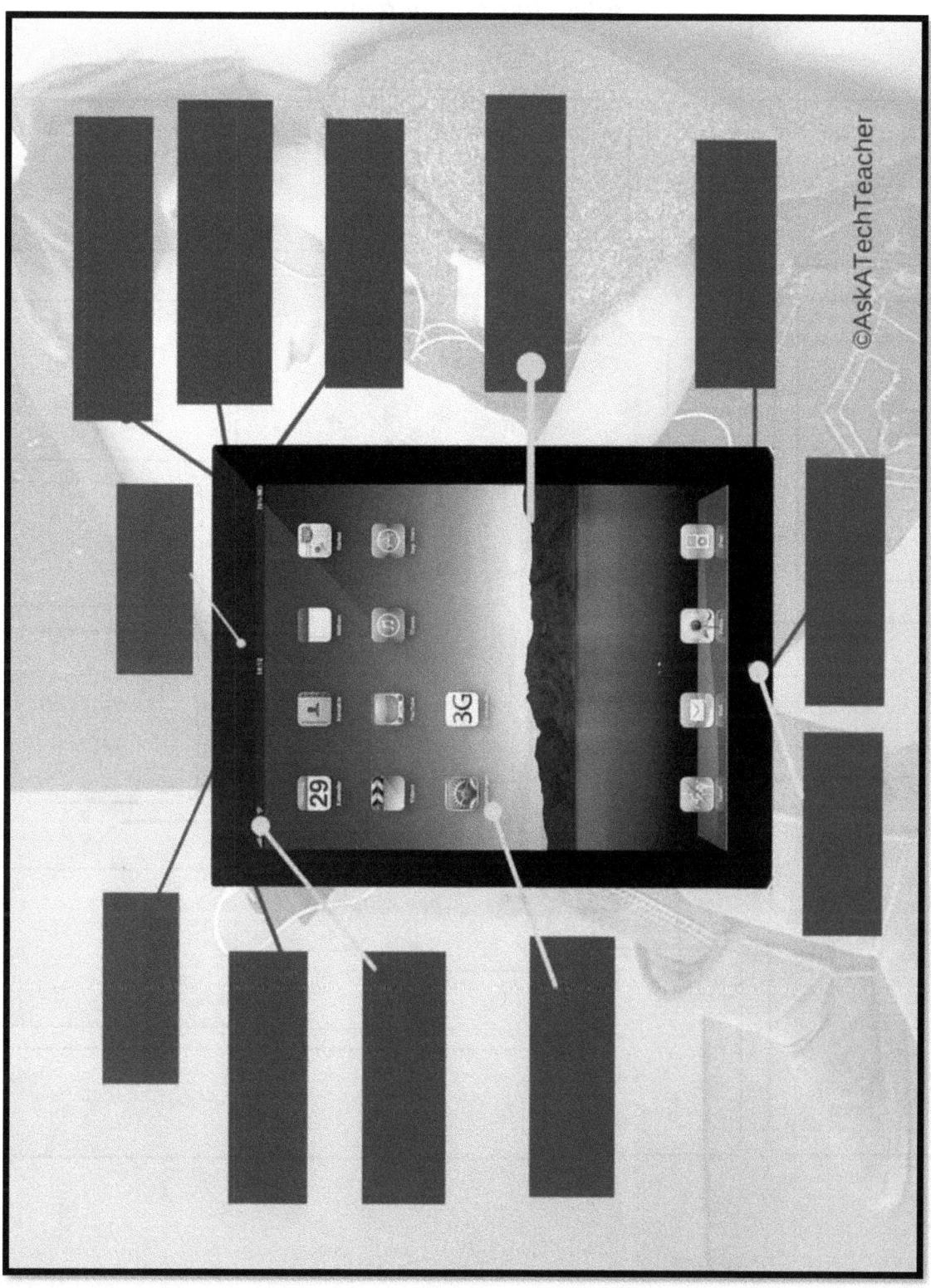

2nd Grade Technology Curriculum: Teacher Manual

Assessment 3—Parts of a Smartphone

PARTS OF THE SMARTPHONE
Adapt this to your needs

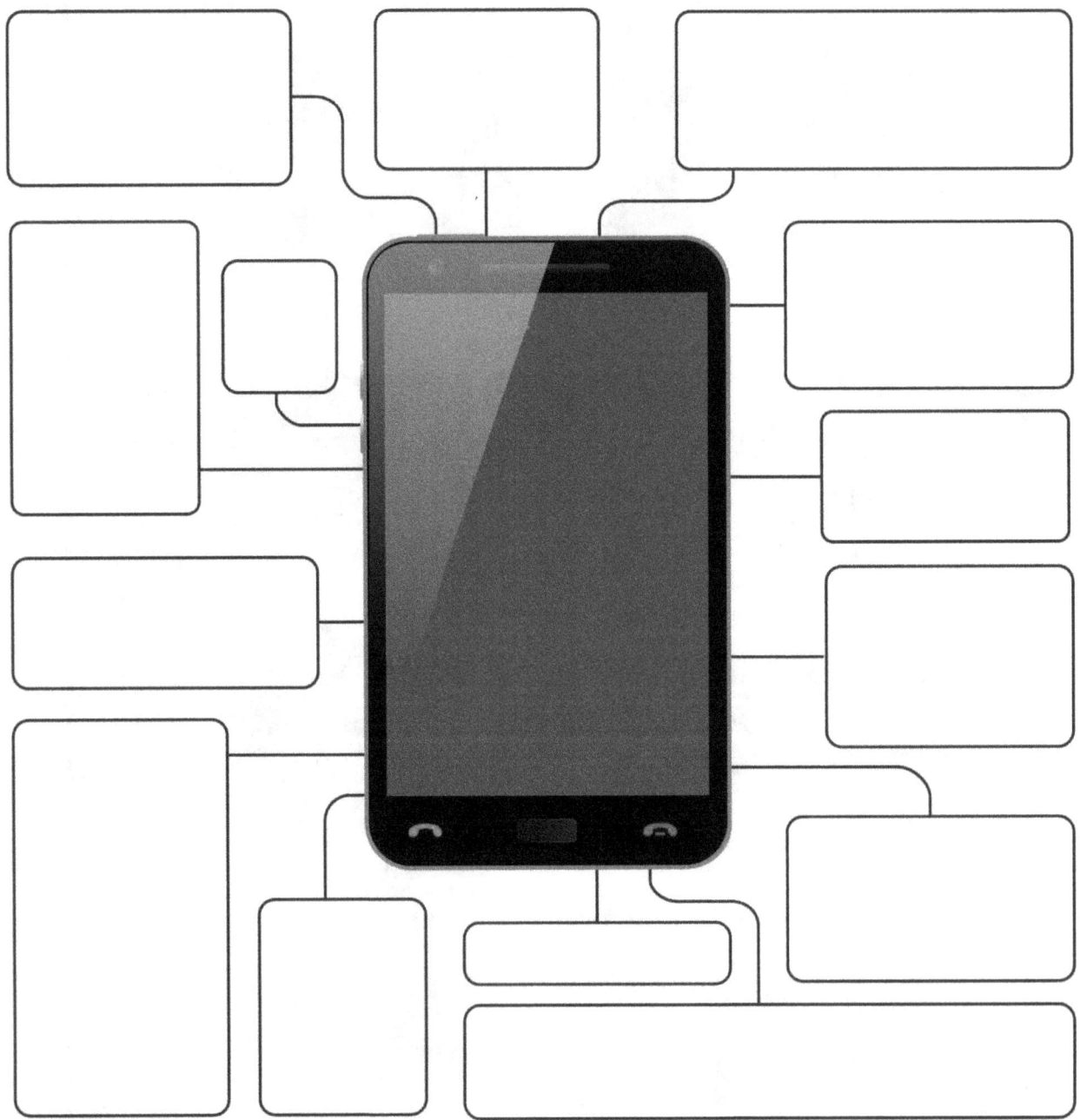

Article 6 "Do you make these 9 mistakes?"

Do You Make These 9 Mistakes?

...with your students/child's technology education?

- Show how to do something rather than allowing her/him to discover
- Do for them rather than let them do it
- Say 'no' too often (or the other enthusiasm-killer, Don't touch!)
- Don't take them seriously
- Take technology too seriously. It's a tool, meant to make life easier. Nothing more.
- Underestimate their abilities
- Over-estimate their abilities
- Give up too quickly
- Think there's only one way to do stuff on the computer

I promise—none of these are necessary to thrive in technology. Children walk in the classroom loving learning. They can't break most computer parts. They *want* to try things out and do it themselves.

Let them. They may discover a Better Mousetrap.

After fifteen years, I still learn from my students. Children are serious about having fun. It's one of their jobs. Technology is how they do this. Feel free to join them. You'll be surprised how much they know.

But, sometimes, they need help. Offer it with a guiding hand.

2nd Grade Technology Curriculum: Teacher Manual

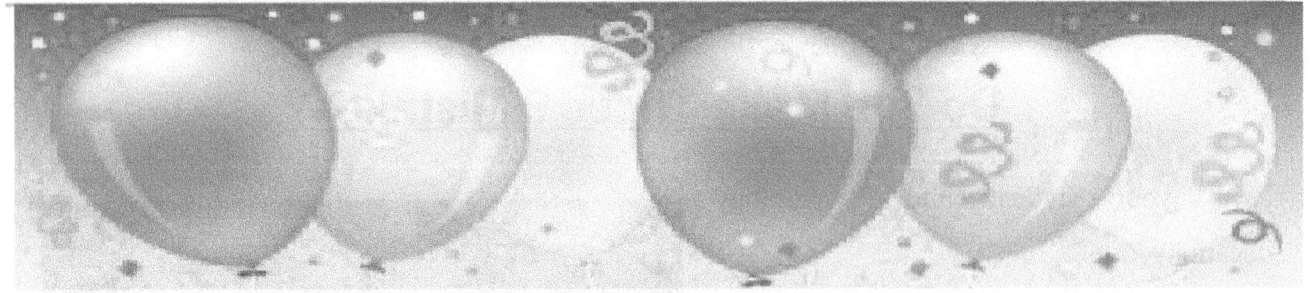

Take Tech into the Classroom

When the classroom teachers feels students are settled into the class routine enough to get started on the class pod of computers, make time to join them for center time and transfer tech class knowledge to the class.

Before going:
- Make sure the class computers work
    - *CPU*
    - *headphones*
- Make sure class computers have all links required for class work. What are the teacher's favorites?
    - *The school website*
    - *Tech lab class internet start page*
    - *Typing practice program*
    - *Starfall*
    - *A math program*
- Make sure they are set up the same as the tech lab (or know where the differences are so you can explain to students

During your visit, go over these with students:
- Same rules that apply in the tech class apply in the classroom (add your rules)
    - *No food or drink by computers*
    - *No fooling around*
    - *No grabbing neighbor's equipment*
    - *No internet except on approved sites*
    - *Try to solve problems before asking for help (especially important because you as tech teacher won't be there to help)*
    - *Read the screen before asking for help*
    - *Leave the station the way you found it*
    - *Print only with permission*
- Practice good habits every time you sit at computer
- Take questions

Lesson #3 Internet and Digital Citizenship

Vocabulary	Problem solving	Skills
• Address • Back button • Bling • Dialogue box • Digital Citizenship • Digital Neighborhood • Tabbed browsing • Toggle	• I can't exit program (Alt+F4) • Screen froze (Is dialogue box open?) • Doc disappeared (check taskbar) • Got off website (use back arrow or Start Page tab on browser) • 'Back' doesn't work (it's at beginning) • It takes a lot of time to follow these rules (it becomes habit)	**New** Plagiarism Digital footprint Fair use, Public domain Image copyrights **Scaffolded** Digital citizenship
Academic Applications Any time students go online	**Materials Required** Internet, keyboarding tool, digital citizenship links, student workbooks (if using)	**Standards** CCSS. ELA-Literacy.CCRA.SL NETS: 1d, 2b, 3a

Essential Question
How do I use the internet so it is as safe as possible?

Big Idea
The internet can be a safe neighborhood if used correctly

Teacher Preparation
- Talk with grade-level team so you tie into conversations.
- Know which tasks weren't completed last week.
- Integrate domain-specific tech vocabulary into lesson.
- Know if you need extra time to complete this lesson.

Assessment Strategies
- Shared evidence of learning
- Completed warm-up, exit ticket
- Joined class conversations
- Decisions followed class rules
- Left room as s/he found it
- Higher order thinking: analysis, evaluation, synthesis
- Habits of mind observed

Steps

Time required: 45 minutes in one sitting or spread throughout the week

Class warm-up: Students visit a website safely (i.e., avoiding ads, staying on assigned link, and as a good digital citizen)

_____Observe students visiting a website and take note of what digital citizenship issues need reinforcing.

_____Three topics will be discussed in this lesson. Cover all of them, but you may break them up among several lessons rather than all at once—especially if you're a grade-level teacher. Mix these in where most relevant with your inquiry:

- *internet*
- *the digital neighborhood*
- *digital citizenship*

Internet

_____ Explain the **meaning of 'Internet'**. Is it *Figure 25* (chaos) or *27b* (an orderly town):

Figure 25a-b—What is the Internet?

_____ Discuss how people use the internet.

_____ Discuss browsers (like Chrome and Firefox). Compare the internet toolbar to other tools students use (i.e., MS Word, Google Docs). Explore the internet toolbar.

_____ Discuss the purpose of 'links' within webpages. Explore what happens when students click a link. Where do students think it takes them?

_____ Have students open internet start page and click on a site. Notice how it opens in a new tab—called 'tabbed browsing' (*Figure 26*). Show how to toggle between class start page and website.

Figure 26—Internet basics

_____ If you're looking for an interactive tutorial on using the internet, try one from the Burlington County Library System.

59

2nd Grade Technology Curriculum: Teacher Manual

The Digital Neighborhood

_____Watch an Internet safety video from BrainPop or from the Ask a Tech Teacher resource pages. Talk about it as a group. Show students how to enlarge a video to fill the screen.

_____Before diving into the internet, discuss '**digital neighborhood**'. What are student thoughts on safe internet use? Discuss *Figure 27* (full size poster in Appendix):

Figure 27—Digital neighborhood

- stay on assigned websites
- don't click ads
- don't get distracted by bling
- don't talk to strangers
- follow netiquette rules (*Figure 31a*)

_____Bring up a website students from class internet start page. Point to warnings in *Figure 28*:

Figure 28—Internet safety

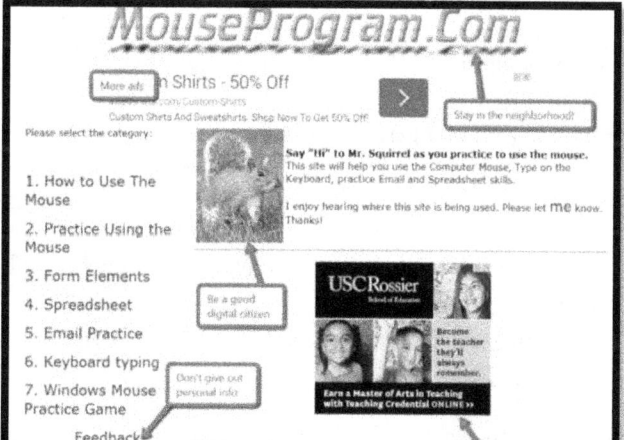

_____Use inquiry-themed sites to practice internet use with students. Encourage them to use links, forward and back buttons, home button.

Digital Citizenship

_____Discuss **digital citizenship**. You'll cover it repetitively throughout the year, as it authentically arises during lessons. Discuss the topics listed in *Figure 29* under 2nd Grade.

Figure 29—2nd grade Digcit topics

Digital Citizenship Topics	K	1	2	3	4	5	6
Cyberbullying	x	x	x	x	x	x	x
Digital citizenship	x	x	x	x	x	x	x
Digital commerce						x	x
Digital communications				x		x	x
Digital footprint and Online presence			x	x	x	x	x
Digital law				x		x	x
Digital privacy			x	x	x	x	x
Digital rights and responsibilities	x	x	x	x	x	x	x
Digital search and research				x	x	x	x
Fair use, Public domain			x	x	x	x	x
Image copyright				x		x	x
Internet safety	x	x	x	x	x	x	x
Netiquette		x	x	x	x	x	x
Online Plagiarism			x	x	x	x	x
Passwords	x	x	x	x	x	x	
Social media						x	x
Stranger Danger	x	x	x				

_____For more detail, see *"How To Teach Digital Citizenship"*, at the end of Lesson.

General discussion of Digital Citizenship

- Review last year's digital citizenship discussion. Solicit ideas from students.
- Discuss X/Twitter (*"13 Reasons to Use Twitter in the Classroom"* article at end of lesson) and hashtags—watch "Hashtag, you're it! (available on YouTube).
- Discuss texting. Watch *Jennette McCurdy's "Chicken" Commercial for Safe Kids USA (available on YouTube).*

Cyberbullying

- What is **cyberbullying**? What does 'cyber' mean? What is the same/different about bullying and cyberbullying?
- Use tools similar to those employed to deal with neighborhood bullies on cyberbullies.
- Watch these videos:
    - *Common Sense cyberbullying*
    - *six videos from kids like you (available on Kids Against Bullying)*

Digital footprint

- Why is it important? (Hint: We are influenced by what we find on a digital footprint.)
- Watch "The Digital Footprint" (available on YouTube).

Digital privacy

- Introduce **Digital Privacy**. Discuss how **passwords** protect privacy. Remind students they never share passwords, even with friends.
- Discuss password guidelines and rules.
- Watch a video on passwords. If you don't have a favorite, check Ask a Tech Teacher's resource pages.

Figure 30—Privacy on the internet

Digital rights and responsibilities

- What are the **digital rights and responsibilities** of a second grader? Watch this "Digital Rights and Responsibilities" YouTube video. Discuss these concepts:

    o *Act the same online as you'd act in your neighborhood.*
    o *Don't share personal information. Don't ask others for theirs.*
    o *Be aware of your surroundings. Know where you are in cyberspace.*
    o *Always show your best side online.*
    o *Anonymity doesn't protect you.*
    o *Share knowledge online.*
    o *If someone is 'flaming', stop it if possible or walk away.*

Netiquette

- What is '**netiquette**' (*Figure 31a*—see full-size poster in appendix)?

Plagiarism

- What does '**plagiarism**' mean? Why give credit to original authors/artists?
- Watch this Common Craft Plagiarism video (available on their website for free).
- Discuss plagiarism concepts like image copyrights, fair use, public domain.

_____ Post the pyramid in *Figure 31b* in your classroom (full-size poster in appendix). Every time you've discussed a topic, mark it off:

Figure 31a—Netiquette rules; 31b—Digcit topics wall chart

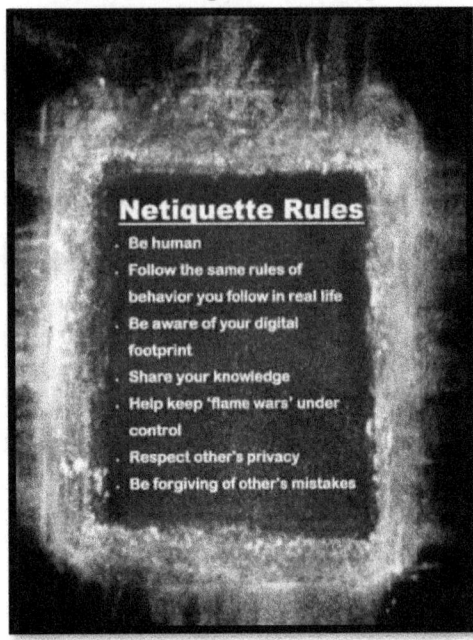
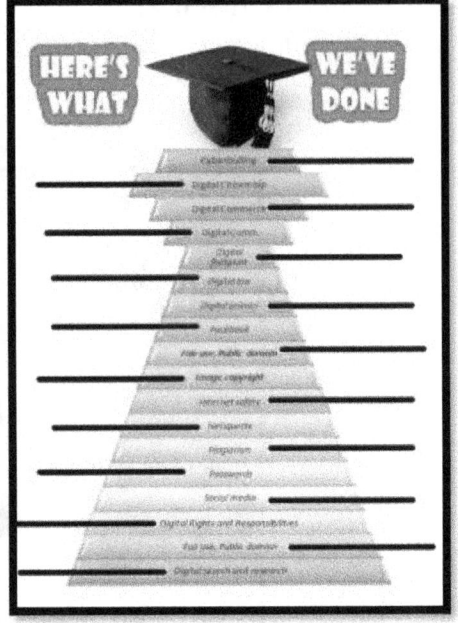

Class exit ticket: ***Using a virtual wall like Padlet (Figure 32) which can be embedded into the class internet start page, have students add an important fact from this lesson. No two students can contribute the same fact.***

Figure 32—Padlet wall on digital citizenship

Differentiation

- *Early finishers: visit class internet start page for websites on digital citizenship.*

Article 7 "How to Teach Digital Citizenship"

How To Teach Digital Citizenship

Common Sense Media named Ask a Tech Teacher as one of the 2014 blogs to watch on the topic of Digital Citizenship. It reminded me what a massive topic this is—at least 19 topics:

1. **Cyberbullying**—Harassment that happens on the Internet
2. **Digital citizenship**—Live in the digital world safely, responsibly, and ethically
3. **Digital commerce**—Electronic buying and selling of goods
4. **Digital communications**—Electronic transmission of info including email, IM, SMS, chatrooms, forums, multi-player games
5. **Digital footprint**—Trail left in cyberspace by the use of digital communication
6. **Digital law**—Legal rights and restrictions governing technology use
7. **Digital privacy**—Protection of information, reputation, and rights while using digital mediums
8. **Digital rights/ responsibilities**—Privileges and freedoms extended to all digital users and behavioral expectations that come with them. (Ribble & Bailey, 2007)
9. **Digital search and research**—Search and research that relies on online sources
10. **Effective Passwords**—Make these easy to remember but hard to guess
11. **Fair use**—Legal use of copyrighted materials without owner permission provided the use is fair and reasonable, does not impair the value of materials, and does not curtail owner profits
12. **Image copyright**—Exclusive legal right to reproduce, publish, sell, or distribute an image
13. **Internet safety**—Security of people and their information when using the Internet
14. **Netiquette**—Electronic 'etiquette' on the net
15. **Online Plagiarism**—Wrongful appropriation of another author's "language, thoughts, ideas, or expressions"
16. **Online presence**— individual's collective existence online
17. **Public domain**—The realm embracing rights to online material that belong to the community at large, are unprotected by copyright or patent, and can be appropriated by anyone
18. **Social media**—Online platforms like Facebook and Twitter by which individuals and communities create and share content
19. **Stranger Danger**—Perceived danger by strangers

Teaching digital citizenship starts young and never ends:

> Start teaching digital citizenship in kindergarten and include it every year through middle school. Select age-appropriate topics and teach them in an age-appropriate way. For example Stranger Danger is a great way to start Kindergartners/1st Graders on cyberbullying and digital privacy. But, I don't start a discussion of Digital commerce until middle school—they don't really get it until then.

A while ago, I collected ideas from my personal learning network on how they teach Digital Citizenship in their classrooms. I think you'll find a lot of good ideas:

Kindergarten (and Pre-K)
- *I briefly discussed Cyber Safety. I don't go into too much detail because they don't understand at that age what passwords/usernames, etc. are. So, I discuss not to use their names online or talk to strangers.*
- *I used Faux Paw and Hector's World.*
- *Like most things I do, I start Digital Citizenship as early as I can, so for my school, that means with our 3-4 yr. olds. I group Digital Citizenship in with the traditional cybersafety as well as learning about the parts of computers, network, how to treat technology, how to use technology appropriately, etc.*
- *So our 3-4 yr. olds learn about washing hands prior to use, cleaning keyboards, mice, headphones after use, and then we do some read alouds throughout the year - Arthur's Computer Disaster, Berenstein Bears Computer Trouble, Computer Teacher from the Black Lagoon, My First Book About the Internet, Goodnight iPad, Franklin & the Computer, Surf Sammy's New Computer.*

1st Grade
- *We watched Professor Garfield via Infinite Learning Labs. We answered the questions together at the end and decided if the answers were part of your "Yappy". You never give out your Yappy, which is your name, address, phone number, personal information, or your plans. There are also great posters that you can use on the site as well.*
- *I used Router's Birthday Surprise at Netsmartz.*
- *Most of the same lessons as K, but we also watch Smart Guy - Strangers on the Net (internet safety), Magic School Bus Gets Programmed (video on computer parts), correctly identifying by matching name and picture for the external parts of the computer (mouse, monitor, keyboard, jump drive, camera, printer, scanner, case, speakers/headphones).*

2nd Grade
- *For 2nd/3rd, I tried to use Netsmartz kids but they found it sort of "corny". My 2nd/3rd graders are more mature and therefore they didn't really like Netsmartz. So, instead, I used BrainPop Jr.'s video on Cyber Safety. We did a Q&A afterwards to make sure they were paying attention. I also printed out the "Talk about it" Worksheet and had them work in partners to write down their own rules for Cyber Safety. Once I used Internet Safety, which is one of Brain Pop Jr.'s free videos*
- *New tier of lessons - still mostly from Common Sense Media. Safe Surfing with Doug (review of what was covered in K-1 about Dig Cit), Keep It Private, Staying Safe Online, Online Communities, Things for Sale, Whose Property Is This? - no longer available online, What's the Big Idea? - no longer available online, add the concept of input and output to parts of the computer, Using Keywords, Finding Good Sites (website evaluation) - no longer available online, Show Respect Online, Screen Out the Mean (cyberbullying), PBS Webonauts. I try to blend the lessons with other projects we are doing. For example, we talk about keywords and website evaluation right before we do our dinosaur research and PowerPoint project.*

For complete article, visit Ask a Tech Teacher's Digital Citizenship resource pages.

Article 8 "11 Ways Twitter Improves Education"

11 Ways X/Twitter Improves Education

A teacher's challenge is to communicate with students in a way they will hear her/him. Twitter might be perfect for your class.

Twitter can easily be dismissed as a waste of time in the elementary school classroom. Students get distracted. They might see inappropriate tweets. How does a teacher manage a room full of Tweeple?

But, you've read a lot about Twitters usefulness in writing skills and sharing information so you—of the Open Minded Attitude—want to try it. Here's ammunition for what often turns into a pitched, take-sides verbal brawl as well-intended educators try to reach a compromise on using Twitter (in fact, many Web 2.0 tools—blogs, wikis, discussion forums, and websites that require registrations and log-ins—can be added to the list) that works for all stakeholders:

You learn to be concise

Twitter gives you limited characters to get the entire message across. *Letters, numbers, symbols, punctuation and spaces all count as characters on Twitter.* Wordiness doesn't work. Twitter counts every keystroke and won't publish anything with a minus in front of the word count.

At first blush, that seems impossible. It's not. It challenges students to know the right word for every situation. People with a big vocabulary are at an advantage because they don't use collections of little words to say what they mean. All those hints from English teachers about picture nouns and action verbs and getting rid of adverbs and adjectives take on new importance to the Twitter aficionado.

Twitter isn't intimidating

A blank white page that holds hundreds of words, demanding you fill in each line margin to margin is intimidating. A tweet isn't. Students learn to whittle back, leave out emotional words, adjectives and adverbs, pick better nouns and verbs because they need the room. Instead of worrying what to say on all those empty lines, they feel successful.

Students learn manners

Social networks are all about netiquette. People thank others for their assistance, ask politely for help, and encourage contributions from others. Use this framework to teach students how to engage in a community—be it physical or virtual. It's all about manners.

Students learn to focus

You can't get off topic or cover tangential ideas. You have to save those for a different tweet. Tweeple like that trait in writers. They like to hear the writer's thoughts on the main topic, not meanderings.

Students learn to share

Start a tweet stream where students share research on a topic. Maybe it's the life cycle of an animal. Have each student share their favorite website (using a #hashtag — maybe #ancientgreece) and you've created a resource others can use. Expand on that wonderful skill learned in kindergarten about sharing personal toys. Encourage students to RT (retweet) posts they found particularly relevant or helpful.

Tweets need to be written knowing that tweeple can @reply

Yes. This is a world of social networks where people read what you say and comment. That's a good thing. It's feedback and builds an online community, be it for socializing or school. Students learn to construct their arguments expecting others to respond, question, and comment. Not only does this develop the skill of persuasive writing, students learn to have a thick skin, take comments with a grain of salt and two grains of aspirin.

#Hashtags develop a community

Create #hashtags that will help students organize their tweets—#help if they have a question, #homework for homework help. Establish class hashtags to deal with subjects you want students to address.

Students learn tolerance for all opinions

Why? Because Tweeple aren't afraid to voice their thoughts. They spit it right out. Because the Twitter stream is a public forum (in a classroom, the stream can be private, visible to only class members), students understand what they say is out there forever. That's daunting. Take the opportunity to teach students about their public profile. Represent themselves well with good grammar, good spelling, and well-chosen tolerant ideas. Don't be emotional or spiteful because it can't be taken back. Rather than shying away from exposing students to the world, use Twitter to teach students how to live in it.

Breaks down barriers to talking to other people

Students are less worried about typing than raising their hand in class, all eyes on them, and having to spit out the right answer. With Twitter, students can type an answer, delete it, edit it, add to and detract from, all before they push send. Plus, it's more anonymous than the class, with no body language or facial expressions. Just words—and not many of those. Students have their say, see how others respond, have a chance to clarify. What could be safer?

Students are engaged

Twitter is exciting, new, and hip. Students want to use it. It's not the boring worksheet. It's a way to engage students in ways that excite them.

X/Twitter is always open

Inspiration doesn't always strike in that 50-minute class period. Sometimes it's after class, after school, after dinner, even 11 at night. Twitter doesn't care. Whatever schedule is best for students to discover the answer, Twitter is there.

2nd Grade Technology Curriculum: Teacher Manual

Lesson #4 Keyboarding

Vocabulary	Problem solving	Skills
• Ctrl+P • Digital • Enter • Flying windows • Home row • Indent • Log-on • Shortkey • Tab • Toolbar • Touch typing	• Dance Mat won't play flash version (does digital device allow Flash?) • Why shortkeys (they're faster, easier) • How fast should I type? • I can't type (that's OK. You're new) • I don't know where the keys are (that's why you practice) • I type fine with two fingers (have you tried all fingers?) • How do I type non-letter keys (with the closest finger)	**New** Which finger, which key? **Scaffolded** Keyboarding Typing posture
Academic Applications All subjects	**Materials Required** keyboard program, student workbooks (if using)	**Standards** CCSS.W.CCR.6 NETS: 1d, 6a

Essential Question

How do I use a keyboard to share ideas?

Big Idea

Students connect keyboarding and classwork authentically

Teacher Preparation

- Set up student keyboard accounts if required.
- Know which shortkeys are important to your 2nd graders.
- Know which tasks weren't completed last week.
- Integrate domain-specific tech vocabulary into lesson.
- Know if you need extra time to complete this lesson.
- Include other members of the grade-level team, school administration, and parents in an effort to build age-appropriate keyboarding skills.

Assessment Strategies

- Anecdotal observation
- Used prior knowledge
- Followed directions
- Completed warm-up, exit ticket
- Joined class conversations
- Decisions followed class rules
- Left room as s/he found it
- Higher order thinking: analysis, evaluation, synthesis
- Habits of mind observed

Steps

Time required: 45 minutes in one sitting or spread throughout the week
Class warm-up: Keyboard homerow using RoomRecess' Popcorn Typer, BBC's Dance Mat Typing, or another tool that focuses on one row. Observe student posture, hand position.

_____Use this lesson to introduce keyboarding as a skill to students, and then spread the activities throughout the school year, 10-15 minutes per lesson. All relevant keyboarding information is collected into this one place so you know where to look when you need it.

_____It is preferable that students practice keyboarding on a traditional keyboard rather than the iPad version. If students question this, suggest they engage in a research study, using the scientific method, to determine if keyboarding is as fast and accurate on an iPad as a traditional keyboard.

2nd Grade Technology Curriculum: Teacher Manual

Keyboarding Overview

_____Talk as a class about why students learn keyboarding. Come up with a list of reasons and compare it to *Figure 33a (full size poster in appendix)*:

Figure 33a—Why learn to keyboard? 33b—Keyboard curriculum map

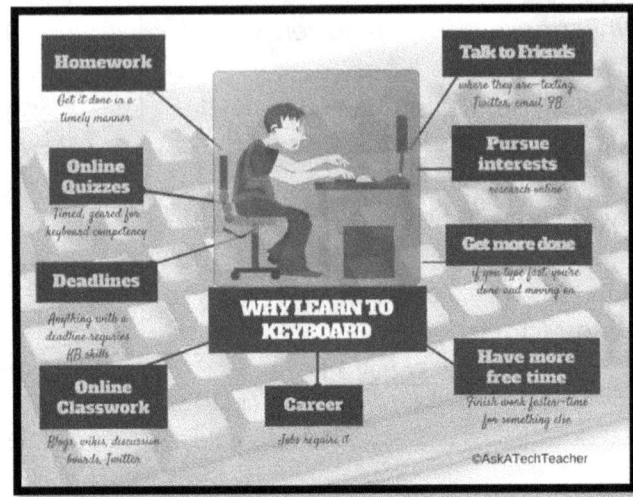
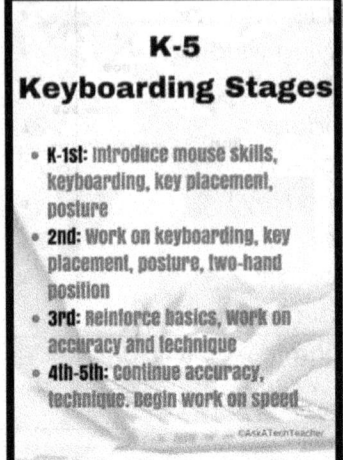

_____This lesson builds on pre-keyboarding skills started in kindergarten, preparing students for two-hand typing and increasing technology demands of education (*Figure 33b*—poster in Appendix).
_____Introduce students to the two programs they will start the year off with:

- *Popcorn Typer*
- *Dance Mat Typing*

_____Students focus on one row at a time.
_____For the first three months of school, spend one month on each row.
_____For months four onward, select a program that uses all keys such as Type to Learn, Typing Web (Google for Addresses). Find options in Ask a Tech Teacher's Keyboarding resource pages.
_____Check several to see which works best for your group. Or, mix them up to keep student interest.
_____Show students what proper hand position should be (*Figure 34*). They won't get this until 5th grade. What you want them to do is think about it:

Figure 34—Hand position

_____Use not only correct hand position, but keep legs in front and elbows at side (*Figure 35a*).

Figure 35a—Keyboard posture; 35b—Keyboarding hints

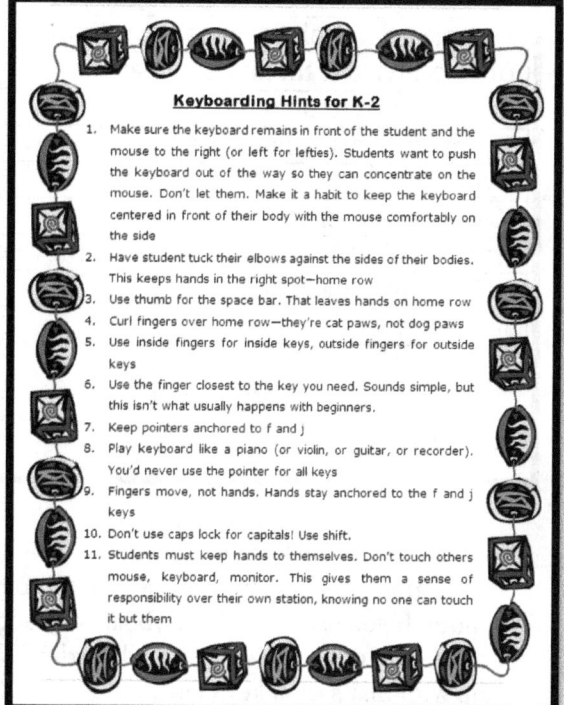

_____As students complete projects throughout the year that require keyboarding (i.e., the slideshow and the word processing report), anecdotally review their:

- *proper posture*
- *speed and accuracy*
- *keyboarding hints in Figure 35b* (full size poster in Appendix)

Keyboard Shortkeys

_____Shortkeys—keyboard shortcuts—for many students are an easier, more efficient method of accomplishing a task. Shortkeys use the keyboard rather than the mouse and tools/toolbars. Many of them work on a variety of platforms—Chromebooks, PCs, Macs, and the internet—meaning once a student has learned the shortkey, that knowledge is transferrable to a variety of situations.
_____Review shortkeys in *Figure 37* (at the end of this Lesson). Every year, students will learn more of these until by the end of 5th grade, they know all of them.
_____See poster, *Use Keyboard Shortcuts. Get Done Faster,* in Appendix.

Keyboarding Assessment

_____**DO NOT EXPECT TOUCH TYPING IN 2nd GRADE**. Earliest: late fourth/early fifth, after several years of keyboarding practice.
_____Assess student keyboarding progress anecdotally and formatively once a month or a few times during the grading period. Evaluate from a technique list such as *Assessment 4*:

Assessment 4—Keyboarding technique

Technique	Date	Date	Date	Date	Date
Feet placed for balance and sits up straight.					
Body centered to the middle of keyboard.					
Eyes on the screen.					
Types with correct fingering.					
Types with a steady, even rhythm.					
Keeps fingers on home row keys.					
Has a good attitude and strives for improvement.					
WPM (words per minute)					
Accuracy percent					

4 pts = Mastery level   2 pts = Partial Mastery level
3 pts = Near Mastery level   1 pt = Minimal Mastery level

_____If your students have just started to practice keyboarding, pick only a few criteria to assess. As the K-1st graders get more practice, they'll come to 2nd grade with a greater facility and you can expect more. If you use iPads for keyboarding, adapt this list to that digital device. There is a small amount of research that shows iPad keyboarding is as fast as traditional—especially when users have grown up with that sort of keyboard.

_____Load *Assessment 4* onto your iPad or mobile laptop. Walk around the room as students practice. Using an annotation tool (i.e., iAnnotate, Notability, Adobe), fill in techniques each student does well and what they need help with. Save under their name or as a screenshot.

Keyboarding Key Knowledge Assessment

_____Besides letter keys, 2nd graders should begin remembering placement of important non-letter keys, such as those in *Figure 36 (full size poster in Appendix)*:

Figure 36—Important non-letter keys

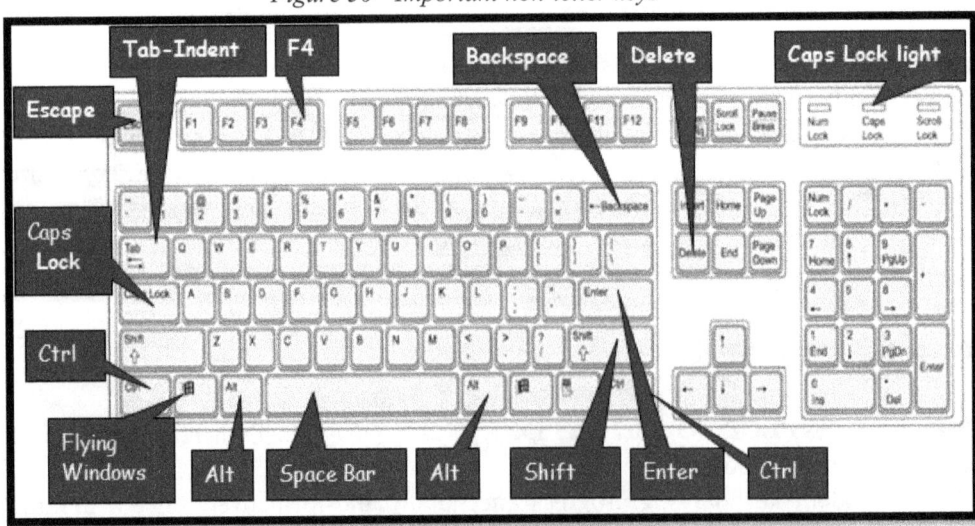

Class exit ticket: *Take three minutes with a neighbor and have students try to name as many of the fifteen important keyboard keys as possible without looking at the keyboard*

Differentiation

- *Early finishers: visit class internet start page for websites that tie into keyboarding.*
- *Review articles at end of Lesson, "Is Keyboarding Dead" and "5 Ways to Make Classroom Keyboarding Fun".*
- *If this lesson doesn't work for your student group, use one from Inquiry-based Teaching with PBL (from Structured Learning). It has 5 additional projects aligned with the SL curriculum.*
- *Offer a Keyboarding Club after school two days a week to accommodate students who want extra practice. Limit it to 45 minutes.*
- *For more depth, follow lessons in K-8 Keyboard Curriculum from Structured Learning.*

"Error, no keyboard — press F1 to continue."

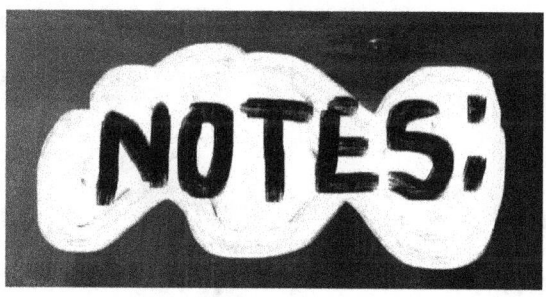

_____

_____

_____

_____

Figure 37—Keyboard shortkeys

KEYBOARD SHORTKEYS

Windows

Maximize window	Double click title bar
Quick Exit	Alt+F4
Date and Time	Shift+Alt+D = Date
	Shift+Alt+T = Time
Show taskbar	WK (Windows key)
Show desktop	WK+M

Ctrl Key

CTRL+

- C: Copy
- CTRL+X: Cut
- CTRL+V: Paste
- CTRL+Z: Undo
- CTRL+B: Bold
- CTRL+U: Underline
- CTRL+I: Italic
- CTRL+P: Print

- CTRL+K: Add hyperlink
- CTRL+E: Center align
- CTRL+L: Left align
- CTRL+R: Right align
- CTRL+P: Print
- CTRL+ : Zoom in Internet
- CTRL- : Zoom out Internet

Fun Keyboard Shortcuts

- < + = + > = ⇔
- — + > = →
- : +) = ☺

Add Your Favorite:

Article 9 "Is Keyboarding Dead?"

Is Keyboarding Dead?

I was on one of my tech teacher forums—where I keep up to date on changes in education and technology—and stumbled into a heated discussion about what grade level is best to begin the focus on typing (is fifth grade too old—or too young?). Several teachers shared that keyboarding was the cornerstone of their elementary-age technology program. Others confessed their Admin wanted it eliminated as unnecessary. Still others dismissed the discussion as moot: Tools like Dragon Speak (the standard in speech recognition software) and iPhone's wildly-popular Siri mean keyboarding will soon be as useful as cursive and floppy discs.

My knee jerk reaction was *That's years off,* but it got me thinking. Is it really? Or are the fires of change about to sweep through our schools? Already, families are succumbing to the overwhelming popularity of touch screens in the guise of iPads. No typing required—just a finger poke, a sweep, and the command is executed. Those clumsy, losable styluses of your parent's era are so last generation. The day kids discover how easy it is to *tell* their phones what they need done (think iPhone 4S)—stick a fork in it; keyboarding will be done.

Truthfully, as someone who carefully watches ed tech trends, a discussion about the importance of keyboarding says as much about national education expectations as typing. Schools are moving away from reports and essays as methods of assessing understanding. Teachers want plays that act out a topic, student-created videos that demonstrate authentic understanding, multi-media magazines that convey a deeper message. Web-based communication tools like Voki, Animoto, and Glogster—all of which have limited typing—are *de rigeur* in every academic program that purports to be tech-savvy. Students are encouraged to use audio, visual, taped vignettes, recorded snippets—everything that ISN'T the traditional MS Word document with a bullet list of comprehensive points to convey the message. For much of what students want out of life—to call a friend, find their location on GPS, arrange a get-together, create a reminder—writing is passé. Email to your middle school and high school children is as anachronistic as snail mail. Even texting is being shunted aside by vlogs and Skype, and note-taking—with the popularity of apps like Evernote—has become something best accomplished with swipes and clicks.

That's what's killing keyboarding.

But it's not dead yet. Certainly, voice commands can activate a software program or bring up the teacher's website to view homework, but how do you quietly talk to a computer during a lecture? Are programs like Dragon Speak and Siri capable of blocking out extraneous sounds and focusing in on the singular human voice? And don't discount the aesthetics of typing. Take me for example. I'm a K-8 technology teacher. I'm in the know about the latest and greatest in technology trends. I'm expected to try them—and use them. I write for a hobby, but I have arthritis. My doctor wants me to stop typing, switch to Dragon Speak. My modern kids are all for it, but Dragon Speak's quirkiness (like mis-typing oh-so-many words) is distracting. Plus, there's a connection between my brain and fingers that helps me think. Maybe it's as simple as I muse at the speed I type. Maybe the clackity-clack of the keys is soothing to my rattled brain. Nothing in my pedagogic or anecdotal research has convinced me it isn't also true for kids. If we eliminate the peaceful predictability of tapping fingers on those little squares, will getting words on paper be more difficult?

I wonder.

I decided to poll my parents. Overwhelmingly, they support age-appropriate keyboard training for children as young as kindergarten. They understand that typing may be antiquated someday, but not today, or tomorrow. Until it is, they want their kids to learn it.

What do you think?

Article 10 "5 Ways to Make Classroom Keyboarding Fun"

5 Ways to Make Classroom Keyboarding Fun

When you teach typing, the goal isn't **speed and accuracy**. The goal is that students type well enough that it doesn't disrupt their thinking.

Let me say that again:

The goal of keyboarding is students type well enough that it doesn't disrupt their thinking.

Much like breathing takes no thought and playing a piano is automatic, students want to be able to think while they type, fingers automatically moving to the keys that record their thoughts. Searching for key placement shouldn't interfere with how they develop a sentence. Sure, it does when students are just starting, but by fourth grade students should be comfortable enough with key placement to be working on speed.

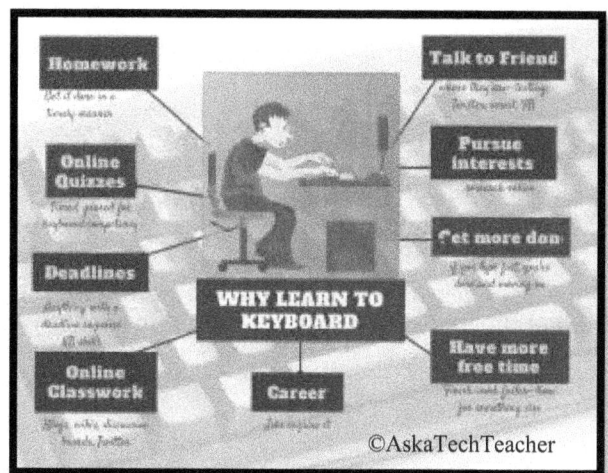

To type as fast at the speed of thought isn't as difficult as it sounds. When referring to students in school, 'speed of thought' refers to how fast they develop ideas that will be recorded. 30 wpm is the low end. 45 wpm is good.

Students used to learn typing in high school, as a skill. Now, it's a tool for learning. So much of what we ask students to do on the way to authentic learning requires typing. Consider the academic need to:

- *write reports*
- *comment on Discussion Boards and blogs*
- *journal in blogs and online tools like Penzu*
- *research online (type addresses into a search bar)*
- *take digital notes (using Evernote, OneNote and similar)*
- *collaborate on Google Apps like Docs, Sheets, Presentations*
- *take online quizzes (like PARCC, SB)*
- *use online tools for core classes (Wordle, Animoto, Story Creators)*

If you're a Common Core state, keyboarding shows up often in the Standards, but can be summarized in these three ways:

- *Keyboarding is addressed **tangentially**–students must be able to type *** pages in a single sitting (see CCSS.ELA-Literacy.W.4.6 for example. The 'pages in a single sitting' starts in 4th grade with one page and continues through 6th where it's increased to three–see CCSS.ELA-Literacy.W.6.6)*
- *By 3rd grade, Common Core discusses the **use** of keyboarding to **produce** work, i.e., CCSS.ELA-Literacy.W.3.6 which specifically mentions 'use technology to produce and publish writing (using keyboarding skills)'*
- *Keyboarding is required to take **Common Core Standards assessments** in the Spring.*

The myth is that students will teach themselves when they need it. That's half right. They will teach themselves, but it won't necessarily be in time for their needs. If you're in a tech-infused school, it's your obligation to teach them the right way to type so they can organically develop the tools to support learning.

Most teachers roll out typing with a graduated program like Type to Learn or Typing Club. In September of the new school year, students start Lesson 1. Sometime around May, they are through all the lessons and considered trained. Everything is on auto-pilot with little intervention from the teacher. That works for about ten percent of students. Those are the ones who are intrinsically motivated to learn and nothing gets in their way.

The other 90% need a little more help. Here are six ideas to make your typing lessons fun and effective:

Drill

Drill is part of every granular typing program. Students must learn key placement, finger usage, posture, and all those other details.

There are a lot of options for this—both free like Typing Web and fee-based like QwertyTown. Students usually start enthusiastically, which wanes within a few months as it becomes more of the same rote practice.

Games

When your organic typing program shows signs of wearing on students, throw in a sprinkling of games that teach key placement, speed and accuracy. Big Brown Bear is great for youngers; NitroTyping for olders, and Popcorn Typer for the in-between grades of 2nd-5th.

Offer games sporadically, not on a schedule. Make it a reward for keyboarding benchmarks.

Team Challenge

Students work in teams to answer keyboard-related questions in a game show format. You can use a Jeopardy template that includes not only keyboard questions, but shortkeys that students use often.

Integrate into Class Inquiry

Within a month of starting a keyboarding program, have students use their growing skills authentically in class projects. This can be book reports, research, a brochure for history class, or a collaborative document through Google Apps. The keyboarding is a tool to communicate knowledge in a subject, much like a pencil, an artist brush or a violin. The better their keyboarding skills, the easier it is to complete the meat of the project, like a blog response, trading cards on characters in a book, or a family tree.

Remind students to use the keyboarding skills they've learned to make this real-life experience easier—hands on their own side of the keyboard, use all fingers, good posture, elbows at their sides. Let their team of grade level teachers know what traits to look for as students research on class computers or in the library. Get parents to reinforce it at home.

Using keyboarding is the most effective way to learn it. It won't take long before keyboarding with good technique will be habit.

ASCII Art

ASCII Art uses keyboarding skills to create artistic representations of class learning. This is a fun way to use keyboarding in other classes. All students do is find a picture that represents the class inquiry topic being addressed, put it as a watermark into the word processing program, type over the washed out image with a variety of keys, then delete the watermark. This takes about thirty minutes usually and always excites students with the uniqueness of their work.

2nd Grade Technology Curriculum: Teacher Manual

Lesson #5 Problem Solving

Vocabulary	Problem solving	Skills
• Ctrl Z • Flying windows • Guess and check • Keyboard shortcuts • Password • Patterns • PW • Shortkeys • Start button • Strategies • Taskbar • UN • User name	• I lost my work (Ctrl+Z or check taskbar) • I can't close a program (Alt+F4) • I can't save (Ctrl+S) • I can't find the tool (use shortkey) • I can't print (where did you print?) • Computer didn't save (did you back up to your digital portfolio?) • How can I guess at an answer if I don't know what it is? • Computer lost part of my project (check folder for more recent save) • My hand's been up five minutes (can you solve the problem yourself?)	**New** Problem solving **Scaffolded** Digital citizenship Keyboarding Problem solving
Academic Applications Academics—all classes	**Materials Required** Problem-solving Challenge, student workbooks (if using), prizes (if using them)	**Standards** CCSS. Std. for Math.Prac. NETS:4a, 5c

Essential Question

How do I use technology when there are so many problems?

Big Idea

Problem-solving in technology often involves common sense and doing what worked in the past

Teacher Preparation

- Know which tasks weren't completed last week.
- Know if you need extra time to complete this lesson.
- Talk with class teacher. Are students experiencing recurring problems on class computers? Favorites: 'Can't print' and 'save didn't work'.
- Integrate domain-specific tech vocabulary into lesson. Expect students to do the same.
- Know what tech problems former 2nd graders had and include those in your problem solving list.

Assessment Strategies

- Followed directions
- Completed warm-up, exit ticket
- Joined class conversations
- [tried to] solve own problems
- Decisions followed class rules
- Left room as s/he found it
- Higher order thinking: analysis, evaluation, synthesis
- Habits of mind observed

Steps

Time required: 45 minutes in one sitting or spread throughout the week with 30 minutes set aside for Problem-solving Challenge

Class warm-up: Keyboard homerow using RoomRecess' Popcorn Typer, BBC's Dance Mat Typing, or another that focuses on one row. Observe student posture, hand position.

_____This Lesson includes three sections:

- *problem solving overview*
- *daily problem solving*
- *Problem-solving Challenge (a game)*

_____Use this time to introduce the topic of 'tech problem solving'. Then, as with keyboarding, mix these up throughout the school year, always returning to tech troubleshooting strategies when students have difficulty.

Problem Solving Overview

_____Reinforce the importance of students solving their own problems.
_____Here are strategies that will help (*Figure 38*—full size poster in Appendix):

Figure 38—How to Solve a Problem

- Act out a problem
- Break problem into parts
- Draw a diagram
- Guess and check
- Never say 'can't'
- See patterns
- Notice the forest and the trees
- Think logically
- Distinguish relevant from irrelevant info
- Try, fail, try again
- Use what has worked in the past

Daily Problem Solving

_____Discuss computer problems with students. Start with a review of hardware-based problems (*Figure 39*). Challenge students to know these:

- *Volume doesn't work—are headphones plugged in? Is volume on?*
- *Computer doesn't work—is power on?*
- *Mouse doesn't work—is light on?*
- *Monitor doesn't work—is power on?*

_____Discuss how understanding hardware helps to solve tech problems.

Figure 39—Hardware and solutions

_____What problems have you noticed during class this year? Last year? Cover those with students.
_____What problems do students run into when they use computers at home or in class? Write them on class screen as students list them:

- *What's user name? What's password?*
- *I can't exit the program (Alt+F4)*
- *Start button disappeared (push 'flying windows' button)*
- *I lost my work (Ctrl+Z)*
- *Program shut down (Is it on taskbar?)*
- *How do I save (Ctrl+S)?*

_____Have a list of the twenty-five most common technology problems your students face between Kindergarten and 5th grade. Students will be expected to know these before graduating to Middle School and they will be included in the Problem-solving Board. *Figure 40* is an example:

Figure 40—Troubleshooting computer problems

TROUBLESHOOTING COMPUTER PROBLEMS

#	Problem	Why	Solution
1	Deleted a file	Deleted by accident	Open Recycle Bin—right-click--restore
2.	Can't exit a program	Can't find X or Quit	Alt+F4
3.	Can't find a program	Shortcut moved	Type 'Word' (or program name) into Search bar
4.	Keyboard doesn't work	Unplugged, lost file	Plug cord into back; reboot
5.	Mouse doesn't work	Unplugged, lost file	Plug cord into back, reboot
6.	Start button is gone	Task bar gone	Push Windows button
7.	No sound	Mute on	Unmute
		Volume down	turn volume up
		Unplugged headphones	plug headphones in
		Lost file	Reboot
8.	Can't find a file	Saved wrong, moved	Start button—Search
9.	Menu command grayed out	You're in another command	Push escape 3 times
10.	What's today's date?	You forgot!	Hover over the clock
11.	Taskbar gone	Student interference	Push Windows button
			Drag border up to expose
12.	Taskbar was moved	Student interference	Drag it to the bottom of screen
13.	Desktop icons messed up	Student interference	Right click on screen—arrange icons
			Too small? Highlight and Ctrl+ to enlarge
14.	Computer frozen	Mouse frozen	Reboot
15.	Program frozen	Dialog box open	Clear the dialog box
		Not selected on taskbar	Click program on taskbar
16.	I erased my document/text	Ooops	Ctrl+Z
17.	Screen says "Ctrl-Alt-Del"	You rebooted	Hold down Ctrl-Alt—push Delete
18.	Program closed down	Ooops	Is it open on the taskbar? If so—click on it
			Reopen program—see if it saved a back-up
19.	Tool bar missing on www	Pushing F11 key	Push F11 key
20.	Internet window too small	Hard to read	Ctrl+ to enlarge; Ctrl- to delarge (or Ctrl+mouse wheel)
21.	Double click doesn't work	Who knows?	Push enter
22.	Shift key doesn't work	Caps lock on	Push caps lock to disengage
23.	I can't remember how to…	So many skills…	Try a right click with the mouse
24.	When I type, it types over	I want to insert text	Push the 'insert' key
25.	The document is 'read only'	I didn't do anything	Just 'save-as' under a new name and all is fixed

_____Throughout the year, encourage students to use shortkeys. For some, this is more efficient, quicker to accomplish a goal. Many are cross-platform meaning they work on Macs, PCs, Chromebooks, and the internet. This means students have a first step to try for figuring out how to solve a problem they've never before solved in a particular situation.

Figure 41-Common shortkeys

Windows	
Maximize window	Double click title bar
Quick Exit	Alt+F4
Date and Time	Shift+Alt+D = Date
	Shift+Alt+T = Time
Show taskbar	WK (Windows key)
Show desktop	WK+M

Ctrl Key			
CTRL+			
C: Copy		CTRL+K:	Add hyperlink
CTRL+X: Cut		CTRL+E:	Center align
CTRL+V: Paste		CTRL+L:	Left align
CTRL+Z: Undo		CTRL+R:	Right align
CTRL+B: Bold		CTRL+P:	Print
CTRL+U: Underline		CTRL+ :	Zoom in Internet
CTRL+I: Italic		CTRL- :	Zoom out Internet
CTRL+P: Print			

2nd Grade Technology Curriculum: Teacher Manual

Problem-solving Challenge

_____Have students play Problem-solving Challenge. Pass out copies of common problems your student group faced last year (see article, *18 Techie Problems Every Student Can Fix*). This list can include hardware problems and shortkeys.

_____Divide class into groups. Give ten minutes to study problem-solving list. Collect papers.

_____If an extra student, make them time keeper.

_____**Go to Group One**. Present a problem. Give them five seconds to solve and then move onto next group. Give that group five seconds and so on until solution is revealed or all groups had a chance. If no one answers, provide the answer.

_____**Go to Group Two** and ask them to solve next problem. Repeat process.

_____Each right answer gets one point.

_____Continue until you run out of time.

_____Prizes? Optional. I give Free's (*Figure 42b*) with prizes they value. You might decide no prizes.

Class exit ticket: *Set up a board on the classroom wall (Figure 42a). Ask each student to post a tech problem anonymously that they have had difficulty with.*

Figure 42a—Problem-solving Board; 42b—FREE sample

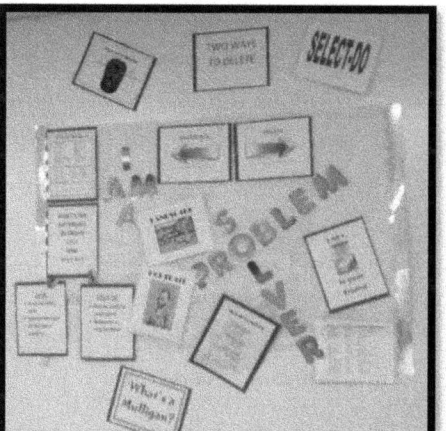

Differentiation

- Put Problem Solving Challenge into a Jeopardy template.
- Leave 'I am a Problem Solver' board up year-round. Ask students to present solutions for classmates when you get 2-3 of the same question.
- For more ideas on teaching problem solving, see the article at the end of the Lesson, *"How to Teach Students to Solve Problems"*.
- For a discussion on how teaching tech requires problem solving skills, read article at end of Lesson, *"The Secret to Teaching Tech: Delegate"*.

18 Techie Problems Every Student Can Fix

Amazingly, there are twenty tech problems that cause about eighty percent of the stoppages. In the next two pages, I'm going to tell you what those are and how to solve them. Trust me. They're easier than you think. I routinely teach them to kindergarten-fifth graders, and then they teach their parents.

I'll first tell you problem, why it occurs, and finally, the most common solution to fix it:

Deleted a file
Why? By accident or changed my mind
What to do: Open Recycle Bin; right-click—restore

Can't exit a program
Why: Can't find X or Quit tool. This happens with pesky internet ads marketers don't want you to exit
What to do: Alt+F4 works 95% of the time. Try that.

Can't find Word
Why: Shortcut moved, was deleted by accident or became inactive
What to do: Right-click on desktop—select 'New'—"Word Document". Or, use 'search' on Start

Keyboard doesn't work
Why: Lost connection
What to do: First check to be sure it actually isn't working by pushing 'Num Lock'. If the 'Num Lock' light goes on/off, the problem is not the keyboard. If it does: Re-plug cord into back of tower or reboot

Mouse doesn't work
Why: Lost connection
What to do: Move it around to see if the cursor moves. If it doesn't, re-plug cord into back or reboot

Start button is gone
Why: Taskbar disappeared
What to do: Push Flying Windows (lower right corner of keyboard)

No sound
Why: Mute is on; volume is down; headphones are unplugged
What to do: Unmute the sound or turn it up; plug headphones in; reboot

Do you notice how often I say reboot? Sometimes, the computer simply gets confused and drops actions out of the queue which means they stop working. All you have to do is restart the system to get things back to normal.

Can't find a file
Why: Saved wrong, moved
What to do: Push Start button—Start search; when you find it, resave in a location you will remember

Menu command grayed out
Why: You're in another command
What to do: Push escape 3 times. This d makes the command you'd like to use available

What's today's date?
Why: You forgot!
What to do: Hover over clock; in Word, use the shortkey Shift+Alt+D

Taskbar was moved
Why: Student interference
What to do: Click on an open part of taskbar; drag to bottom of screen (or where you prefer it to be)

Desktop icons messed up
Why: Student interference; you added more icons and now everything's confused
What to do: Right click on screen—select 'Sort by', select method you'd like icons arranged

Computer frozen
Why: Mouse frozen; keyboard frozen, dialogue box open
What to do: Check solutions in this list. If nothing works, reboot

Program frozen
Why: Dialog box open; not selected on taskbar
What to do: Look around screen for dialogue box wanting input. Answer. Or click program on taskbar

I erased my document/text
Why: Ooops
What to do: Ctrl+Z

Screen says "Ctrl-Alt-Del"
Why: You rebooted
What to do: Hold down Ct+Alt—then push Delete. This will bring you to log-in screen or desktop

Program closed down
Why: Ooops
What to do: If on taskbar, click. If not, reopen—see if right sidebar shows a back-up and open that

Toolbar missing at top of www
Why: Unknown
What to do: Push F11 key

Article 12 "How to Teach Students to Solve Problems"

How to Teach Students to Solve Problems

Of all the skills students learn in school, **problem solving** arguably is the most valuable and the hardest to learn. It's fraught with uncertainty—what if the student looks stupid as he tries? What if everyone's watching and he can't do it—isn't it better not to try? What if it works, but not the way Everyone wants it to? When you're a student, it's understandable when they decide to let someone tell them what to do.

But this isn't the type of learner we want to build. We want risk-takers, those willing to be the load-bearing pillar of the class. And truthfully, by a certain age, kids want to make up their own mind. Our job as teachers is to provide the skills necessary for them to make wise, effective decisions.

It's not a stand-alone subject. It starts with a habit of inquiry in all classes—math, LA, history, science, any of them. I constantly ask students questions, get them to think and evaluate, provide evidence that supports process as well as product. Whether they're writing, reading, or creating an art project, I want them thinking what they're doing and why.

Common Core puts problem solving front and center. It comes up in ELA ("*Students will be challenged and asked questions that push them to refer back to what they've read. This stresses critical-thinking, problem-solving, and analytical skills that are required for success in college, career, and life.*"), but is inescapable in Math. In fact, students cannot fully meet the Math Standards without understanding how to effectively approach the unknown. Consider the Standards for Mathematical Practice that overlay all grade levels K-12. Don't they sound like great strategies for everything, not just math? How about deciding what classes to take in Middle School? Or whether to make a soccer or basketball game on the weekend? Or which college to attend? Using these eight tools strategically, with precision, and tenaciously is a great first step.

The question becomes: How do students **learn to use them**? Certainly, as they accomplish their grade-level math curriculum, you as teacher remind them they aren't doing a multiplication problem (or an Algebra one); rather they're reasoning abstractly or using appropriate tools strategically, or expressing regularity in repeated reasoning, but for deep learning, hands-on authentic experience is required. Let's say, for example, the class is investigating the purchase of an MP3 player. Should they purchase an IPod, a smartphone, a dedicated use MP3 player, or a different option? How do students arrive at a decision—solve that problem? Ask students to work through the steps below as they address a decision. Ask them to note where they accomplish one or more of the Standards for Mathematical Practice above:

1. What do you want in an MP3 player? Should it play music, show videos, pictures, communicate with others, be a phone also? Make that list so you know how to evaluate information as you collect it **(compare/contrast)**.

2. What do you know about the topic (**evidence**)? Have you seen some you liked or didn't like? What have you heard about those on your list? You are a good resource to yourself. Don't discount that. You'll be surprised how much you know on a variety of topics. This step is important to college and career. Future employers and schools want you to think, to use your intelligence and your knowledge to evaluate and solve problems.

3. What advice do knowledgeable friends have (**perspective taking, collaboration**)? You want the input of MP3 users. Your friends will think whatever they own is the best, because they're vested in that choice, but listen to their evidence and the conclusions they draw based on that. This is important to a team-oriented environment. Listen to all sides, even if you don't agree.

4. **Dig deeper (close reading)**. Check other resources (**uncover knowledge**). This includes:
    o *people who don't like the product*
    o *online sources. Yep, you might as well get used to online research if you aren't yet. Statistics show more people get their news from blogs than traditional media (newspapers, TV) and you know where blogs are.*
    o *your parents who will bring up topics friends didn't, like cost, longevity, reliability*
5. **Evaluate your resources (integration of knowledge)**. How much money do you have? Eliminate the choices that don't fit your constraints (money, time, use, etc.) If there are several choices that seem to work, this will help you make the decision. You might have to save money or get a job so you can afford the one you've chosen. Or, you might decide to settle for a cheaper version. Just make sure you are aware of how you made the choice and are satisfied with it.
6. What are the **risks involved** in making the decision (**reflection**)? Maybe buying an MP3 player means you can't do something else you wanted. Are you comfortable with that choice?
7. **Make a decision (transfer learning)**. That's right. Make a decision and live with it knowing you've considered all available information and evaluated it logically and objectively.

Optionally, you might have students evaluate problem solving in their favorite game, say, Minecraft. All it requires is that as they play--and think about what they're doing:

- *What is the goal of Minecraft? How is it best achieved*
- *What does the student know about playing the game that can be used in achieving the goal?*
- *Does working with friends and gaining feedback make life easier in Minecraft?*
- *How does experience in the game affect progress?*
- *and so on...*

This is how students become the problem solvers required of their Future. When the day comes that how they solve a problem affects the direction their life takes (college, career, marriage, children, a tattoo), they'll be happy to have strategies that make it easier.

Article 13 "The Secret to Teaching Tech: Delegate"

The Secret to Teaching Tech: Delegate

There's a secret to teaching kids how to use the computer. It's called 'delegate'. I don't mean slough off teaching to aides or parents. I'm referring to empowering students to be problem-solvers, and then expect it. Here's how:

- Computers are only hard to learn if kids are *told* they are. Don't. Compare keyboarding to piano—a skill lots of kids feel good about—or one that relates to your particular group. Remove fear.
- Teach students how to do the twenty most common problems faced on a computer (more on that as they get older). Expect them to know these—do pop quizzes if that's your teaching style). Post them on the walls. Do a Problem-solving Board. Remind them if they know these, they'll have 70% less problems (that's true, too) than kids who don't know how to solve these. If they raise their hand and ask for help, play Socrates and force them to think through the answer. Sometimes I point to the wall. Sometimes I ask the class for help. Pick a way that works for you. The only solution you *can't* employ is to do it for them
- Teach students keyboard shortcuts. Does that sound like an odd suggestion? It isn't. Students learn in different ways. Some are best with menus, ribbons and mouse clicks. Some like the ease and speed of the keyboard. Give them that choice. If they know both ways, they'll pick the one that works best for them. Once they know these, they'll be twice as likely to remember how to exit a program (Alt+F4) or print (Ctrl+P).
- Let neighbors help neighbors. I resisted this for several years, thinking they'd end up chatting about non-tech topics. They don't when sufficiently motivated and interested. They are excited to show off their knowledge by helping classmates.

Lesson #6 Tools and Toolbars

Vocabulary	Problem solving	Skills
• Alt • Ctrl • Double-click • Enter • Icon • Log-on • Palette • Port • Shortkeys • Spacebar • Toolbars • Tools	• My mouse doesn't work (wake it) • My volume doesn't work (are headphones plugged in?) • Double-click doesn't work (enter) • Students turn monitors off because they can't close programs? Have them leave monitors on at class end. • Trouble remembering tools? Use shortkeys. • I can't close the program (Alt+F4) • My drag-and-drop doesn't work (use left mouse button, not right)	**New** **Scaffolded** Tools/toolbars Hardware problems Important keys Shortkeys Keyboarding Symbols
Academic Applications Math, tech, relationships, compare-contrast	**Materials Required** Internet, drawing program, keyboard program, student workbooks (if using)	**Standards** CCSS.St. for Math.Pr #2 NETS: 1d, 5c

Essential Question

How do tools and toolbars help me use technology?

Big Idea

Use symbols to share ideas faster and more efficiently

Teacher Preparation

- Talk with grade-level team to tie into symbols.
- Know which tasks weren't completed last week.
- Integrate domain-specific tech vocabulary into lesson.
- Know if you need extra time to complete this lesson.

Assessment Strategies

- Anecdotal observation
- Completed warm-up, exit ticket
- Joined class conversations
- [tried to] solve own problems
- Decisions followed class rules
- Left room as s/he found it
- Higher order thinking: analysis, evaluation, synthesis
- Habits of mind observed

Steps

Time required: 45 minutes in one sitting or spread throughout the week with 20 minutes set aside for Symbols lesson

Class warm-up: Keyboard homerow with Popcorn Typer, Dance Mat Typing, or another that focuses on one row.

_____Review important keys (poster in Appendix) students should know by year-end.

_____Review parts of the digital devices used in your class—CPU, monitor, keyboard, mouse, headphones, volume, printer, power buttons, USB ports, peripherals. Show how they connect to the device. Discuss troubleshooting hardware problems:

- *If volume doesn't work, check headphones and volume control.*
- *If mouse doesn't work, is it lit up (which means mouse works)?*
- *If keyboard doesn't work, does NumLock work (which means keyboard works)?*

- *If headphones don't work, are they plugged in? In correct CPU?*
- *If monitor doesn't work, is it on? Is mouse awake?*
- *If computer doesn't work, is it on? Is it hibernating?*

_____Review shortkeys students are familiar with:

- *Ctrl+P*
- *Ctrl+S*
- *Alt+F4*
- *Ctrl+V*
- *Ctrl+C*
- *Alt+Tab*

_____Remind students of the pictures they drew in 1st grade (if they used the SL tech curriculum last year) to symbolize their homeland (for example, students thought *Figures 43a-b* symbolize America).

Figure 43a-b: Pictures as symbols

_____What do the images in *Figures 44a-d* symbolize to you (or pick symbols relevant to your inquiry)?

Figure 44a-d: Common symbols

_____Discuss the idea a picture is worth a thousand words. What does that mean? Is a picture a symbol of words and thoughts?

_____Discuss math signs (*Figure 45a*) and numbers (*Figure 45b*). How are these symbols? Why are 'numbers' symbols?

Figure 45a-b: Mathematical symbols

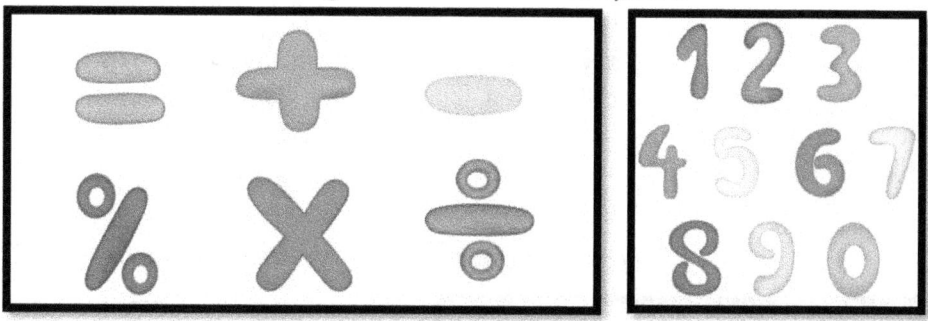

_____What are tools? Toolbars? How do they symbolize an action (*Figures 46a-b*)?

Figure 46a—Toolbar symbols; 46b—desktop icon symbols

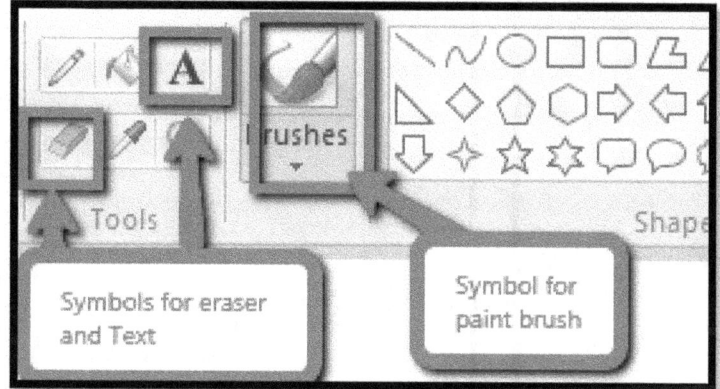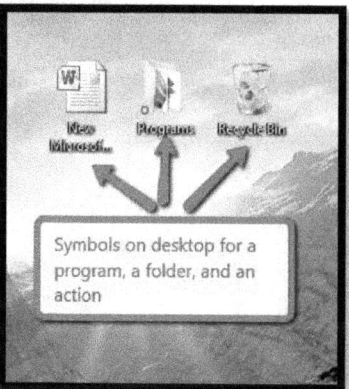

_____Open drawing program (KidPix, TuxPaint, ABCYa, other) in the digital device you use. Allow students to explore the tools and toolbars that are available.
_____If you use multiple digital devices in your classroom (say, Chromebooks and iPads), compare toolbars and tools in both. Discuss differences and reasons.
_____Draw a symbol that visually represents an idea, words, or something else.

Class exit ticket: *Create a poll with a word that can be interpreted many ways. Ask students to vote on what they think the meaning is. See article at the end of Lesson on* The Power of Symbols—What does 'Turkey' mean?

Differentiation

- *Replace this lesson with one from Inquiry-based Teaching with PBL (from Structured Learning)).*

Article 14 "The Power of Symbols—What Does 'Turkey' Mean?"

The Power of Symbols–What Does 'Turkey' Mean?

As a summation to your discussion with students on symbols, idiomatic expressions, geography, farms, or another topic, post this on your class screen. The poll includes lots of definitions for the word 'turkey'–from objective to idiomatic. Have each student come up some time during the day (or class) and make pick all those they are familiar with.

Figure 47a—Symbols poll; 47b—result of poll

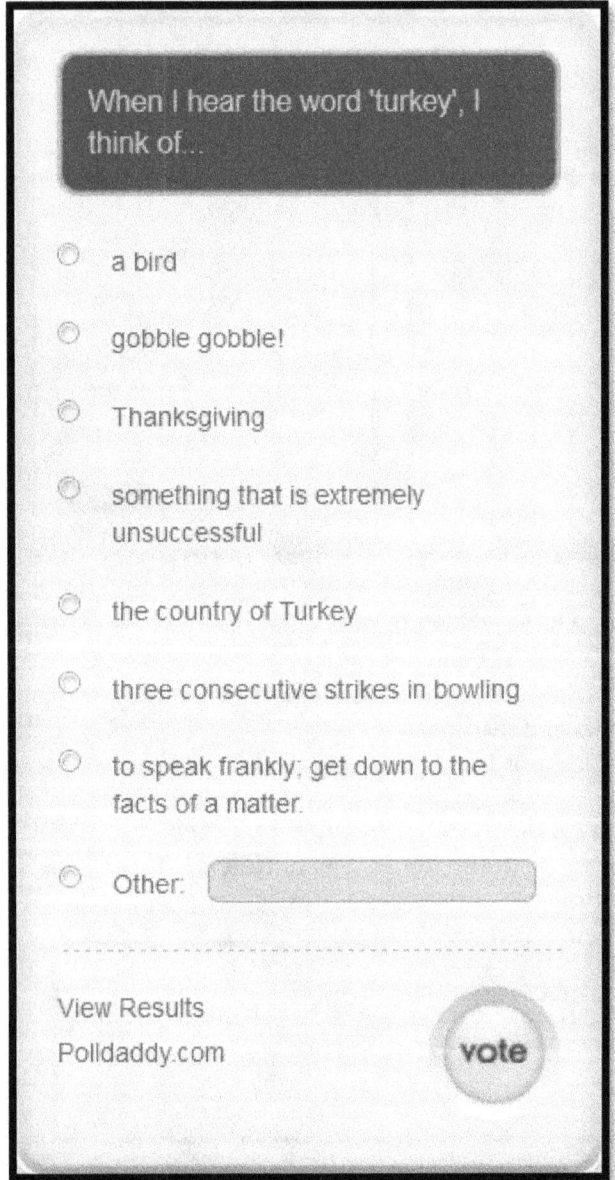
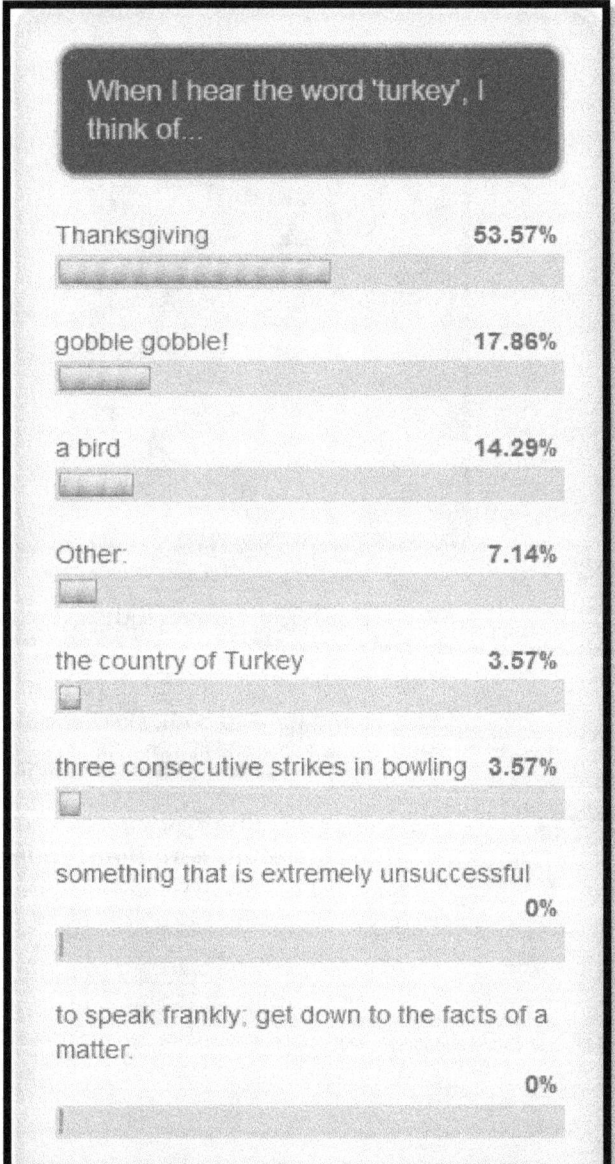

2nd Grade Technology Curriculum: Teacher Manual

Lesson #7 Coding

Vocabulary	Problem solving	Skills
• Animation • Coding • Debug • Hour of code • Programming • Screenshot • Sequence • Symbolism	• I don't know how to use the programming tool (experiment; be a risk-taker) • I don't like coding (why?) • My partner does lots of the work (that's OK if you do your part) • I couldn't debug my program (start at the beginning)	**New** Coding/programming Animation Screenshots **Scaffolded** Problem solving
Academic Applications Math, critical thinking, habits of the mind	**Materials Required** Coding links, membership in onsite program (i.e., Code.org)	**Standards** CCSS Stds for Math. Practice NETS: 4a-b, 5c-d

Essential Question
How do I use a program I've never seen before?

Big Idea
By thinking critically, I can create something new and useful.

Teacher Preparation
- Have all coding/programming tools ready to use.
- Talk with grade-level team so you tie into conversations.
- Know which tasks weren't completed last week.
- Integrate domain-specific tech vocabulary into lesson.
- If doing Hour of Code, try to get additional time—at least 75 minutes—with each class to complete the activities.

Assessment Strategies
- Followed directions
- Anecdotal observations
- Joined class conversations
- [tried to] solve own problems
- Worked well with a partner
- Decisions followed class rules
- Left room as s/he found it
- Higher order thinking: analysis, evaluation, synthesis
- Habits of mind observed

Steps

Time required: 75 minutes—60 for the Hour of Code activity and 15 minutes for set-up
Class warm-up: None

_____Discuss critical thinking and problem solving. Does this apply to, say, Minecraft?

_____The reasons educators embrace coding are simple: **It teaches children to think.** Discuss fundamental programming concepts:

- ***abstraction and symbolism**—*variables are common in math, but also in education. Tools, toolbars, images—these all represent something bigger.
- ***creativity**—*think outside the box; develop solutions no one else has
- ***debugging**—*write-edit-rewrite; when you make a mistake, don't give up or call for an expert. Look at what happened and fix where it went wrong.

- ***if-then thinking**–actions have consequences*
- ***logic**–follow a problem from A to Z, understand the predictability of movements*
- ***sequencing**–know what happens when; mentioned in CCSS for grades 1 through 5*

_____Share this with students and get their thoughts:

> ***"In 1997, the New York Times reported, 'It may be a hundred years before a computer beats humans at Go.' It took 16 years."***

_____December will host the **Hour of Code**, a one-hour introduction to coding, programming, and why students should love it. It's designed to demystify code and show that anyone can learn to be a maker, a creator, and an innovator.

_____Coding is a great tie-in to Common Core Math Standards. Any time you show students how to use math skills outside of math, it surprises them. They don't expect a discussion on problem solving or modeling to come from math.

_____Review the Common Core Standards for Mathematical Practice. If you are not a Common Core school, review the similar guidelines from your Standards:

- CCSS.Math.Practice.MP2
  Reason abstractly and quantitatively
- CCSS.Math.Practice.MP3
  Construct viable arguments; critique reasoning of others
- CCSS.Math.Practice.MP4
  Model with mathematics
- CCSS.Math.Practice.MP5
  Use appropriate tools strategically
- CCSS.Math.Practice.MP6
  Attend to precision
- CCSS.Math.Practice.MP7
  Look for and make use of structure
- CCSS.Math.Practice.MP8
  Look for and express regularity in repeated reasoning

_____Most students think programming looks like *Figure 48a* when it actually looks like *Figure 48b*:

Figure 48a-b: Which is programming?

 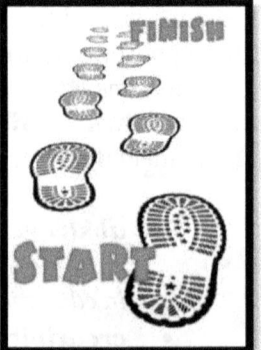

2nd Grade Technology Curriculum: Teacher Manual

_____Do students remember coding activities from previous years—*Figures 49a-c*:

Figure 49a—Kodable; 49b—Hopscotch; 49c—Tynker

 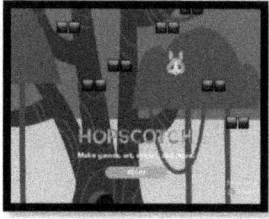 

_____This lesson presents four approaches to coding. Pick one that works for your student group:

1. *Hour of Code lessons*
2. *miscellaneous coding websites*
3. *sequencing*
4. *animation*

_____These can be done individually or in small groups. They may be done any time during the school year.

Follow one of the free online Hour of Code programs

_____Websites like Code.org (Google for web address) offer full lesson plans for Hour of Code. This is the easiest way to get involved in programming as they do all the planning for you. This may be exactly what you need.
_____Before starting, review digital citizenship–especially privacy.

Miscellaneous coding websites

_____Here are some great coding/programming websites 2nd graders find exciting:

- Minecraft Edu
- ScratchJr.
- Tinkercad–fee–perfect for 3D printing

_____Find a list of coding websites by grade level on Ask a Tech Teacher's resource pages.
_____Here are apps that take coding to iPads if you're a 1:1 iPad school:

- Cargo-Bot—logic iPad game
- Hopscotch (for up to intermediate–more complicated than Kodable)
- Kodable
- Tynker

_____For an in-depth discussion on three iPad programming apps, read the article at the end of the Lesson, *Want to Code on an IPad? Here are 3 Great Apps.*

Sequencing

_____Create a series of sequenced activities using slides that students must rearrange. These can be simple or involved, and might tie into inquiry taking place in the classroom. For example, enter life cycle slides into a slideshow tool like PowerPoint or Google Slides, share with students, and have them arrange in the correct order. In *Figures 50a-c*, what's the correct order for the slides? _____This can be done as a class or in small groups.

Figure 50a-c: Correct sequence

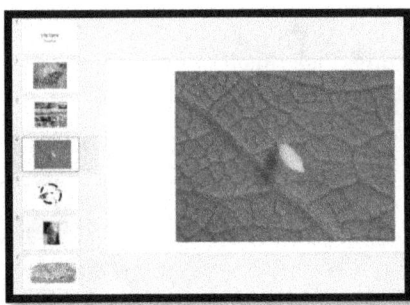  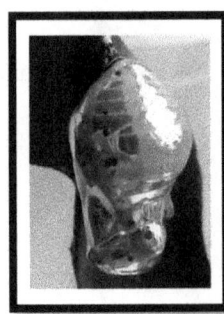

Animation

_____Use a free program like Pivot Animator (find it by searching the Internet) to program a stick figure. It's simple and students love making their own creative animated stories.

Figure 51a-c—Stick figure animation

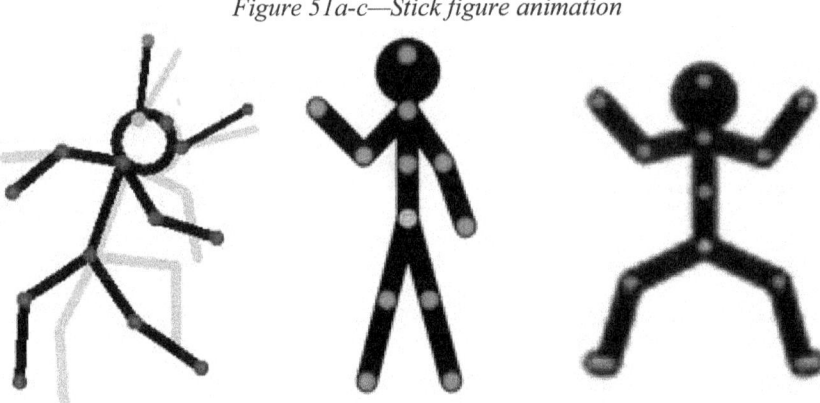

_____In *Figures 51b-c*, the red dots show places where the figure can be bent. Each frame, students make a minor adjustment to the figure. By the time they finish and play the animation, the figure appears to be moving.

_____Pivot Stick Figure is a downloaded program. If you have IPads, try the apps Stick Nodes or Scribble Movie. If you use Chromebooks, try one of the other Coding options.

_____Save a screenshot (explain why this will not save the animation) to digital portfolios with student last name and project name. Here are options, depending upon your digital device:

- **Windows:** *Snipping Tool*
- **Chromebook:** *hold down control key and press window switcher key*
- **Mac:** *Command Shift 3 for a full screenshot; Command Shift 4 for partial*

- **Surface tablet**: hold down volume and Windows button
- **iPad**: hold Home button and power button at same time
- **Online**: a screenshot tool like Jing, Nimbus, or Snagit

_____Throughout class, check for understanding.

Class exit ticket: None

Differentiation

- If you struggle with programming because you've never taught it before, read the article at the end of this Lesson, *"How do I Teach a Program I Don't Know How to Use"*
- If this lesson doesn't work for students, use one from How to Jumpstart the Inquiry-based Classroom. It has 5 projects aligned with curriculum.

Is Windows a virus?

No, Windows is not a virus. Here's what viruses do:

1. **They replicate quickly** - okay, Windows does that.
2. **Viruses use up valuable system resources, slowing down the system as they do so** - okay, Windows does that.
3. **Viruses will, from time to time, trash your hard disk** - okay, Windows does that too.
4. **Viruses are usually carried, unknown to the user, along with valuable programs and systems.** - Sigh. Windows does that, too.
5. **Viruses will occasionally make the user suspect their system is out of date and the user will buy new hardware.** - Yup, Windows does that, too.

But there are fundamental differences: Viruses are well supported by their authors, are running on most systems, their program code is fast, compact and efficient and they tend to become more sophisticated as they mature.

So Windows is not a virus. It's a bug.

Article 15 "Want to Code on an iPad? Here are 3 Great Apps"

Want to Code on an IPad? Here are 3 Great Apps

Coding has become the poster child for a tech-infused classroom. So many teachers took students to Code.org's curriculum offerings, the website crashed.

So what is 'coding'? According to the Urban Dictionary, it's another word for 'programming' which means:

The art of turning caffeine into Error Messages

Let's go to Webster's definition instead:

The act or job of creating computer programs

Not much better. To techies, 'programming' or 'coding' is

a series of symbols, used synonymously as text and grouped to imply or prompt the multimedia in the games and programs that happen on computers, websites, and mobile apps.

According to Computer Science Education Week:

- There will be 1 million more computing jobs than students over the next 10 years (adding up to $500 billion in salaries)
- More than 50 percent of all projected math and science occupations are in computing occupations.
- Computing occupations are among the highest-paying jobs for new graduates. Yet fewer than 3% of college students graduate with a degree in computer science.

When kids learn to code, they also learn to thrive in the 21st Century world. No surprise the United Kingdom took the bold step of adding coding to the core school curriculum.

Most programming classes, training, and games take place on websites, but with the popularity of iPads, developers created apps to put the learning where kids live. As I evaluated three to share with you today, I measured them against the minimum standards for any app—be it coding or reading—used for education. These guidelines include:

- *support the '4 C's'—creativity, critical thinking, communication, collaboration*
- *offer compelling content ('compelling' varies teacher-to-teacher and student-to-student)*
- *are not distracting or overwhelming in colors, music, or activity*
- *offer levels that differentiate for student needs*
- *include few ads—and those that are there do not take up a significant portion of the screen*
- *are intuitive to use with a short learning curve*
- *don't collect personal information other than user credentials or data required to operate the app*
- *rated 'for everyone' or 'low maturity'*
- *include no in-app purchases or billing*

Based on these criteria, here are my top three:

Kodable

Kodable bills itself as a programming curriculum for grades K-2 that can be accomplished in twenty minutes a week. The main character is a chinless blue fuzzball with big eyes and a small mouth. The goal is to move him/her along a short track littered with coins by providing commands to indicate which direction the creature should go. Players use logical thinking and sequencing to complete the maze and win gold coins. As they improve, they level up, adding if-then analysis to their decision matrix, and the course gets more complicated.

It's colorful, active, self-directed, and requires no programming experience. It's fun music and kid-friendly animation makes it intuitive to use and easy to keep playing. Audio directions and a helping hand show what needs to be done if students get stuck. There are minimal tutorials, making this app about exploring, trial-and-error, and an adventurous spirit.

Hopscotch

Hopscotch teaches basic computer programming concepts to children between the ages of 8 and 12. It uses no typing or syntax, just drag and drop blocks. The interface is simple, colors vibrant, and moves intuitive (at least as you start). Using it, students create games, animations, drawings and more while learning to make their characters do simple (and not-so-simple) moves.

When students open the program, they start with a blank canvas or a pre-made project ranging from easy to difficult. Once they make their selection, they receive visual prompts to program their project, often as text and images, but sometimes in the form of a video that walks them through what will be required. When completed, students view their project, debug (edit) it as needed, and then publish it to the Hopscotch community where it is shared with other enthusiasts.

Tynker

Tynker, both the website and the companion app, teaches programming with puzzles to ages 3-8. You get twenty puzzles with the free app and can purchase more as needed. They are solved by stringing together commands in sequences using a drag-n-drop interface. No internet connectivity is required. When students open the app, they choose 'Create' or 'Play':

- *To build a new game, choose 'Create', and then choose 'New project', 'Game Kit' or 'Sample.*
- *To play an existing game, choose 'Play'*

Tynker uses fundamental coding concepts—sequencing, logic, critical thinking—to solve a puzzle. It follows the popular Scratch pictorial model of snapping together coded pieces rather than writing out intimidating words and symbols.

There are a lot of coding apps available besides these three—Codea, Pyonkee, Lightbot, Tickle App, and Scratch Jr. Coding is a transformative tool for the 21st Century classroom. Expect lots more entrants and upgrades to existing offerings before this year's December Hour of Code.

Article 16 "How Do I Teach a Program I Don't Know How to Use?"

How Do I Teach a Program I Don't Know How to Use?

I am constantly finding new programs I think would be perfect in the classroom. I might see colleagues using them or my PLN raves about them so loudly, I figure I better try them out. Because I'm a technology teacher, I can usually unravel how to use them pretty quickly. Sometimes a few minutes. Usually, less than fifteen. Am I special? Do I have a magical skill that tells me how to use what I've never before seen without training? Is this something only I can do and other teachers need to take a class or spend hours struggling, me at their elbow?

Not at all. In fact, anyone can learn a new program, app, tool quickly and efficiently with just a little inside knowledge and a few secrets. The first secret: **It's more about problem solving than tech.**

Before I share the second secret, let's talk about knowing how to quickly learn new web tools is important. If you're a teacher, you know there's no shortage of Favorite Tech Tools in the minds of colleagues, students, parents, or admin. Here's my list from last month: Edmodo (I'm the only teacher in my PLN who isn't wrapped around this amazing digital portfolio tool), Tellagami, Haiku Deck, Smores, and Canva. I learned all of them in the past thirty days except one. Next month, it will be Storify, Storyjumper, Hemingway App, Diigo, Teach Your Monster To Read, and Sumdog.

This plethora of web tools gives many teachers I know technophobia. There's no way to stay on top of the learning curve so why even begin. In fact, it's one of the biggest complaints from teachers in my school—that every time I suggest a tech project, it includes a tool they've never heard of and don't have time to learn.

You know what? They're right. But there is a way to make it easy. That's my second secret: Most tools are intuitive. That means they are constructed in a way that's similar to all other tools—

- *they use common commands—file, exit, save*
- *they use common symbols and shortkeys—red squiggly line for spelling, Ctrl+F to find a word on the page*
- *their toolbars and tools look like lots of other programs—bold, alignment, links, indent*
- *program layout looks familiar—toolbars at the top*
- *right click brings up relevant commands*
- *big start button somewhere obvious*

When you're faced with a new tool, trust that this will be the case. In fact, using it as a teachable moment with students and try the new tool out in front of them. Show them how you learn. That means you don't need to spend a lot of time preparing. Budget five minutes to review the canvas and experiment with a few clicks, but leave the heavy lifting—the real experimenting—for class, with your students. Let them see how you learn a new tool.

Let's test this out on a program I taught myself quickly and it has since become one of my favorites for creating posters—Smore.

The screen opens like this:

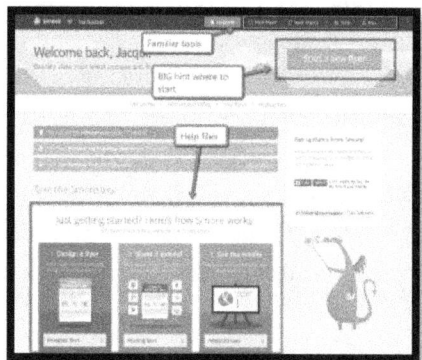

1. *Familiar toolbar at the top, helpful videos to explain details, a big BOLD Start button*

Where do you go first? Here's the next screen:

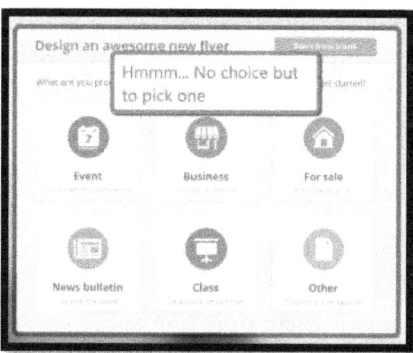

2. *Six choices. No other options.*

If you make the wrong choice, use the back arrow to return to this screen. Here's the next screen:

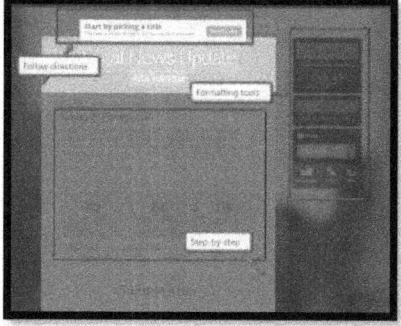

3. *Step-by-step directions for filling out the flier; easy formatting tools*

Once the flier is created, it continues to be a standard process to save/export/share.

You might think this is easier than other web tools, but it isn't. Most web tools try to be intuitive, easy to figure out. They want to be understood so you return.

Which brings us back to Secret #1: Using a new web tool is no different than the problem solving we teach students, often wrapped around the **Common Core Standards for Mathematical Practice** (which I've slightly reworded below):

- *Make sense of a program [look around the screen and see what looks familiar] and persevere in solving it [believe you can do it]*
- *Construct viable arguments [what's a logical approach to using the tool?]*
- *Use appropriate tools strategically [which tools, toolbars have you used in other circumstances to solve a problem?]*
- *Attend to precision [carefully follow steps in prescribed order; for example, screen 3 above]*
- *Look for and make use of structure [look for patterns of use, familiar from other web tools]*
- *Look for an make use of repeated reasoning [notice how the web tool works and trust that it will continue to work the same way]*

Note: If you're thinking back to Microsoft's upgrade from Office 2003's drop down menus to Office 2007's ribbon, I agree—that was a nightmare. I have no idea what they were thinking. That boondoggle of an upgrade was the single biggest boost to Google Apps.

That's it. Those are my secrets:

- *look around the screen*
- *notice what's familiar*
- *trust yourself*
- *keep putting one virtual foot in front of the other*

If you have a web tool you'd like to learn and aren't sure how to get started, drop me a note in the comments. I'll give you suggestions or we can work through it together.

Lesson #8 Google Earth

Vocabulary	Problem solving	Skills
• 3D • Digital portfolio • Google Earth • Mashup • Screenshot • Search engine • Street view • Toolbar • Zoom	• How do I use Street View (click SV guy and see which streets light up) • Why can't I use Street View (it's not available everywhere) • Buildings aren't 3D (is 3D layer selected? All buildings aren't 3D) • Difficult dragging globe (use arrows) • Difficult changing perspective (use tool on right side of screen)	**New** Mash-up of tools **Scaffolded** Digital citizenship Digital tools Google Earth Drawing tool Image editor
Academic Applications Writing, geography	**Materials Required** Google Earth on computers, drawing program, keyboard website, student workbooks (if using)	**Standards** CCSS.ELA-Literacy.RI.2.7 NETS: 1c, 6a

Essential Question

How can I use technology to explore my world?

Big Idea

Use multiple technologies to identify questions to investigate

Teacher Preparation

- Have Google Earth (or alternative) and class drawing program ready to use.
- Talk with grade level team to tie into inquiry.
- Know which tasks weren't completed last week.
- Integrate domain-specific tech vocabulary into lesson.
- Know whether you need extra time to complete lesson.

Assessment Strategies

- Followed directions
- Completed warm-up
- Understood how programs work together in project
- Explored Google Earth
- Joined class conversations
- [tried to] solve own problems
- Decisions followed class rules
- Left room as s/he found it
- Habits of mind observed

Steps

Time required: 45 minutes in one sitting or spread throughout the week with 30 minutes set aside for Google Earth lesson

Class warm-up: Keyboard homerow using RoomRecess' Popcorn Typer, BBC's Dance Mat Typing, or another that focuses on one row. Observe student posture, hand position.

_____Open Google Earth. Discuss how this program contributes to understanding of a topic:

- easily see a country's relationship to the world
- zoom in or out to get a better perspective
- drop into Street View to see firsthand what the world looks like

_____Students used it in Kindergarten (*Figure 52a*—virtual field trip) and 1st (*Figure 52b*—symbols)--if they used the SL tech curriculum:

2nd Grade Technology Curriculum: Teacher Manual

Figure 52a-b: Google Earth projects in K/1

_____Open Google Earth. Ask a volunteer to review program for class—zoom in/out, drag map, street view, tour 3d buildings, and use arrows.

_____Demo today's project. It is done by mashing up multiple programs. Before beginning, discuss this concept with students—the usefulness of using various tools for one project. Have they done this before? Discuss the report they'll do at the end of the school year that will 'mash up' text and images from a word processing program and the internet.

_____Review today's project—*Figures 53a-c:*

Figure 53a-c: Mashup using Google Earth and drawing program

- *Find country of origin on Google Earth. Explore using Street View and 3D layer.*
- *Adjust view so country is recognizable on screen. Zoom in/out and drag map with the mouse to display country nicely.*
- *Take a screenshot in Google Earth and save to student digital portfolio.*
- *Open class drawing program. Expect students to remember how to use programs from prior years.*
- *Add the saved image to the canvas.*
- *Add the flag for the student country of origin (sticker or drawn in). If the drawing program doesn't come with clipart for flags:*
    - o *show how to search for a flag on a search engine; upload to the drawing program (this is how the flag was inserted in Figure 53b)*
    - o *have students draw it in (as was done in Figure 53c)*
    - o *If going online for the flag, review digital rights and responsibilities (from earlier lesson)*
- *Add student name with ABC tool or handwritten.*

2nd Grade Technology Curriculum: Teacher Manual

_____Discuss which steps are from Google Earth and which from the drawing program used in class.
_____Have students find their country of origin using Google Earth. Zoom in and adjust to preference, then save the image to the student digital portfolio. Don't worry if it's not perfect.
_____Throughout class, check for understanding.
_____When done, save to digital portfolios with student last name and project name; print/share/publish, as desired. If your drawing tool doesn't allow saving, try a screenshot:

- **Windows**: *the Snipping Tool*
- **Chromebook:** *hold down the control key and press the window switcher key*
- **Mac**: *Command Shift 4 to take a partial screenshot*
- **Surface tablet**: *hold down volume and Windows button at the same time*
- **iPad**: *hold Home button and power button at same time*
- **Online**: *a screenshot tool like Jing, Nimbus, or Snagit*

_____Why is it important to put student name in file name? Demonstrate a search for students of their name. See how their files show up even if they didn't save it right—as long as they saved it to network? Putting a last name in file name makes it harder to lose work.

Class exit ticket: **None**

Differentiation

- Use upcoming field trip instead of country of origin. Show route, measure distance, enter buildings if 3D available, travel streets if Street View available. Very fun.
- Use a geographic location that ties into classroom discussion instead of country of origin. As above, use 3D buildings and Street View to extend learning.
- Explore other locations using Google's World of Wonder.
- Explore Universe or underwater by switching to Google Earth and Google Sky.
- Use time of day tool to show sunrise/sunset around globe.
- If class is discussing a historic event, use Time Slider tool to change date.
- If this lesson doesn't work for students, use one from How to Jumpstart the Inquiry-based Classroom. It has 5 projects per grade level aligned with SL curriculum.

2nd Grade Technology Curriculum: Teacher Manual

Lesson #9 Intro to Word Processing

Vocabulary	Problem solving	Skills
• Column • Ctrl • Cursor • Edit • Font • Format • Menu • Number Square • Ribbon • Row • Screen • Show/hide • Word processing • Wrap	• How do I open a program (double click icon)? • How do I close a program (Alt+F4)? • What's the difference between backspace and delete (see Appendix)? • What's the difference between 'save' and 'save-as' (see poster in Appendix)? • What's the difference between 'edit' and 'format'? • What's the difference between menu, ribbon, and toolbar? • I didn't finish the Number Square (that's OK, as long as you worked hard) • Why must I have my name in file name?	**New** Number square Word processing Spreadsheets (if using this option) Annotate workbooks (if using these) **Scaffolded** Text skills Keyboarding Problem solving
Academic Applications math	**Materials Required** Number Square template, word processing program, student workbooks (if using), Google Earth (maybe),	**Standards** CCSS.ELA-Literacy.W.2.6 NETS: 1d, 6a, 6c

Essential Question

How do I use technology for math?

Big Idea

Develop an awareness of how tech tools help learning

Teacher Preparation

- Ask math teacher if students know the Number Square.
- Have Number Square file available for download.
- Know which tasks weren't completed last week.
- Integrate domain-specific tech vocabulary into lesson.
- Know if you need extra time to complete this lesson.

Assessment Strategies

- Made connections between tens, digits, rows, columns
- Saved project to digital portfolio
- Annotated workbook (if using)
- Completed warm-up, exit ticket
- Joined class conversations
- [tried to] solve own problems
- Left room as s/he found it
- Higher order thinking: analysis, evaluation, synthesis
- Habits of mind observed

Steps

Time required: 45 minutes in one sitting or spread throughout the week with 30 minutes set aside for Number Square

Class warm-up: Keyboard QWERTY row using RoomRecess' Popcorn Typer_or another that focuses on one row. Observe student posture, hand position.

_____Students who haven't finished the **Google Earth** project, do so while other students are warming up on keyboarding.

_____This unit starts a series to familiarize students with word processing programs. It includes:

2nd Grade Technology Curriculum: Teacher Manual

- *Intro to basics (this Lesson)*
- *3 writing projects*
- *1 graphic organizer*
- *1 comprehensive report*

_____By the end of this Lesson, students will know word processing basics that will get them through much of what is required in second grade.

_____Open class word processing program on class screen; review layout and demonstrate pieces:

- *appearance of screen*
- *tools and toolbars*
- *menus students will use*
- *cursor: tells user where they are*

_____Open **Number Square** (full-size *Assessment 5* at the end of the Lesson) on class screen. What is a number square? Is it familiar to students? Do they see how each row is a bundle of 10 (see *Figure 54*)? How many is a bundle of ten tens? Discuss the place value of each digit in a number. Notice how each column is laid out.

Figure 3--Number Square

_____Demonstrate how to type student and teacher name into blanks. If not in typeover, it will push line out. Demonstrate this and how to fix.

_____Review basics students will use today:

- *show where font size/color/type tools are*
- *discuss the difference between backspace and delete*
- *discuss the difference between format and edit*

_____Adjust instructions to match class word processing tool. Delete steps as needed or add your own.

_____If necessary, review math concepts—like 'multiples' that are referred to in the directions.

_____Add student and teacher name. If students have a student workbook, help them use the annotation tool available in your school to mark up their PDF.

_____Demo first line of Number Square (*Assessment 5*):

- *fill in missing numbers*
- *change fonts as required in directions*
- *change colors as required in directions*
- *change font sizes as required in directions*

_____Don't expect students to finish project. The goal is to get comfortable using word processing tools, changing fonts, and formatting a document. These are skills they will use often.

_____ Throughout class, check for understanding.

_____ Save to digital portfolio either as a stand-alone document or a screenshot of the student workbook page. Include student last name and project name in the file name.

_____ Why is it important to include student last name in file name? Demonstrate a search for students of their name. See how their files show up even if they didn't save it right—as long as they saved it to the network? Putting a last name in file name makes it harder to lose work.

_____ Occasionally when students have difficulty doing what you are teaching, ask why—and listen carefully to the answer. It may not be what you expect.

Figure 55—Number Square in a spreadsheet

Class exit ticket: **Have neighbor verify that student saved/printed/ published/shared number square correctly.**

Differentiation

- Show students how to align text in cells, add borders and pictures as in Assessment 5, cell 99.
- Do this exercise in a spreadsheet program rather than a word processor (see Figure 55). Early finishers can visit number square websites such as NRICH's Build a number square
- If this lesson doesn't work for students, use one from Inquiry-based Teaching with PBL (from Structured Learning).

2nd Grade Technology Curriculum: Teacher Manual

Assessment 5—Number Square

Number Square

Name: _____ Teacher_____

Directions:

1. Fill in missing numbers
2. Color every multiple of 2 red
3. Change font on numbers that end in 7 to **Comic Sans**
4. Color every multiple of '3' blue
5. Change font size for all multiples of 9 to **24**

1	2	3				7			10
	12			15	16				20
		23		25		27		29	
	32		34	35		37			40
41	42	43			46		48	49	
51	52				56	57			60
				65				69	70
71		73			76				
	82	83						88	
91			94						100

108

Lesson #10 Holiday Story

Vocabulary	Problem solving	Skills
• Borders • Clipart • Edit • Font • Format • Heading • Insert • Menu bar • PDF • Red/green squiggles • Taskbar • Title • Wrap	• How do I move down a line (enter) • My picture went in the wrong spot (did you mark spot with cursor?) • What's the difference between 'edit' and 'format'? • What's the difference between a heading and a title? • Where's 'font color'? (Remember skills from Number Square) • Why can't I highlight word to change font (you can—clicking once is faster) • Why triple click? (to select sentence) • My picture won't move (change wrap)	**New** Stories in word processing Importance of titles Wrapping text Using rubrics Compare-contrast **Scaffolded** Digital citizenship Word processing skills Collaboration Annotate workbooks
Academic Applications Writing, language	**Materials Required** word processing program, story rubrics, student workbooks (if using)	**Standards** CCSS.ELA-Literacy.W.2.6 NETS: 1d, 6c, 6d

Essential Question

Can color and visual help me share ideas?

Big Idea

Students use multi-media technology to communicate ideas thoroughly and clearly

Teacher Preparation

- Reinforce writing rules taught in core class.
- Students bring pre-written story (if using this option).
- Have classroom digital tools ready to use.
- Know which tasks weren't completed last week.
- Integrate domain-specific tech vocabulary into lesson.
- Know if you need extra time to complete this lesson.

Assessment Strategies

- Used good keyboarding habits
- Saved project to digital portfolio
- Wrote an interesting title
- Followed writing conventions
- Completed warm-up, exit ticket
- Annotate workbook (if using)
- Worked well with a partner
- Completed project, rubric
- Joined class conversations
- [tried to] solve own problems
- Left room as s/he found it
- Higher order thinking: analysis, evaluation, synthesis
- Habits of mind observed

Steps

Time required: 60 minutes in one sitting or spread throughout the week with 15 minutes set aside to type story and 15 minutes to format

Class warm-up: Keyboard QWERTY row using Popcorn Typer or another tool that focuses on one row. Observe student posture and hand position.

_____Discuss writing. What strategies have students learned for success in writing? With student input, develop a list of skills students will use during this exercise.

_____What is the difference between writing by hand and keyboarding? Consider 1) trying to remember where keys are, 2) typing while thinking, 3) hand gets tired, 4) handwriting is slow 5) typing is slow in 2nd grade. Discuss how all of these might change as they get older.

_____Discuss difference between typing from a written copy and typing from thoughts in student's head. Which is harder? The students' answers may surprise you. You may use either option for this Lesson. If typing from copy, it will take students about 10-15 minutes. If typing from thoughts, give students about 15 minutes.

_____Use a word processing program like MS Word, Google Docs, Open Office, or another your school uses. Review the layout in *Figure 56* and adapt it to your program. For example, where would you find the menu bar on yours?

Figure 56—Word processing start-up page

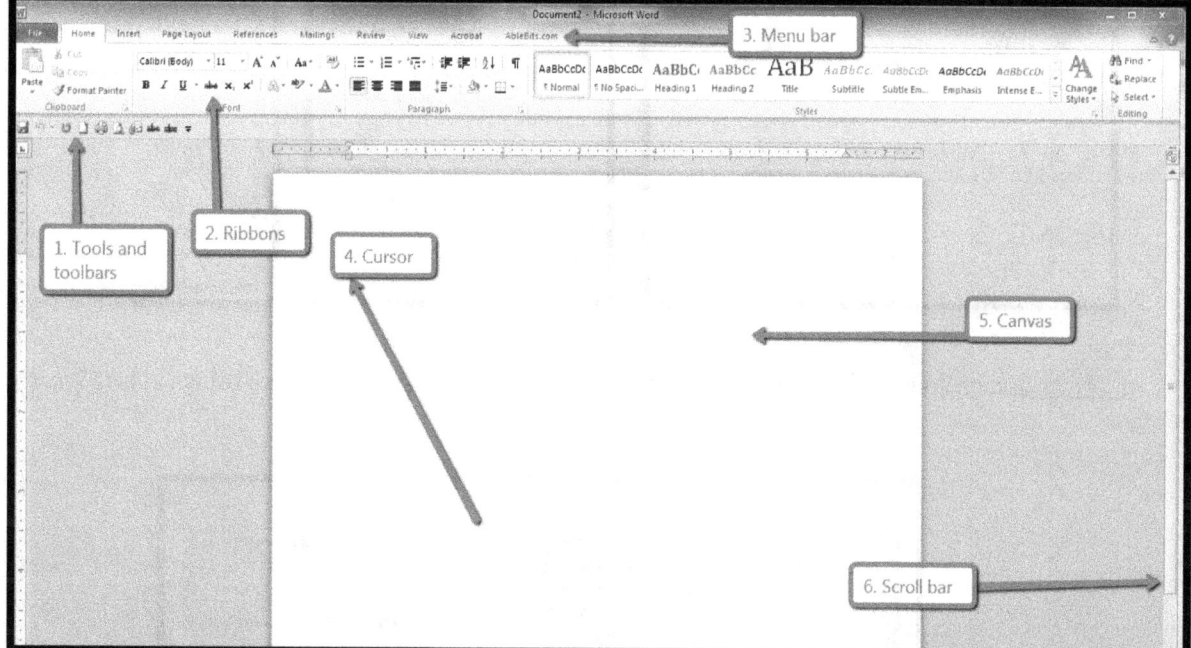

_____Review projects students did in kindergarten and first grade (if they used the SL tech curriculum) that practiced writing skills using digital tools. *Figures 57a-c* were done in drawing tools rather than a word processing tool:

Figure 57a-c—Word processing projects in K, 1

_____How does this **compare-contrast** to writing in word processing? Consider:

- *word processing focuses on text; drawing program focuses on art*
- *word processing has many more ways to format text than a drawing program (because of the prior point)*

_____Show *Figures 58a-c* (two in Google Docs and one in Word). Students always get excited by the colors, fonts, clipart. They don't believe they'll be able to do this!

Figure 58a-b—Story in Google Doc; 58c—in Word

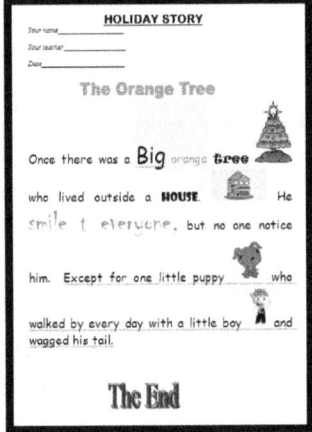

_____Every time students sit at computer, remind them to use good keyboarding skills (*Figure 59*):

Figure 59—Proper keyboarding posture

_____Review skills learned with Number Squares: fonts, sizes, insert, tools, and toolbars.
_____Remind students they will use same writing skills here they use for class literacy projects.
_____Add heading at top (name, teacher, date). Why a heading? Add two enters to leave room for the title. That will be added later.
_____Change font to 48.
_____Follow class strategies for story writing (i.e., Bold Beginning, Mighty Middle, Exciting Ending).
Remember: **Students are still learning to use the word processing tool.** They will have

difficulty juggling writing and typing skills so if you want to grade this project on the quality of the writing, have them bring a completed story to class that they simply type into their word processing program.

_____Sentence starts with capital, ends with period; space after period/comma. What other writing rules did class come up with that should be used today?

_____Correct red (spell-check) and green (grammar) squiggly lines. When do students use backspace or delete to make corrections? What are the blue squiggly lines—can students figure that out?

_____Work with a neighbor. Read through each other's story and suggest edits.

_____With the story written, have students add title. How do they know the title? Discuss how it comes from story. Discuss that it draws reader in and makes them want to continue. Have neighbor read the story and sum it up into two-three words that suggest the title.

_____Done? Format the story as follows (see *Figures 60a* and *60b* for two examples):

Figure 60a-b—Story in word processing program

 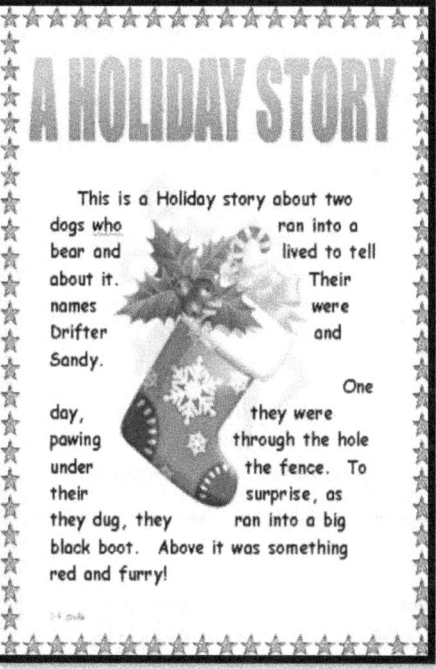

- *Change font of three words by clicking inside word (not highlighting) and selecting tool from ribbon. For example: Use 'Chiller' for 'haunted house'. Show students how to change font to a different one if they change their mind.*
- *Change size of three words by clicking inside word (not highlighting) and selecting tool from ribbon.*
- *Change color of three words by clicking inside word (not highlighting) and selecting tool from ribbon. Match color to word, i.e. make 'pumpkin' orange.*
- *Add a festive border that fits the holiday. Be sure it's a 'page border' (if available).*
- *Add three pictures by clicking where picture should go. Notice blinking cursor. That's where image will go. Insert from clipart. Use handles to resize. Show students how to delete a picture they change their mind about.*
- *Alternatively: Show students how to add one picture and wrap the text around it (Figure 60b). Use handles to resize.*

_____ Check to be sure story fits. If the story is longer than a page, resize font/images.

_____ With neighbor, have students check rubric (*Assessment 6* at the end of the Lesson) to ensure the project has required elements. If using student workbooks, students can annotate the blank rubric in their workbook using a tool like iAnnotate or Adobe, then print that one page or take a screenshot and print that.

_____ Save with or without assistance with student last name and project name (why student name?); print (Ctrl+P, File-print), publish, or share as is done in your classroom.

_____ Ask students: What digital tools are used in this project? (Hint: software, printer). What else could be used? (Hint: online images, email, pdf). How would they create this story without digital tools?

Class exit ticket: **Turn in rubric before leaving class.**

Differentiation

- Use this as a formative assessment of word processing, remembering text skills learned in kindergarten and first grade.
- Students use a story they've already written. In that case: Focus on keyboarding skills.
- Students work in pairs to edit their stories.
- Instead of a word processing tool, students use an audio tool like AudioBoom, a comic creator (like ReadWriteThink, or a multimedia tool like VoiceThread. Note: This may change time required to complete this lesson.
- Publish stories via PDF to class website so students can share with parents.
- If you need extra time for this project, you can shorten the Letter Writing Lessons (next two).
- Show students how to search Google images, find a picture that fits their story, copy-paste where cursor is blinking.
- If students have word study, practice on SpellingCity.
- If this lesson doesn't work for students, use one from Inquiry-based Teaching with PBL (from Structured Learning).

"Pencil and paper: archaic information storage and transmission device that works by depositing smears of graphite on bleached wood pulp. Requires operator skilled at '*handwriting*' technique."

Assessment 6—Story rubric

Name_____   Teacher's Name_____

HOLIDAY STORY GRADING RUBRIC

1. Heading with name, date, teacher   _____
2. Title stands out, centered   _____
3. Several lines of story   _____
   a. 3 different fonts   _____
   b. 3 different size fonts   _____
   c. 3 different colors   _____
   d. Spell-check   _____
   e. Grammar-check   _____
4. 1-3 inline pictures   _____
5. A festive border   _____
6. Story fills one page but not more   _____
7. Professional appearance   _____

Name_____   Teacher's Name_____

HOLIDAY STORY GRADING RUBRIC

1. Heading with name, date, teacher   _____
2. Title stands out, centered   _____
3. Several lines of story   _____
   a. 3 different fonts   _____
   b. 3 different size fonts   _____
   c. 3 different colors   _____
   d. Spell-check   _____
   e. Grammar-check   _____
4. 1-3 inline pictures   _____
5. A festive border   _____
6. Story fills one page but not more   _____
7. Professional appearance   _____

Lesson #11 Holiday Letter I

Vocabulary	Problem solving	Skills
• Alignment • Body • Closing • Fonts • Format • Heading • Hover • Icon • Letter • Red/green squiggles • Tool • Wrap	• Caps stuck (is caps lock on?) • How do I log on (do you know user name and password?) • What's today's date? (hover over clock) • Which alignment tool is center (hover over tools) • What's the difference between grammar and formatting? • What's the difference between save and 'save-as'? • What's the difference between letters and other writing?	**New** Letter writing in word processing tool **Scaffolded** Word processing Digital letter writing Keyboarding
Academic Applications Writing, language	**Materials Required** word processing program, spelling words (if using this activity), student workbooks (if using)	**Standards** CCSS.ELA-Literacy.L.2.1 NETS: 3c, 6d

Essential Question
How do I use technology to write a letter?

Big Idea
Use technology to improve letter-writing skills

Teacher Preparation
- This two-week project can be flipped with Lesson 13 and 14, depending upon timing of holiday.
- Talk with grade team about which grammar rules they are discussing and student foundation in letter writing.
- Know spelling words for week if using this option.
- Have required digital tools ready to use.
- Know which tasks weren't completed last week.
- Integrate domain-specific tech vocabulary into lesson.
- Know if you need extra time to complete the lesson.

Assessment Strategies
- Followed directions
- Saved to digital portfolio
- Worked well with neighbor
- Strengthened letter by revising and editing
- Practiced writing conventions from class and Common Core
- Completed warm-up, exit ticket
- Joined class conversations
- [tried to] solve own problems
- Decisions followed class rules
- Left room as s/he found it
- Higher order thinking: analysis, evaluation, synthesis
- Habits of mind observed

Steps

Time required: 45 minutes in one sitting or spread throughout the week with 30 minutes set aside for letter

Class warm-up: Keyboard QWERTY row with Popcorn Typer or another tool that focuses on one row. Observe student posture and hand position.

_____ This is a two-week project in word processing, to teach formatting skills while reinforcing classroom study on grammar, spelling and elements of a letter.

_____Students wrote letters in kindergarten and first grade (if they used the SL tech curriculum):

Figure 61a-c—Letters from Kindergarten and 1st grade

_____Discuss what makes a letter different from a story (i.e., greeting, closing, content, development).
_____Open word processing program used in your school (Word, Google Docs, Notes, Open Office or similar) as independently as possible. Students will write letters similar to *Figures 62a-c*:

Figure 62a-c—Three levels of letter writing complexity

_____If you use Chromebooks or iPads, you may use the apps for Office 365, Notes, Pages, or Google Drive (Google for addresses). Whatever tool you use, you want it to focus on writing, not images or design. This lesson is to develop student skills within word processing.
_____Type heading (name, teacher, date—enter between each line). Explain alignment, that this is left aligned. Show Word's alignment tools.
_____Discuss letter writing skills students have learned in class, such as:

- *open with a greeting*
- *describe actions, thoughts, and feelings where required*
- *use temporal words to signal event order where required*
- *end with a closing*

_____Type a letter to parents about why students are thankful (or another topic that works for your student group). Use font size 14-16. Adjust font look as learned in earlier lessons. Remind students that text wraps to next line—no need to push *enter*.

2nd Grade Technology Curriculum: Teacher Manual

_____As students type, reinforce keyboarding skills such as elbows at sides, hands on homerow, and legs in front of body. Remind students: Every time they use computer, practice good habits.

_____Check grammar/spelling; clear red/green squiggles.

_____Students won't format the letter this week—that'll be next week. When done, work with neighbor to insure:

- *sentence fluency*
- *good grammar and spelling*
- *proper letter writing style*
- *achieve the purpose of the letter*

_____Continually throughout class, check for understanding.

_____Save (or should they 'save-as'?) with last name in file name (why?).

Class exit ticket: *Have neighbor verify that student saved letter to their digital portfolio, with their last name in the file name.*

Differentiation

- *If students need help with letter writing, try ABCYa.*
- *Students who finish: Practice spelling words on SpellingCity.*
- *Students who finish: Visit internet start page for websites that go with classwork.*
- *Replace this lesson with one from Inquiry-based Teaching with PBL (from Structured Learning).*

"A printer consists of three main parts: the case, the jammed paper tray and the blinking red light"

-Anonymous

Lesson #12 Holiday Letter II

Vocabulary	Problem solving	Skills
• Ctrl+Z • Edit • Format • Handles • Resize • Rubric • Save as • Start button • Taskbar • Undo	• I can't find my letter (search) • Deleted letter by accident (Ctrl+Z) • How do I change word color/font/size? (click inside word; pick tool) • What's the difference between backspace and delete? • What's the difference between 'format' and 'edit'? • How do I clear red and green squiggly lines?	**New** Letter writing in word processing tool **Scaffolded** Word processing Digital letter writing Keyboarding Annotate workbooks
Academic Applications Writing, language	**Materials Required** word processing program, rubric, keyboarding program, student workbooks (if using)	**Standards** CCSS.ELA-Literacy.L.2.1 NETS: 3c, 6d

Essential Question

How do I use technology to write a letter?

Big Idea

Use technology to improve letter-writing skills

Teacher Preparation

- This two-week letter-writing project can be flipped with Lesson 13/14, depending upon timing of holidays.
- Talk with class teacher about grammar rules and letter writing being discussed in class.
- Have class digital tools ready to use.
- Know which tasks weren't completed last week.
- Integrate domain-specific tech vocabulary into lesson.
- Know if you need extra time to complete this lesson.

Assessment Strategies

- Followed directions
- Completed letter, rubric
- Understood digital tools
- Completed warm-up, exit ticket
- Able to annotate workbook (if using workbooks)
- Worked well with a partner
- Joined class conversations
- [tried to] solve own problems
- Decisions followed class rules
- Left room as s/he found it
- Higher order thinking: analysis, evaluation, synthesis
- Habits of mind observed

Steps

Time required: 45 minutes in one sitting or spread throughout the week with 30 minutes set aside for letter project

Class warm-up: Keyboard Lower row using Popcorn Typer or another tool that focuses on one row. Observe student posture, hand position, and good typing habits.

_____This is second of two-week word processing project to teach formatting skills as well as reinforce classroom study on grammar, spelling and elements of a letter.

_____Open student letter started last week as independently as possible. Can't find it? Try these suggestions (*Figure 63*):

- *Did you save to the computer's local drive (i.e., 'My Documents')? Never save there.*
- *If you saved with your name in the file name, go to Start>Search. Type your last name in. It'll populate with all files that include your name.*
- *Were you sitting somewhere else? Start>Search can only find files on the network. Maybe you saved on the local drive where you were sitting. Check last week's seat.*

Figure 63—I can't find my file

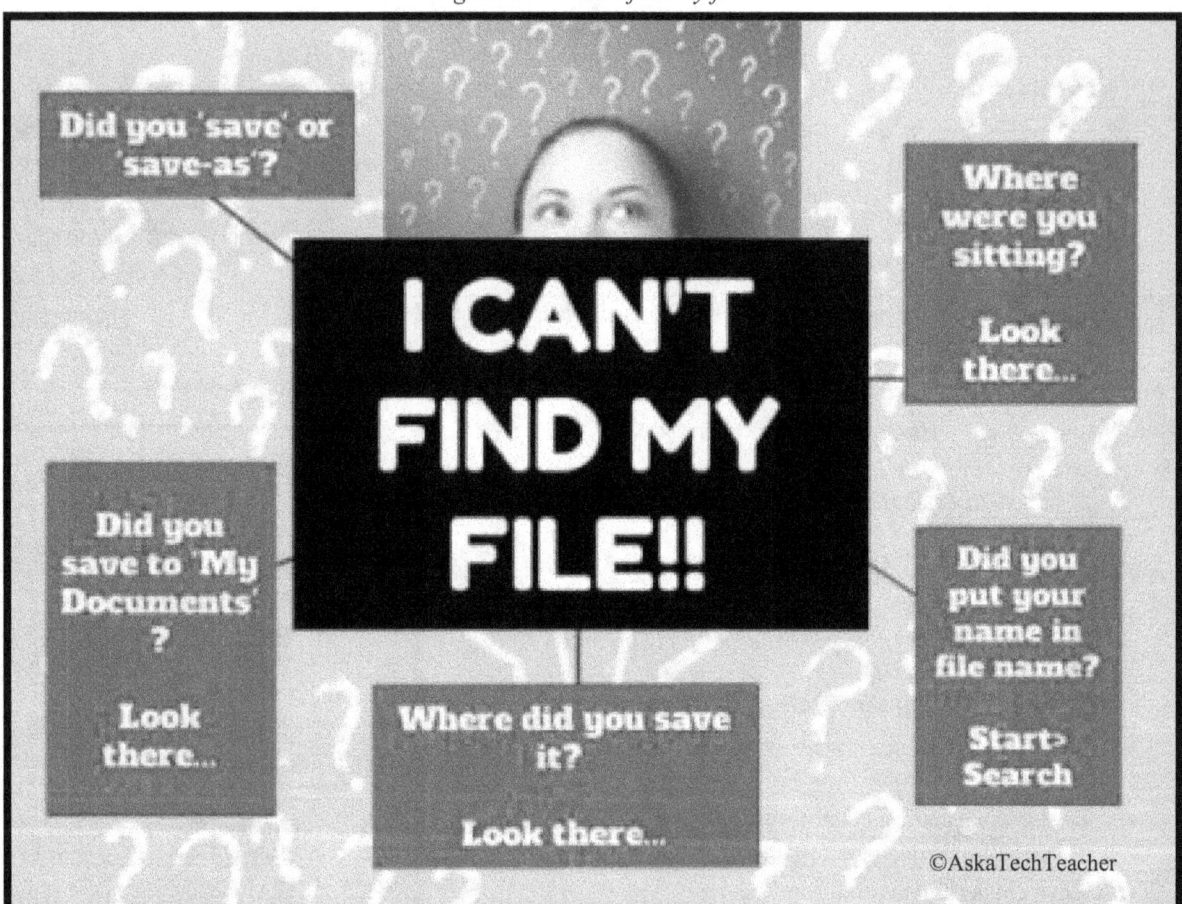

_____Students won't write their letter today (unless you give them the warm-up time to do this). Today, they'll format what they've written.

- *Change font color, look, and size by clicking inside word (students will remember this from Number Square).*
- *Add three pictures to body of letter (not heading or closing) using word processing program native clip art or a collection you make available for student use. Resize as needed so letter fits one page.*
- *Add festive border.*

_____Show students how to check page count to see if letter fits one page. Adjust font and picture sizes as needed.
_____Remind students: Every time they use computer, practice good habits.
_____Figures 64a-c are examples of completed letters:

Figure 64a-c—Student letters

_____Continually throughout class, check for understanding.
_____Have students work with a partner to complete the rubric (*Assessment 7*) to be sure all required elements are included.
_____If using student workbooks, students can annotate the blank rubric in their workbook using a tool like iAnnotate or Adobe.
_____Save and print/share/publish without assistance. Should students save or save-as?

Class exit ticket: *Submit rubric and letter via print, screenshot, and/or share.*

Differentiation

- *Those who finish: Practice keyboarding or visit holiday websites.*
- *If this lesson doesn't work for students, use one from How to Jumpstart the Inquiry-based Classroom. It has 5 projects aligned with curriculum.*

- **What do you call a computer superhero?**

  A Screen Saver.

- **Why did the computer cross the road?**

  To get a byte to eat.

- **What do you get if you cross a computer with an elephant?**

  Lots of Memory.

- **What do you get when you cross a dog and a computer?**

  A machine that has a bark worse than its byte.

- **Why was the computer so angry?**

  Because it had a chip on its shoulder.

- **Why did the computer get glasses?**

  To improve its websight.

- **Why did the computer sneeze?**

  It had a virus.

Assessment 7—Letter writing rubric

*Name*_____

*Teacher's Name*_____

LETTER WRITING RUBRIC
2nd *Grade*

1. Heading with name, date, teacher　　　_____

2. Greeting　　　_____

3. Closing　　　_____

4. Several lines of a letter　　　_____

　　a. Different fonts　　　_____

　　b. Different size fonts　　　_____

　　c. Different colors　　　_____

　　d. Spell-check　　　_____

　　e. Grammar-check　　　_____

5. Inline pictures—all the same size　　　_____

6. A festive border　　　_____

7. Story fills one page but not more　　　_____

8. Professional appearance　　　_____

2nd Grade Technology Curriculum: Teacher Manual

Lesson #13 Reading on the Internet

Vocabulary	Problem solving	Skills
• Address bar • Back button • Bling • Browser • Desktop • Escape • Hand • Internet neighborhood • Internet start page • Scroll • Search engine • Toolbar	• Program's gone (check taskbar) • I don't like stories on this page (use back key or start page tab) • Webpage text too small (Ctrl++ to zoom) • I clicked X, but internet didn't close (is a dialogue box open?) • I clicked bling! (exit with back arrow) • I can't find link (where cursor becomes a hand) • I hear sounds not from story I'm reading (close tab it's coming from)	**New** Using browsers Tabbed browsing **Scaffolded** Digital citizenship Digital tools Reading on the internet Keyboarding
Academic Applications Reading, internetting	**Materials Required** Internet, story websites, iPads (if using), student workbooks (if using), keyboarding program	**Standards** CCSS.ELA-Literacy.RF.2.4 NETS: 1d, 2b-c

Essential Question

How do I use technology to read?

Big Idea

Reading on the internet enables connections print books don't

Teacher Preparation

- Have log-ins for online library such as RAZ Kids or Subtext (if available).
- Have a list of story websites on class internet start page.
- Talk with grade-level team so you tie into conversations.
- Know which tasks weren't completed last week.
- Integrate domain-specific tech vocabulary into lesson.
- Know whether you need extra time to complete this lesson with your student group.

Assessment Strategies

- Followed directions
- Completed warm-up
- Shared understanding of story with classmate
- Joined class conversations
- [tried to] solve own problems
- Decisions followed class rules
- Left room as s/he found it
- Higher order thinking: analysis, evaluation, synthesis
- Habits of mind observed

Steps

Time required: 45 minutes in one sitting or spread throughout the week with 20 minutes set aside for internet reading

Class warm-up: Keyboard Lower row using Popcorn Typer or another tool that focuses on one row. Observe student posture and hand position.

_____Before students read an internet story, discuss internet neighborhood. How should they stay safe in this unknown world? (See flier in appendix):

- *Stay on assigned link.*

- *If you get off of it, use back arrow or start page tab.*
- *Only go to websites teacher has approved.*
- *Don't talk to strangers.*

Figure 65—Safe online reading

_____Watch these two videos on safe internet use:

- *BrainPop Jr—Internet Safety*
- *My Online Neighborhood (available on YouTube)*

_____Want more? Watch this Internet Safety for Kids K-3 (available on YouTube).
_____Model how to 1) access internet, 2) find class start page, and 3) go to links being used today. Point out ads to be avoided. Point out bling.
_____When pursuing 'reading' on the internet, expect 'close reading' as defined by PARCC:

A significant body of research links the close reading of complex text—whether the student is a struggling reader or advanced—to significant gains in reading proficiency and finds close reading to be a key component of college and career readiness. (Partnership for Assessment of Readiness for College and Careers, 2011, p. 7)

_____What can students get from an internet story they can't from a print story? (Answers: click links for enrichments, take a pile of books wherever they go, not worry about ripping pages—anything else?).

Figure 66—Why read digital books

_____Open browser—what's a 'browser'? How does it help students find websites? Use tabs on browser to move between class internet start page and approved links.

_____Access online stories from class list using your favorite online story website or find some on Ask a Tech Teacher's resource pages for *Reading*.

_____Demonstrate how to use at least one site—toolbars, links, 'hand' that identifies link, back/forward button, home button, address bar, and browser tabs. Clarify where students can go on a site and where they can't (i.e., ads, any link out of teacher-provided one).

_____If you use an online reading program like Subtext, RAZ Kids, Goodreader, Shelfari, or another web-based library (Google for addresses), show students how to access books through these tools and how to use them to collaborate, share, comment, and respond to each other.

_____Set students up with a reading buddy. They share details of a story, help decode affixes and unknown words, discuss the plot and characters. Remind them to follow rules for conversations (speak one at a time, listen to each other with care, gain floor in respectful ways).

_____Now set students lose to read!

_____As they're reading, encourage students to access the vocabulary decoding tools you've provided:

- *Kids Wordsmyth*
- *Merriam-Webster for Kids*
- *One created by prior students*—they find an unknown word, add it with a definition to a webpage you've set up for that purpose (maybe on the class blog or website)

_____Throughout class, check for understanding.

_____For more on close reading online, read the article, *"3 Digital Tools to Encourage Close Reading"*, at the end of the Lesson.

Class exit ticket: None

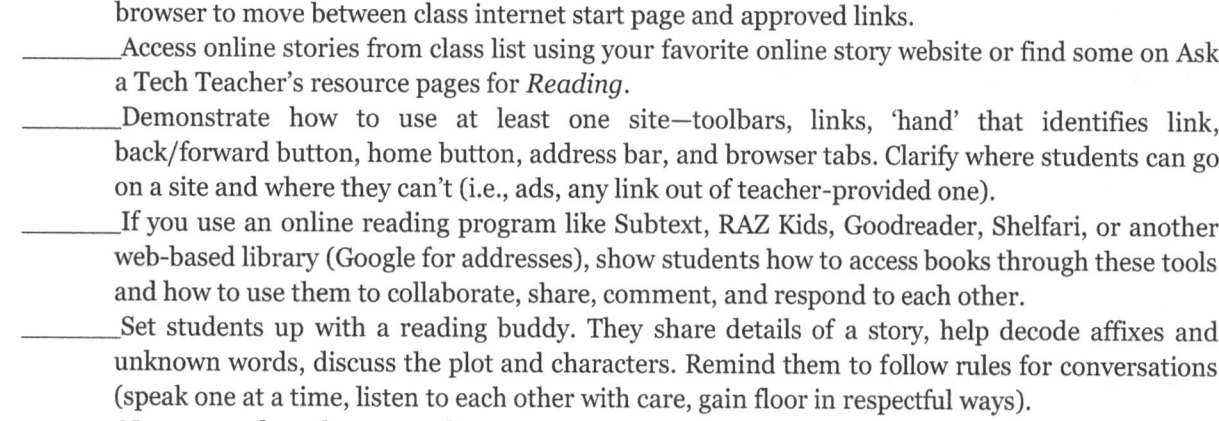

Article 17 "3 Digital Tools to Encourage Close Reading"

3 Digital Tools to Encourage Close Reading

'Close reading' entered the teacher's lexicon with this Common Core literacy anchor standard:

> ***Read closely*** *to determine what the text says explicitly and to make logical inferences from it; cite specific textual evidence when writing or speaking to support conclusions drawn from the text.*

Dr. Doug Fischer defines close reading this way:

> *Close reading is a careful and purposeful re-reading of the text.*

If you're looking for a longer definition, the Partnership for Assessment of Readiness for College and Career (PARCC) defines it this way:

> *Close, analytic reading stresses engaging with a text of sufficient complexity directly and examining meaning thoroughly and methodically, encouraging students to read and reread deliberately. Directing student attention on the text itself empowers students to understand the central ideas and key supporting details. It also enables students to reflect on the meanings of individual words and sentences; the order in which sentences unfold; and the development of ideas over the course of the text, which ultimately leads students to arrive at an understanding of the text as a whole. (PARCC, 2011, p. 7)*

...and explains its importance:

> *A significant body of research links the close reading of complex text—whether the student is a struggling reader or advanced—to significant gains in reading proficiency and finds close reading to be a key component of college and career readiness. (Partnership for Assessment of Readiness for College and Careers, 2011)*

It's not just getting kids to read that's important; it's getting them to read with understanding and memory that matters. This is not instinctual. Students need to be taught *how* to read complex texts.

First, don't be intimidated by the word 'complex'. For many, that term conflates with 'complicated' and 'advanced'. It isn't. In fact, complex text is the most beneficial to learners because it's chock full of meaning, evidence, and connections. **Close reading is a great approach to turning 'complex' into 'simple' by providing concrete steps to decode material**.

Here are three approaches to evaluating whether students have closely-read the complex text:

- *ask questions that are open-ended and require evidence*

- *ask questions that require students to think and understand what they're reading*
- *ask questions that plumb the depths of the text being read while considering only information contained there, not from outside sources*

Three tools make these happen:

- iAnnotate
- Snap! Learning
- Reading A-Z

iAnnotate

IAnnotate enables students to read, mark up, and share PDF, DOC, PPT and image files. It is a feature-rich app (80+ tools including a highlighter, text and notes, images, underline, and cross out) that makes it easy to indicate confusing sections, evidence for a point being made, or specific issues to be covered in more depth. A document can be opened from within the app, an email, or a wide variety of cloud locations like Dropbox and Google Drive.

Snap! Learning

Created by Sullivan Learning Centers, Snap Learning provides a Close Reading Program for grades 2-8 with a series of interactive exercises that guides students in reflecting on the meaning of words and sentences, the sequence in which these sentences are arranged, and how ideas are developed over the course of the text. All content is Common Core-aligned.

Reading A-Z

Reading A-Z's 2500+ K-6 books (in English, Spanish and French) provide 27 levels of developmentally appropriate texts for students to practice the skills and strategies of close reading. Close reading materials include:

There are a lot of tools out there to assist with close reading. These three are a great starting point, but whatever you pick, be sure it works well for your unique student group.

For a more in-depth look, check out this article on Ask a Tech Teacher.

2nd Grade Technology Curriculum: Teacher Manual

Lesson #14 Graphic Organizers

Vocabulary	Problem solving	Skills
• Clipart • Diagram • Doc • Formatting • Graphic organizer • Heading • Print preview • Ribbon • SmartArt • Template • Visual learning • Visual organizer	• There's not enough room in the graphic organizer to type what I need to (resize font) • Still not enough room (evaluate what's written, edit to be concise) • Program disappeared (check taskbar) • My computer doesn't work (wake mouse up, check power) • My project takes two pages • My graphic organizer is on top of title (drag it down)	**New** Graphic organizer **Scaffolded** Digital citizenship Digital tools Digital portfolio Keyboarding
Academic Applications Any subject that requires curating, organizing	**Materials Required** Internet, word processing program, keyboard program, graphic organizer	**Standards** CCSS.ELA-Literacy.W.2.6 NETS:4b, 6a-d

Essential Question

How can I communicate information quickly and clearly—and in a way that's appropriate to my audience?

Big Idea

Share information visually to make it more exciting and clear

Teacher Preparation

- Talk with grade level team so you tie graphic organizer into their conversations
- Have graphic organizer ready to use.
- Know which tasks weren't completed last week.
- Integrate domain-specific tech vocabulary into lesson.
- Know if you need extra time to complete this lesson.

Assessment Strategies

- Followed directions
- Saved to digital portfolio
- Completed project
- Understood digital tools used
- Used good keyboarding habits
- Worked well with a partner
- Completed warm-up, exit ticket
- Joined class conversations
- [tried to] solve own problems
- Decisions followed class rules
- Left room as s/he found it
- Higher order thinking: analysis, evaluation, synthesis
- Habits of mind observed

Steps

Time required: 45 minutes in one sitting or spread throughout the week with 30 minutes set aside for graphic organizer

Class warm-up: Keyboard Lower row using Popcorn Typer or a tool that focuses on one row. Observe posture, hand position, and other good typing habits.

_____ This is the last project in the word processing unit. After this, expect students to use this tool with nominal assistance for projects.

_____ From 2nd through 5th grade, students create a project that communicates an idea using graphic organizers. This project is the first.

127

2nd Grade Technology Curriculum: Teacher Manual

_____What is a graphic organizer (visual organizer)? How does it communicate? Show students examples from last year's 2nd, 3rd, 4th, and 5th grade classes. Is the message clear? What task might be particularly appropriate for this form of communication? And what audience?
_____Today, working in groups if desired, students will create a graphic organizer.
_____Here are examples students completed prior years--if they used the SL curriculum:

Figure 67a-b—Graphic organizers from kindergarten, 1st grade

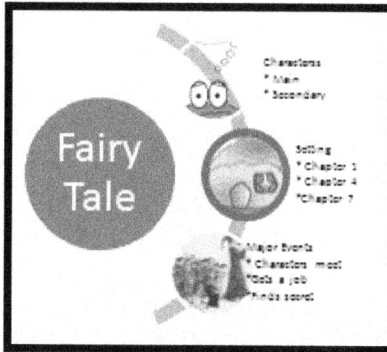 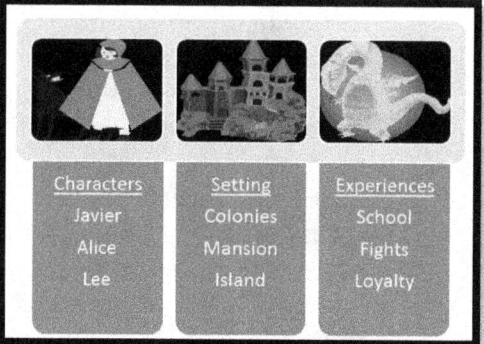

_____*Figures 68a-d* are projects students will do between 2nd and 5th grade (in the SL curriculum):

Figure 68a—Graphic organizer in 2nd grade; 68b—3rd grade; 68c—4th grade; 68d—5th grade

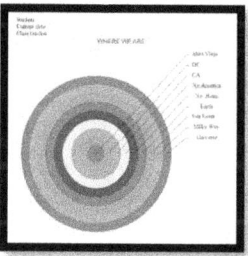  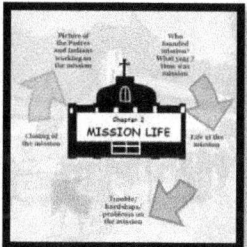 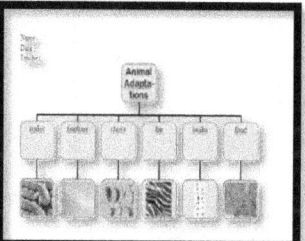

_____This can be done in any word processing program that supports graphic organizers, i.e., Word or Docs. We use SmartArt but graphic organizer templates are available from online sites:

Figure 69a-c—Online graphic organizers

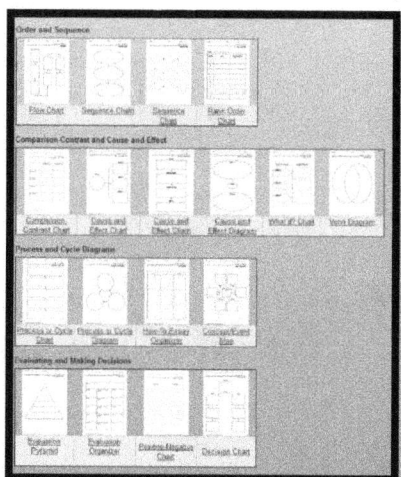 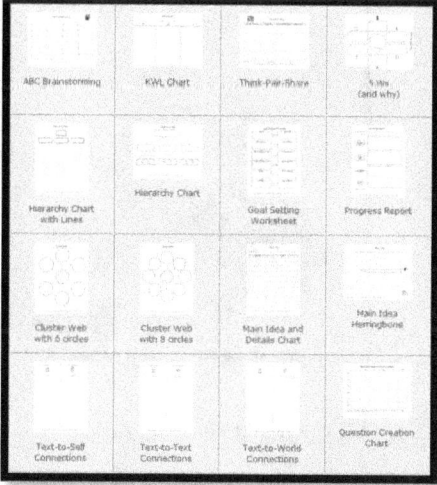

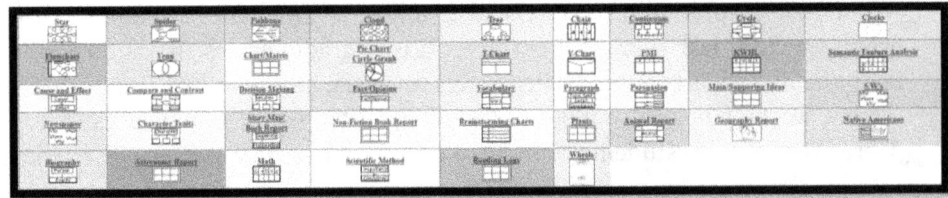

- Holt Interactive Graphic Organizers (from HRW)
- Teacher Vision's Graphic organizers--all topics
- Graphic organizers from Enchanted Learning
- Scholastic's Graphic Organizers—for reading

_____If students are going to access an online site, review proper digital citizenship.

_____Demonstrate project for students (*Figures 70a-b*). Adapt as needed for your tool:

Figure 70a—Graphic organizer with MS Word; 70b—with Google Draw

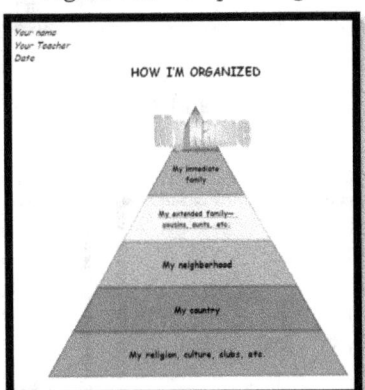
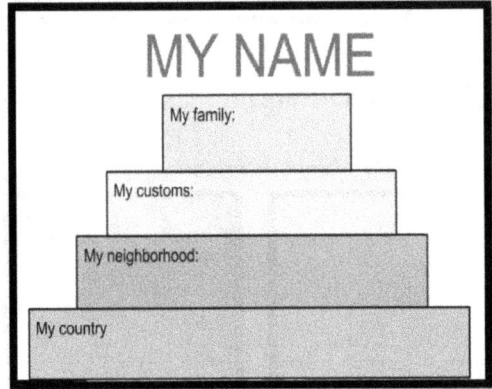

_____Open the word processing tool used in your class. Show students how to load either the graphic organizer you've selected or one native to your word processing program.

Figure 71a-b—How I'm Connected (with or without images)

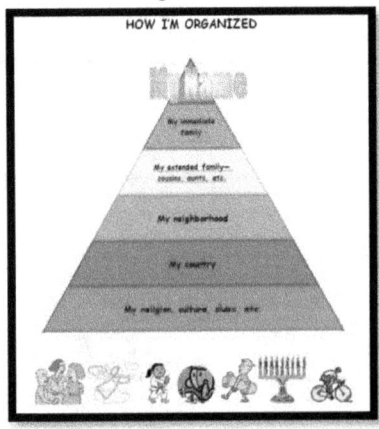
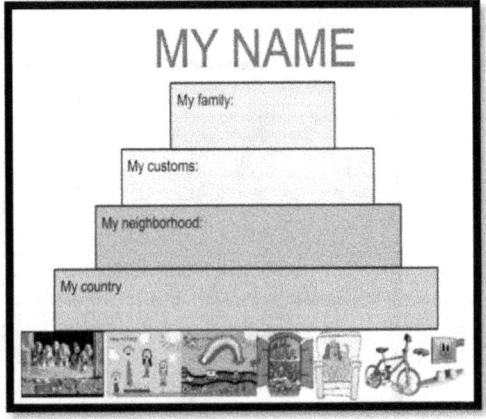

_____Add heading. Why a heading?

_____Add title (i.e., *How I'm Organized*) font size 16, centered and bold. Push enter so graphic organizer will appear underneath.

_____Insert the graphic organizer of your choice (like the pyramid in *Figures 70a-b*). Once selected, add shapes to get six (or number needed for your topic).

_____Add text to each layer as fits topic. Format with 'change colors' and 'SmartArt Styles'.

_____Add student name at pinnacle with WordArt.

_____Have students review project with a neighbor to be sure it's clear and readable.

_____Save to digital portfolio; save-as to flash drive (if available). What's the difference between save and 'save-as'? Why include student last name in the file name?

_____Print/share/publish, as is the custom in your classroom.

_____Continually throughout class, check for understanding.

Class exit ticket: *Have a poll available as students leave class, asking what digital tools they used today. Choices include: software, internet, online tools, and printer. They can select as many options as fit.*

Differentiation

- Add event pictures at bottom (Figures 71a-b); resize so they are consistent and fit in one row.
- Replace this lesson with one from Inquiry-based Teaching with PBL (from Structured Learning)).

_____

_____

_____

_____

Lesson #15 3 Ways to Send Greetings

Vocabulary	Problem solving	Skills
• Canvas • Desktop publishing • Flier • Font • Graphics • Greeting cards • Image • Online tool • QR code • Scheme • Software • Template • Text box	• Can't exit program (Alt+F4) • Document disappeared (check taskbar) • Can't write on card (insert text box) • I deleted picture by accident (Ctrl+Z) • I can't change to a different page (use left panel) • How do I print all pages (push print once; they all print) • I printed—it came out weird (fold) • My QR code can't be read (check edges—are all parts of code included?) • Card template doesn't fold	**New** QR codes Folding cards **Scaffolded** DTP Digital tools Keyboarding
Academic Applications Writing, art, digital citizenship	**Materials Required** desktop publishing tool, keyboarding program, QR creator, student workbooks (if using)	**Standards** CCSS.ELA-Literacy.W.2.6 NETS: 6a, 6d, 7a

Essential Question

What technology is best for sharing holiday greetings?

Big Idea

I can share a celebration with technology

Teacher Preparation

- Have QR code builder ready to use.
- Have QR scanner on iPads or other digital device.
- Talk with grade-level team so you tie into conversations.
- Know which tasks weren't completed last week.
- Integrate domain-specific tech vocabulary into lesson.
- Know if you need extra time to complete this lesson.
- Know senior center students can make cards for (if doing this option).

Assessment Strategies

- Completed project
- Understood use of digital tools to produce and share project
- Used good keyboarding habits
- Completed warm-up, exit ticket
- Joined class conversations
- [tried to] solve own problems
- Decisions followed class rules
- Left room as s/he found it
- Higher order thinking: analysis, evaluation, synthesis
- Habits of mind observed

Steps

Time required: 45 minutes in one sitting or spread throughout the week with 30 minutes set aside for project

Class warm-up: Keyboard Lower row using Popcorn Typer or a tool that focuses on one row. Observe student posture, hand position, and typing habits.

_____**Compare-contrast** software and online tools. Which are digital? (Hint: Both—why?). Put *Figure 72* table on class screen, but not filled in. Have students suggest data to complete cells:

Figure 72—Compare-contrast software vs. online tool

	SOFTWARE	ONLINE TOOL
Examples	MS Office, KidPix, Type to Learn, Reader Rabbit	Google Drive apps, ABCYa, Dance Mat Typing
Access	Accessible only from where you installed the software	Accessible from any computer with an internet connection
Compatibility	Varies	Most are compatible across platforms
Control	You control	Someone else controls—may be removed without permission
Daily use	Depends upon whether compatible with computer	Depends upon whether your internet connection works
Limitation	Don't run on iPads, Chromebooks	Run on most computer systems
Maintenance	If it breaks, you have to fix it	If it breaks, someone online fixes it.
Updates	You do these	Managed by website; always up to date
Where it lives	On your computer (or network)	On the internet
Collaborate	Difficult	Easy
Cost, security, set-up, speed		

_____Throughout the year, we complete greeting card projects as an authentic formative assessment of student knowledge. Most kids love to make greeting cards for family and friends so will work hard to be sure they have the text accurate, the best pictures, and an effective design.

_____Today we are creating holiday greeting cards using either software or an online tool. Pick any or all of the three projects:

- *Holiday Drawings*
- *Greeting Card Creator*
- *QR Code Holiday Wish Lists*

Holiday Drawings

_____Remember designing cards in Kindergarten and 1st grade (if they used the SL tech curriculum) using drawing software like KidPix, TuxPaint, Pixie, or Paint (*Figures 73a-c*)

Figure 73a-c—Holiday drawings in K-1

_____...or an online tool for iPads and Chromebooks like Paint Sparkles Draw (*Figure 74a*), ABCYaPaint (*Figure 74b*). Google for webtool addresses:

Figure 74a-c: Holiday card on iPads and Chromebooks

 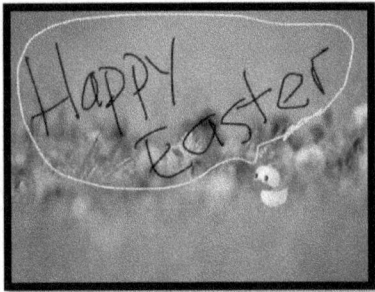 

_____If using an online template, remind students of good digital citizenship when using the internet.
_____Open your card tool. Students can draw the picture (*Figure 75a*) or use a prepared image (*Figure 75b*). Review how to use the tool but don't reteach. Expect students to apply previous knowledge to this exercise.

Figure 75a-b—Holiday cards

_____Ask students to write two sentences that express their holiday sentiment to a family member.
_____Print/share/publish, as is the norm in your classroom.

Greeting Card Creators

_____Open the greeting card creator used in your school. Compare-contrast this tool's toolbars and canvas with another program students are using, say the word processing program used last lesson. What's the same? What's different?
_____Use Publisher (*Figure 76a*), MS Word (*Figure 76b*), Open Office (*Figure 76c*), or another tool of your choice:

Figure 76a—Greeting card in Publisher; 76b—Word; 76c—Open Office; 76d—Avery

 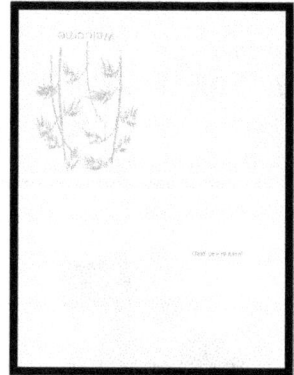  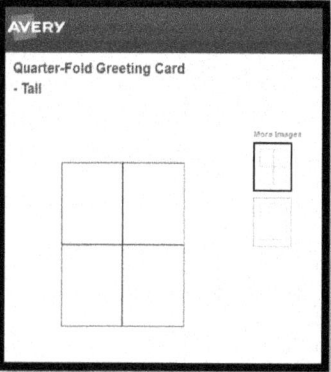

_____If you're an iPad school, consider sending digital-only greetings using apps. These are environmentally-friendly, no printing, and quick. Just create, email and you're done.

Figure 77—IPad greeting cards (online)

_____This is a student-directed project, an opportunity to be risk-takers and critical thinkers. They are familiar with these skills. Encourage them to transfer prior knowledge; help where necessary.

_____Walk students through the tool's opening screen—task pane, page layout, middle work area, ribbons, menus.

_____Find templates for 'Holiday cards' (what's a template?). Select one as well as whatever options are available. For example Publisher allows students to select color and font schemes.

_____Once the card template shows up:

- **Page 1** (cover): Edit text, but don't add new text. Also, don't change fonts, sizes, etc.
- **Page 2** (left side when card is open): Add one or more images.
- **Page 3** (right side when card is open): Edit text if desired or make no changes.
- **Page 4** (back of card): Add student name.

_____If students are new to cards: Don't change text; add only one picture.

_____Continually throughout class, check for understanding.

_____Save (Ctrl+S) to student digital portfolio. Print/share/publish as is done in your school.

_____ If students need help folding, follow *Figure 78*:

- *Fold top down, keeping white sides together*
- *Fold side-to-side, with cover on outside*

Figure 78—Fold a printed card

_____ Consider: How does technology help students to share exactly what they mean, rather than a card bought in the store?

QR Code Holiday Wish Lists

_____ Students write a Christmas list and encode it into a QR code. They then add it to a picture they have drawn and see if classmates can guess whose list it is by the clues in the drawing.

_____ Discuss a 'QR code' (Quick Response code). It is a barcode scanned by a camera on a smart phone (or similar device) that takes you to specific information like a website, contact information, or text.

_____ Where have students seen them? Have examples from stores and magazines available to show. What is the benefit of this approach (lots of information in a small space, can provide a direct link to a website without having to type in the complicated address)?

_____ Open one of the many QR creators available on the internet (such as Kaywa). I like GoQR because it's simple enough for a second grader. QR Stuff allows colored codes. Google *QR creators* for addresses.

_____ First, type the student name, followed by student holiday shopping list.

_____ As they type, students will see the QR code develop. The more data they add, the denser the squiggles. What else do students notice about the QR Code (for example, what's with the corners?)

_____ Check spelling.

2nd Grade Technology Curriculum: Teacher Manual

_____Once the QR code is created, save to student digital portfolio with a screen shot.

_____Open class drawing program. Students draw a picture with clues for classmates about whose holiday list this is. For example, if student likes pets, include a dog (*Figures 79a-c*).

_____Add the QR code artistically on the drawing. Be sure the entire code is copied or it won't work.

Figure 79a-c—QR code cards

_____Print and add to a bulletin board on the classroom wall. Students walk around and try to guess whose picture belongs to whom before scanning the QR code.

_____Show students how to use the Scan tool on iPads or Smartphones to read the QR data. Give students lots of time to scan classmates' codes.

_____When done, ask students to reflect on this exercise. What was difficult, easy? What did they learn?

Class exit ticket: Read QR codes of several classmates if you did that project.

Differentiation

- *Create QR Codes about a book being read in class. Post these in the library corner of the classroom. Students can scan them for ideas on which book they'd like to read.*
- *Use a program like QR Voice to translate the QR code into an audio file that plays when you scan it. This is particularly exciting for Language B teachers.*
- *Save cards as PDF and email to family/friends.*
- *Create holiday cards for a community service project?*
- *Instead of holiday cards, create a flier—very simple.*
- *If this lesson doesn't work for students, use one from How to Jumpstart the Inquiry-based Classroom. It has 5 projects aligned with curriculum.*

2nd Grade Technology Curriculum: Teacher Manual

Lesson #16 Around the World I

Vocabulary	Problem solving	Skills
• Annotate • Continents • Digital tools • Drill down • Legend • Network • Poles • Resize • Rubric • Template • Text box • Workbook	• Can't import template into drawing program (is it right file type, i.e., jpg?) • How do I print (Ctrl+P) • How do I save (Ctrl+S) • Fill flowed out of section I wanted to color (connect edges) • Label's in the wrong spot (drag to right spot) • Why can't I save to 'My Documents' (It's not part of school network) • How do I write in my student workbook?	**New** Using templates Annotating workbook **Scaffolded** Digital tools Digital portfolio Mash-up Keyboarding Annotate workbooks (if using these)
Academic Applications Geography or another topic that uses templates	**Materials Required** Topic-specific template, drawing program, keyboarding program, student workbooks (if using)	**Standards** CCSS.ELA-Literacy.RI.2.7 NETS: 3a, 3d, 5b

Essential Question

How can I use an interactive site to share information?

Big Idea

Visual representation of data is sometimes clearer than text

Teacher Preparation

- Know which tasks weren't completed last week.
- Know if you need extra time to complete this lesson.
- Integrate domain-specific tech vocabulary into lesson.
- Have template on school network so students can access.
- Know what image format is required to display template.
- Have rubrics for early finishers (end of next Lesson).
- Talk with grade level team so you tie into conversations on planet, oceans, and continents.

Assessment Strategies

- Followed directions
- Understood digital tools used
- Completed warm-up, exit ticket
- Annotate workbook (if using)
- Worked well with a partner
- Joined class conversations
- [tried to] solve own problems
- Decisions followed class rules
- Left room as s/he found it
- Higher order thinking: analysis, evaluation, synthesis
- Habits of mind observed

Steps

Time required: 45 minutes in one sitting or spread throughout the week with 30 minutes set aside for project

Class warm-up: Keyboard all rows on an online keyboarding site or dedicated software. Remind students of good typing habits.

_____Discuss planet's continents, oceans. What are students discussing in class?

_____'Around the World' project takes two weeks. Open drawing program on class screen and demonstrate. Import template to be used.

_____If students have workbooks, they complete project with the PDF annotator. In fact, it's a good practice of the annotation tools.

_____Before students start a project, ask them to notice what digital tools they are using. Consider others that might accomplish the required goals. A word processing tool like Word? DTP like Publisher? This is a good opportunity to transfer knowledge.

_____Open template in your class drawing program. If you use Chromebooks, try ABCYaPaint or Google Draw (*Figure 80a*). If you're an iPad school, use Drawing Box Free, Doodle Buddy, or the Google Draw app (*Figure 80b*).

Figure 80a—Annotatable template on laptop; 80b—iPad

_____Add student name with text tool.

_____Type or write in continent and ocean names. Show how to resize text boxes to fit provided lines if necessary. Watch grammar. Check spelling against sample on next pages.

_____When done, save to digital portfolio to finish next week. Make sure student last name is in file name. Why?

_____Throughout class, check for understanding.

Class exit ticket: ***Have neighbor verify that student saved this project to their digital portfolio, to finish next week.***

Differentiation

- *As you teach, mention shortkeys as often as possible. For many students, they are easier to use. Once comfortable with these key combinations, tech will be more fun.*
- *Do project as a group—you on class screen, students at their computers.*
- *Time tight? Have students label only continents or oceans.*
- *If this lesson doesn't work for students, use one from Inquiry-based Teaching with PBL (from Structured Learning).*

Assessment 8a-b—Around the World Template

'Around the World' Samples
Top: template with directions
Bottom: completed example

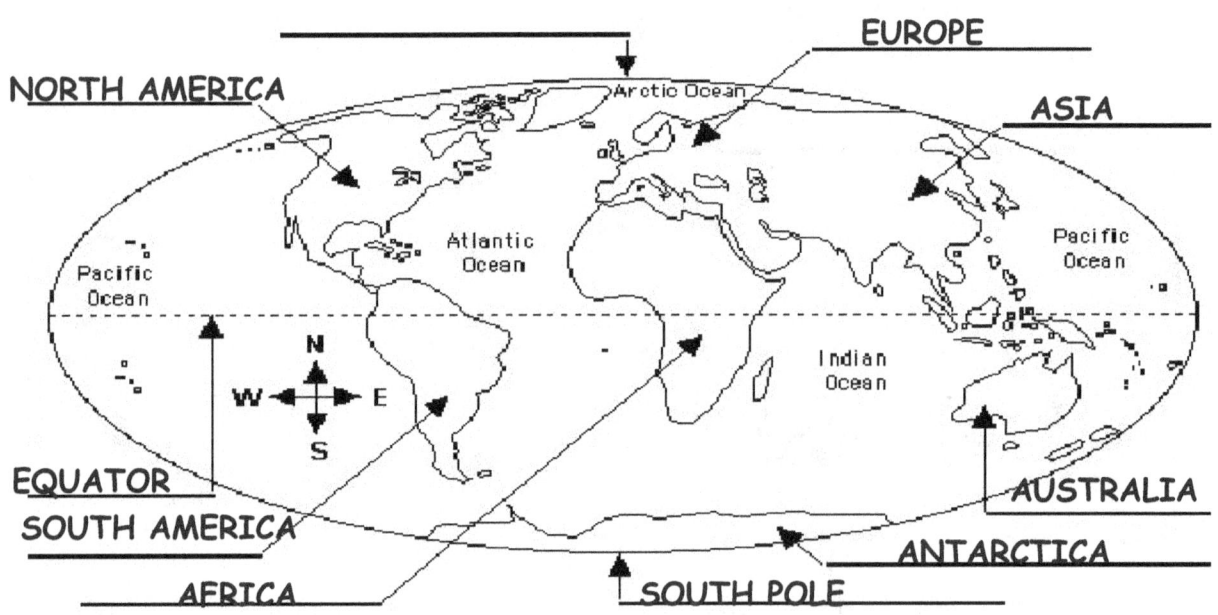

Template credit: Enchanted Learning

1. Color Africa green
2. Color Antarctica white
3. Color Asia
4. Color Australia brown
5. Color Europe red
6. Color No. America orange
7. Color So. America pink
8. Color oceans blue

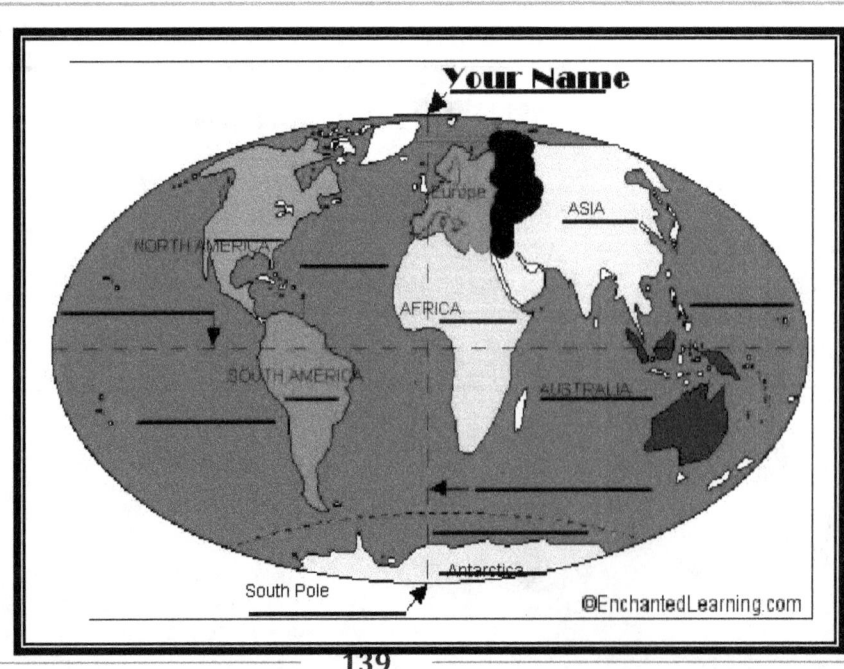

Lesson #17 Around the World II

Vocabulary	Problem solving	Skills
• Fill • Legend • Network • Paint bucket • Resize • Rubric • Template • Text box	• Fill flows into other parts of template (edges aren't snugged—connect). • Can't find project (did you save early save often? Search by last name) • What's the difference between 'export' and 'save' ('export' saves project in a format to be viewed in other programs) • How do I print?	**New** Templates **Scaffolded** Digital tools Drawing program Keyboarding Annotate workbooks
Academic Applications Geography or any topic that requires a template	**Materials Required** Internet, template and rubric, keyboard program, workbooks (if using)	**Standards** CCSS.ELA-Literacy.RI.2.7 NETS: 3a, 3d, 5b

Essential Question

How can I use an interactive site to share information?

Big Idea

Visual representation of data is sometimes clearer than text

Teacher Preparation

- Talk with grade level team so you tie into their inquiry on planet, oceans, and continents.
- Have rubrics available.
- Know which tasks weren't completed last week.
- Integrate domain-specific tech vocabulary into lesson.
- Know if you need extra time to complete this lesson.

Assessment Strategies

- Followed directions
- Finished project, rubric
- Used good keyboarding habits
- Completed warm-up, exit ticket
- Joined class conversations
- Annotate workbook (if using)
- Worked well with a partner
- [tried to] solve own problems
- Decisions followed class rules
- Left room as s/he found it
- Higher order thinking: analysis, evaluation, synthesis
- Habits of mind observed

Steps

Time required: 45 minutes in one sitting or spread throughout the week with 30 minutes set aside for project

Class warm-up: Keyboard all keys on class typing program. Remember: Hands curved over home row, good posture; keyboard in front of body, mouse to right.

_____This is week two of Around the World. Today, students color continents and oceans labeled last week. Use a legend--what's a legend? What have students discussed in class about 'legends'?

_____Open the drawing program used in your school (the same one used Week #1 of this project) and Around the World project. If students have trouble finding it, try these:

- Did you save it to the local drive on your computer (i.e., **'My Documents'**)?
- Go to **Start>Search**. Type your last name. This only works if student saved with their last name in the file.

- Can't find it? Were you **sitting somewhere else**? Check last week's seat.

_____Use paint bucket tool to color as directed on legend at end of prior lesson. If color flows into ocean or wrong continent, undo and connect the black lines that separate sections.

Figure 81—Using templates

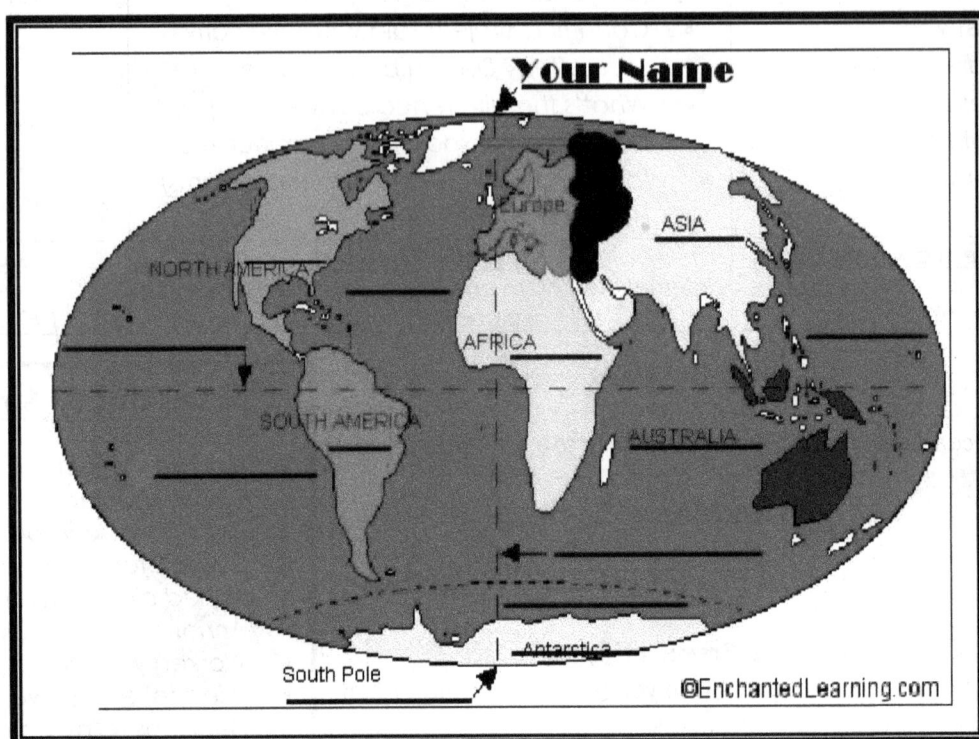

_____If using student workbooks, students can complete the project from PDF format using a tool like iAnnotate or Adobe.
_____Check rubric checklist with a neighbor for details (see *Assessment 9*). Students complete and submit today.
_____Export/save so picture can be used in Open House slideshow. If printing, use shortkey Ctrl+P.
_____If students forget to print, show them how to access their digital portfolio or network folder to find the file name, then right click and print.
_____Continually throughout class, check for understanding.

Class exit ticket: ***Answer a poll on digital tool they used to create this project.***

Differentiation

- Add a compass rose to map; discuss what this is; tie into class discussion.
- Add country flags. Make student country of origin largest.
- If this lesson doesn't work for students, use one from *How to Jumpstart the Inquiry-based Classroom*. It has 5 projects aligned with curriculum.

Assessment 9—Around the World rubric

Around the World
Grading Rubric

Your name: _____ Teacher: _____

1. Map colored as required	__5 points__
a. Oceans blue	_____
b. Continents per legend	_____
2. Continents labeled	__5 points__
a. In correct spot	_____
b. Readable	_____
c. Fonts/sizes correct	_____
3. Your name on project	__5 points__

Around the World
Grading Rubric

Your name: _____ Teacher: _____

1. Map colored as required	__5 points__
a. Oceans blue	_____
b. Continents per legend	_____
2. Continents labeled	__5 points__
a. In correct spot	_____
b. Readable	_____
c. Fonts/sizes correct	_____
3. Your name on project	__5 points__

2nd Grade Technology Curriculum: Teacher Manual

Lesson #18 Valentine Greeting

Vocabulary	Problem solving	Skills
• Border • Export • Font • Format • Greeting • Handles • Heading • Image • Tools • Word processing • Wrap	• I can't exit (Alt+F4) • I can't print (file-print or Ctrl+P) • How do I get text on next line (let it wrap by itself) • How do I know letter fits one page (does bar at bottom of page say '1 of 1'?) • How do I resize an image (handles) • How do I fix spelling (right click on word and select correct spelling) • Why do I learn word processing)?	**New** Screenshots (maybe) Annotation (maybe) **Scaffolded** Digital tools Digital citizenship Word processing formatting skills Letter (or story) writing Keyboarding
Academic Applications Writing, letter-writing, story writing	**Materials Required** word processing program, keyboard website, kid-safe image websites, student workbooks (if using)	**Standards** CCSS.ELA-Literacy.L.2.1 NETS:4b, 6a

Essential Question

Why is word processing the best choice for a letter or story?

Big Idea

It's important to pick the right technology for the intended purpose and audience

Teacher Preparation

- Have digital tools ready to use.
- Talk with grade level team to understand what students know about letter writing, grammar at this point in year.
- Have samples of prior letter writing.
- Know which tasks weren't completed last week.
- Integrate domain-specific tech vocabulary into lesson.
- Know whether you need extra time to complete lesson.

Assessment Strategies

- Followed directions
- Completed project
- Used proper grammar/spelling
- Annotate workbook (if using)
- Worked well with a partner
- Completed warm-up, exit ticket
- Joined class conversations
- [tried to] solve own problems
- Decisions followed class rules
- Left room as s/he found it
- Higher order thinking: analysis, evaluation, synthesis
- Habits of mind observed

Steps

Time required: 45 minutes in one sitting or spread throughout the week with 30 minutes set aside for letter (or story)

Class warm-up: Keyboard all keys using the class typing program. Observe student posture, hand position.

_____This lesson circles back on word processing skills learned earlier in the year, in preparation for the end-of-year report. This project can be a letter as presented, or it might be a story or some other sort of greeting.

_____Today, students will create a Valentine letter in a word processing program, as ongoing preparation for the summative end-of-year report requiring word processing competency. By circling back on basic skills several times, students gain confidence in their ability.

_____Use the program available in your school—Word, Google Docs, Notes, Open Office or another.

_____Remind them of letters they've written in the past. *Figures 82a-c* are three examples of complexity, depending upon student skill level and writing style:

Figure 82a-c—Letters written in 2nd grade

_____*Figures 83a-c* are three complexity levels as applied to this Valentine letter. These reflect as much the student skill level editing and formatting with word processing tools as they do writing skills. In fact, excellent writers may struggle with word processing and end up with a letter like *Figure 83a*:

Figure 83a-c—Valentine letters in 2nd grade

_____If you use Chromebooks or iPads, you may use the apps for Office 365, Notes, Pages, or Google Drive (Google for addresses). Whatever tool you use, you want it to focus on writing, not images or design. This lesson is to develop student skills within word processing.

2nd Grade Technology Curriculum: Teacher Manual

_____Before beginning: Ask students: Why word processing? Why not a desktop publisher? Discuss how to select the right program for particular needs.

_____Discuss writing skills with students. What writing style is appropriate when composing a letter? Who is the audience?

_____Students know the basics of the word processing program being used so plan to assist rather than teach. You may want to use this as a formative assessment of their progress.

_____Open the word processing program. Write a letter that includes:

- *heading*
- *greeting*
- *body—three to five sentences*
- *closing, including student name*
- *festive border (if available)*
- *at least three different fonts*
- *at least three different colors of fonts*
- *at least three different sizes of fonts*
- *at least three images to communicate the same message as text. If student finds images online, review digital citizenship.*

_____Suggest a large font for those who write short letters (i.e., *Figures 83a-b*), a smaller font for longer letters (i.e., *Figure 83c*). Use any font and color. Include student name in closing or at top.

_____Done? Work with neighbor to check:

- *Are grammar and spelling good—red and green squiggles? What's the blue line?*
- *Does letter fit one page? If not, resize images.*
- *Is everything included? If not, edit.*

_____With neighbor, complete the rubric at the end of the lesson (*Assessment 10*). If students have student workbooks, they can complete this with class annotation tool and then send you a screenshot or print just the one page.

_____When done, print/save/share without help. Back-up to flash drive if appropriate.

_____Continually throughout class, check for understanding.

_____Those who finish: Practice keyboarding on online program.

Class exit ticket: *Have neighbor verify student saved correctly to digital portfolio.*

Differentiation

- *If students need help with letter writing, try ABCYa.*
- *Instead of a letter, write a story of about the same length with multiple images, border (if available), and fonts.*
- *Create this letter using a desktop publishing tool like Publisher (Google for address). Which did students like better? What were the differences?*
- *If this lesson doesn't work for students, use one from Inquiry-based Teaching with PBL (from Structured Learning.*

Assessment 10 Valentine letter rubric

Name_____

Teacher's Name_____

LETTER WRITING RUBRIC
2nd Grade

1. Heading with name, date, teacher _____
2. Greeting _____
3. Closing _____
4. Several lines of a letter _____
    a. Different fonts _____
    b. Different size fonts _____
    c. Different colors _____
    d. Spell-check _____
    e. Grammar-check _____
5. Inline pictures—all the same size _____
6. A festive border (if available) _____
7. Story fills one page but not more _____
8. Followed rules of a good digital citizen _____
9. Professional appearance _____

Lesson #19 About Me: A Summative Project

Vocabulary	Problem solving	Skills
• Alt+F4 • Drag-drop • Export • Fills • Open House • Slides • Slideshow • Screenshot • Tools/toolbars	• How do I close a program (Alt+F4) • Typing is hard (it gets easier) • Why is 'transfer' so important (tech skills help you excel in life) • Drawing program won't save (take a screen shot) • I can't log in (what's your UN/PW?) • What's the difference between edit and format?	**New** **Scaffolded** Digital tools Drawing Digital storytelling Keyboarding
Academic Applications Writing, storytelling	**Materials Required** drawing program, keyboarding program, student workbooks (if using)	**Standards** CCSS.ELA-Literacy.L.2.1 NETS: 1d, 4b, 6b-d

Essential Question

Can knowledge of language conventions help me tell my story?

Big Idea

It is easier to communicate ideas when using good language conventions and visual representations

Teacher Preparation

- Have class digital tools ready to use.
- Talk with grade-level team so you tie into conversations.
- Know which tasks weren't completed last week.
- Integrate domain-specific tech vocabulary into lesson.
- Know if you need extra time to complete this lesson.
- Talk with grade level team so you tie into their teaching on grammar and spelling.
- Discuss story construction (i.e., 'Brilliant Beginning, Mighty Middle, and Exciting Ending').

Assessment Strategies

- Followed directions
- Completed project
- Saved/exported successfully
- Demonstrated command of class and/or Common Core writing conventions
- Used good keyboarding habits
- Completed warm-up, exit ticket
- Joined class conversations
- [tried to] solve own problems
- Decisions followed class rules
- Left room as s/he found it
- Higher order thinking: analysis, evaluation, synthesis
- Habits of mind observed

Steps

Time required: 45 minutes in one sitting or spread throughout the week with 10 minutes set aside to discuss word processing editing and 20 minutes for project
Class warm-up: Keyboard 10-15 minutes using class typing tool

_____Today's project starts a four-scene (four week) story—about eight sentences—students will prepare for Open House. It will follow class writing guidelines and be presented as a slideshow. It celebrates tech skills accomplished during second grade.

_____Students will create four slides that tell a story. Each slide will include a picture and text that follows class grammar, spelling and story writing conventions:

- **1st slide**: *introduce themselves with a picture and two well-structured, grammatically-correct sentences. Think of this as an introduction to the main character (Figure 84):*

Figure 84—Slide 1 in story

- **2nd slide**: *develop setting and characters. It might describe actions, thoughts, feelings, with temporal words to signal event order. Think of this as the setting and additional characters (Figure 85):*

Figure 85—Slide 2 in story

- **3rd slide**: *establish the problem the main character must solve or a wish s/he has. This is action and drama—a chance to make the reader feel the worry, fear, or concern the character feels about completing this task. Think of this as the plot, crises (Figure 86):*

Figure 86—Slide 3 in story

- ***4th slide***: *solve the problem; provide a happy ending and sense of closure. Think of this as the resolution of the plot (Figure 87):*

Figure 87—Slide 4 in story

_____Before beginning, write a run-on sentence on the class screen, such as:

onceuponatimetherewasagirlnamemeagshehadadog

_____Confusing, isn't it? Ask a volunteer to show on the class screen where to place:

- *capitalization*
- *punctuation*
- *spaces between words*

_____Ask student if s/he edited with backspace or delete?
_____Done? Open drawing tool (KidPix, Paint, TuxPaint, Pixie, or another used in your school).
_____If you're a Chromebook school, try *ABCYa Paint* or *SumoPaint* (find them on the Internet).
_____If you're an iPad school, try Drawp for School or the app, Doodle Buddy.
_____Demonstrate on class screen: Draw a picture using five colors. Use thick pencil so it will stand out from a distance. Add two sentences to introduce the student.

Figure 88a-b—Scene on in slideshow story

_____Now students draw a picture and add their own two sentences to introduce themselves.

_____ Encourage them to complete this project as independently as possible. They've used the tools before. Remind rather than teach. Leave sample on class screen (*Figures 88a-b*).

_____ Save/export picture with minimal assistance. Why export rather than save?

_____ If necessary, students can take a screenshot and save that to their digital portfolio. Depending upon your digital device, here are screenshot options:

- ***Windows***: *Snipping Tool*
- ***Chromebook:*** *hold down control key and press window switcher key*
- ***Mac***: *Command Shift 3 for a full screenshot; Command Shift 4 for a partial*
- ***Surface tablet***: *hold down volume and Windows button*
- ***iPad***: *hold Home button and power button at same time*
- ***Online***: *a screenshot tool like Jing, Nimbus, or Snagit*

_____ Those who finish: Practice keyboarding using class typing tool.

_____ Continually throughout class, check for understanding.

Class exit ticket: ***Have neighbors check each other's stations to be sure they are left neatly and as they were when class entered.***

Differentiation

- This can be a summative or formative assessment as it uses skills already learned.
- The important part of this lesson is building a four-picture story where text and image deliver the same message. Some students may prefer a tool like Chatterpix that adds voice or PicSay where students annotate a photo.
- To practice short stories (such as this 4-slide story), have students write a X/Twitter story and post it to the class Twitter feed. Here is an example (see the article *"How to Write a Novel in Minimal Characters"* at the end of the Lesson for more):

    He closed the door. Frowning. So strange, no one there. A creeping chill. A prickle of fear. The slithering sounds increased. He looked up. It would be his final action.

- Anytime you can inject tech into the class, do it! Students love seeing gadgets in action. For example—take a video of students at their computers and upload to class website/blog/wiki.
- Those who finish early: Practice spelling/site words on SpellingCity.
- If this lesson doesn't work for students use one from Inquiry-based Teaching with PBL (from Structured Learning.

Article 18 "How to Write a Twitter Novel"

How to Write a Novel with Minimal Characters

I'm a teacher, have been for 35 years. I teach a lesson to my Middle School students that uses X/Twitter to improve their writing skills. There's a lot this popular social media tool can bring to the education world:

- it's non-intimidating. Anyone can get through a atweet
- it forces students to focus on concise, pithy writing. Wasted, fluff words are not an option
- it's fun. Students want to try it because it's the 'forbidden fruit'.

I also have a class that kickstarts the author in students, getting them set up to write and digitally publish the book that festers inside of them (well, statistics say 73% of us have a book inside kicking and screaming to get out).

What I haven't done is blend the two: **Write a novel on Twitter**.

Anna over at Imaginette reminded me that I should. She's not the only one, either, who thinks Twitter is an excellent forum for novel writing. Japan popularized it as the *microblogging novel* or the *micro novel*. Wikipedia defines it as:

> *...a fictional work or novel written and distributed in small parts*

Just to be clear: We're talking about squeezing all those novel parts that we writers slave over…

- plot
- pacing
- character development
- theme
- story arc
- scene

…to name a few must be accomplished in a tweet. Is that even possible? I'd croak a resounding 'No!', but the Guardian persuaded twenty-one accomplished authors to try their hand at this. Here's a sampling:

James Meek

'He said he was leaving her. "But I love you," she said. "I know," he said. "Thanks. It's what gave me the strength to love somebody else."

Ian Rankin

I opened the door to our flat and you were standing there, cleaver raised. Somehow you'd found out about the photos. My jaw hit the floor.

Blake Morrison

Blonde, GSOH, 28. Great! Ideal mate! Fix date. Tate. Nervous wait. She's late. Doh, just my fate. Wrong candidate. Blond – and I'm straight.

David Lodge

"Your money or your life!" "I'm sorry, my dear, but you know it would kill me to lose my money," said the partially deaf miser to his wife.

Jilly Cooper

Tom sent his wife's valentine to his mistress and vice versa. Poor Tom's a-cold and double dumped.

Rachel Johnson

Rose went to Eve's house but she wasn't there. But Eve's father was. Alone. One thing led to another. He got 10 years.

Andrew O'Hagan

Clyde stole a lychee and ate it in the shower. Then his brother took a bottle of pills believing character is just a luxury. God. The twins.

AL Kennedy

It's good that you're busy. Not great. Good, though. But the silence, that's hard. I don't know what it means: whether you're OK, if I'm OK.

Jeffrey Archer

"It's a miracle he survived," said the doctor. "It was God's will," said Mrs. Schicklgruber. "What will you call him?" "Adolf," she replied.

You can get ideas by searching #twitternovels.

2nd Grade Technology Curriculum: Teacher Manual

Lesson #20 Develop Details

Vocabulary	Problem solving	Skills
• Characters • Color (detail) • Conventions • Edit • Grammar • Network • Palette • Plot • Sentence fluency • Setting • Voice	• Capital stuck (check caps lock) • What's my user name? (check with teacher) • What's the difference between backspace and delete? • What's the difference between edit and format? • Do I save or export? (it depends upon the purpose) • Do I save or 'save-as'? • Where's the network?	**New** **Scaffolded** Digital tools Editing skills in word processing Keyboarding
Academic Applications Writing	**Materials Required** word processing program, keyboarding program, story from a first grader, student workbooks (if using)	**Standards** CCSS.ELA-Literacy.W.2.3 NETS: 5b

Essential Question

How does detail enhance the power of a story?

Big Idea

Recount exciting detail about characters, setting, and plot

Teacher Preparation

- Have digital tools ready to use.
- Know which tasks weren't completed last week.
- Know if you need extra time to complete this lesson.
- Integrate domain-specific tech vocabulary into lesson.
- Talk with grade level team to understand what students know about adding detail to a story.
- Have a story written by students in 1st grade (anonymously).

Assessment Strategies

- Recognized growth in writing between 1st and 2nd grade
- Followed directions
- Worked well with a partner
- Completed warm-up, exit ticket
- Joined class conversations
- [tried to] solve own problems
- Decisions followed class rules
- Left room as s/he found it
- Higher order thinking: analysis, evaluation, synthesis
- Habits of mind observed

Steps

Time required: 45 minutes in one sitting or spread throughout the week with 30 minutes set aside for project

Class warm-up: Keyboard all keys on class typing tool. Observe students using good keyboarding habits such as posture, hand position, and eyes on screen

_____Show students a story written by them in first grade (such as *Figure 89*). What makes this story sound immature? For example:

- *insufficient detail*

- *words are too simple*
- *words are repetitive*

Figure 89—1st grade story example

_____Remind students their writing skills have grown since last year. They now know to provide the detail and color that makes a story interesting.

_____Show this story on class screen (without yellow bubbles). Ask students how they would make Mr. Coyote and the large tree more interesting to the reader?

> *Coyote was very old. His fur was mangy and falling out in spots. And his bright white teeth had yellowed with the diet of grasses he ate. He had...*

"Mr. Coyote *was getting very* old *and had to be more careful for his own safety. He had been* walking *for hours and hours through a* beautiful *valley when he came upon a large* tree. *Mr. Coyote was very tired and wanted to* rest *but he also needed to be safe. He kindly asked the tree, "Please open up so I can rest safely in your care".*

> *Its trunk was craggy and thick, and its arms spread wide over the grass as though welcoming Mr. Coyote.*

_____Look at this picture from last week (*Figure 90*). The yellow bubbles show how the student might add detail to these two sentences:

Figure 90—Story with insufficient detail

_____Ask for a volunteer to read it aloud for classmates:

Once upon a time, there was a girl named ***. She had a dog.

_____In this story, who is the girl (*hint: character*)? Who is the dog (*hint: another character*)?
_____Are students pulled into the story? What else would they like to know? Make suggestions that add detail such as is included in the yellow bubbles:

- *tell more about the girl*
- *tell more about the dog*

_____What changes do students suggest? For example:

- *sentence fluency*
- *word choice*
- *voice*
- *writing conventions*
- *organization*
- *idea development*

_____As students make suggestions, write them on class screen. When done, add them to the story. Are students more intrigued by the edited story?
_____If you feel students need practice, have them open a word processing program with a partner. Copy this short story from the class screen:

I play basketball. I love to play basketball. I like to play against my brother. He told me when you stop dribbling, you can't start dribbling again.

_____Discuss as a class how this story might be 'fixed' so it is more exciting:

- *Why does s/he love to play basketball?*
- *Why does s/he like to play against her/his brother?*
- *What was the importance of 'dribbling'?*
- *What does it feel like to play basketball?*
- *How can student add variety to the words 'play', 'dribbling', and 'basketball'?*

_____Have students type the story and edit with partner (should they use backspace or delete?). If necessary, review class guidelines for speaking and listening with a partner:

- *listen to partner with care*
- *speak one at a time*
- *build on others' talk by linking to their remarks*
- *ask for clarification and further explanation as needed*

_____When done, have groups share changes they made with class. Is anyone surprised by how different everyone's changes are?

_____Finally, have students return to last week's story starter (Slide #1 of the Open House slideshow) and edit it based on what they've learned today.

Class exit ticket: ***Have neighbor verify that student saved changes to their story starter (if any).***

Differentiation

- *Practice site words in SpellingCity.*
- *If this lesson doesn't work for students, use one from Inquiry-based Teaching with PBL (from Structured Learning.*

Helpdesk:	Double click "My Computer"
User:	I can't see your computer.
Helpdesk:	No, double click "My Computer" on your computer.
User:	Huh?
Helpdesk:	There is an icon on your computer labeled "My Computer". Double click it.
User:	What's your computer doing on mine?

Lesson #21 Where I Live

Vocabulary	Problem solving	Skills
• Detail • Digital tool • Edit • Export • Format • Icon • Mashup • Palette • Punctuation • Red squiggles • Setting	• Drawing program won't save (take a screen shot and save) • How do I capitalize (shift key) • Cap won't go off (check caps lock) • What's the difference between 'save' and 'export'? • What's the difference between backspace and delete? • How do I exit? (Alt+F4) • How do I use more than one digital tool at a time?	**New** **Scaffolded** Digital citizenship Editing in word processing Keyboarding
Academic Applications Writing	**Materials Required** drawing program, keyboarding program, student workbooks (if using)	**Standards** CCSS.ELA-Literacy.W.2.3 NETS: 1d, 4b, 6b-d

Essential Question

How does detail enhance the power of a story?

Big Idea

Words and pictures deliver a powerful picture

Teacher Preparation

- Talk with grade level team so you tie into their teaching on the basics of story construction.
- Have digital tools ready.
- Know which tasks weren't completed last week.
- Integrate domain-specific tech vocabulary into lesson.
- Know if you need extra time to complete this lesson.

Assessment Strategies

- Followed directions
- Worked well with a partner
- Used good keyboarding habits
- Completed warm-up, exit ticket
- Able to open student workbook independently (if using these)
- Joined class conversations
- [tried to] solve own problems
- Decisions followed class rules
- Left room as s/he found it
- Higher order thinking: analysis, evaluation, synthesis
- Habits of mind observed

Steps

Time required: 45 minutes in one sitting or spread through the week with 20 minutes set aside for project

Class warm-up: Keyboard all keys. Observe good keyboarding, posture, hand position.

_____Today's project continues a four-drawing series students are preparing for Open House. These celebrate tech skills learned this year (tools, toolbars, fills, drag-and-drop, backgrounds, clipart and more.

_____Be prepared to allow students one week to practice, one to save, if necessary.
_____Open drawing software (i.e., KidPix, Paint, TuxPaint, or other).
_____If you're a Chromebook school, try:

- *ABCYa Paint*
- *SumoPaint*

_____If you're an iPad school, try:

- *Drawp*
- *Doodle Buddy*

_____Students have already created the Brilliant Beginning and introduced themselves to readers. Today, they'll discuss the setting with two well-structured, grammatically-correct sentences.
_____Demonstrate on class screen as you illustrate setting and character development (*Figure 91*):

Figure 91—Slide two with writing suggestions

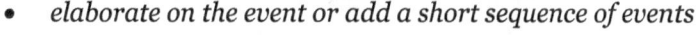

_____Write first sentence. Does it tell students enough? What else would they like to know? Think back to last lesson.
_____Add detail about the characters.
_____How should this story be punctuated?
_____Now students draw their own picture. Feel free to change the color of trees, grass, etc. with the color palette or other tools available for that purpose.
_____Write two sentences about the setting in font 48. Try different fonts and colors.
_____Work with neighbor to:

- *elaborate on the event or add a short sequence of events*
- *add detail to describe actions, thoughts, feelings*
- *add temporal words to signal event order*

_____When done, it might look like *Figure 92a* or *92b*:

Figure 92a-b—Slide 2 examples

_____You might decide students can upload and annotate pictures of their house (*Figure 93*):

Figure 93—Slide 2 using image

_____Remind students *Figure 93* is a mash-up of tech tools.
_____Export to student digital portfolio. Use Alt+F4 to exit.
_____Done? Practice keyboarding with correct posture and hand position, elbows at side.
_____Continually throughout class, check for understanding.

Class exit ticket: **Students check neighbor's drawing to be sure words match the picture.**

Differentiation

- *Instead of their house, students can build a Dream House.*
- *Replace lesson with one from Inquiry-based Teaching with PBL (from Structured Learning).*

Lesson #22 My Body

Vocabulary	Problem solving	Skills
• Align • Default • Dialogue box • Export • Form • Handles • Resize • Server • Template • Text box	• Program disappeared (check taskbar) • Text box is too big (resize) • Didn't print (select correct printer?) • Drawing program won't save (take screenshot) • Text is too big (reduce font size) • I can't find template (try server) • I can't find server (follow directions) • My text boxes overlap (resize) • Where's the camera roll?	**New** Camera roll **Scaffolded** Digital citizenship Using templates Digital tool mash-up Keyboarding Annotate workbooks (if using these)
Academic Applications Health, human body, other inquiry requiring labels	**Materials Required** human body template, keyboarding program, human body websites, student workbooks (if using)	**Standards** CCSS.ELA-Literacy.RI.2.7 NETS: 1c, 3c-d, 4b

Essential Question

How can a form I fill out help me remember information?

Big Idea

Typing into a form helps me to remember what I'm studying

Teacher Preparation

- Have classroom digital tools ready.
- Place human body template where students can access.
- Have list of human body websites on start page.
- Decide whether this is practice or assessment.
- Integrate domain-specific tech vocabulary into lesson.
- Know which tasks weren't completed last week.
- Know if you need extra time to complete this lesson.
- Talk with grade level team to use the same terminology.

Assessment Strategies

- Followed directions
- Completed project
- Used good keyboarding habits
- Completed warm-up
- Annotate workbook (if using)
- Worked well with a partner
- Joined class conversations
- [tried to] solve own problems
- Decisions followed class rules
- Left room as s/he found it
- Higher order thinking: analysis, evaluation, synthesis
- Habits of mind observed

Steps

Time required: 45 minutes in one sitting or spread throughout the week with 20 minutes set aside to label and format human body template

Class warm-up: Keyboard all keys on class typing program.

_____For this lesson, students will label a digital document with its parts. In past lessons, we used the world (continents and oceans). In this lesson, we'll use the human body as an example. You can label a life cycle, parts of a story, or anything else being studied in the classroom.

_____Introduce the unit. For the human body, start with a video and discuss as a group. If you don't have a favorite, try one from the Ask a Tech Teacher resource pages.

2nd Grade Technology Curriculum: Teacher Manual

_____This lesson provides three approaches to supporting inquiry using:

- *Fill-in-the-blank template*
- *Label student picture*
- *Label an avatar as though it was human*

Fill-in-the-blank Template

_____Ask students to fill in a digital worksheet (see *Assessment 11*):

Figure 94a-b: Fill in the blank templates of human body

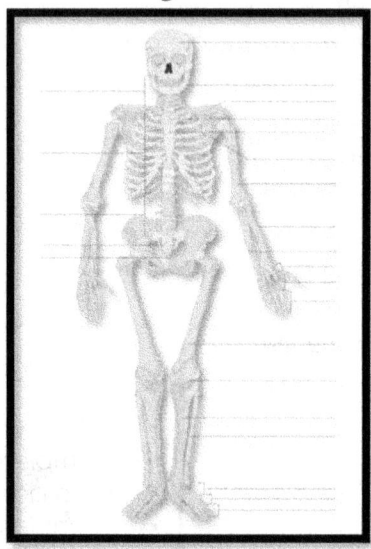
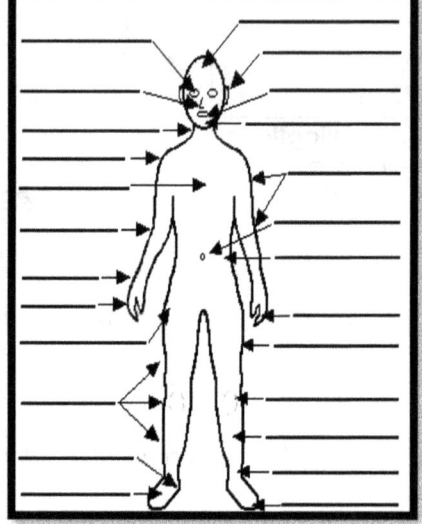

_____If you have desktop computers, you might use KidPix, Paint, or Google Draw. You can even use a word processing program like Google Docs or MS Word.
_____If you're a Chromebook school, try ABCYa Pain or SumoPaint.
_____If you're an iPad school, try these:

- *Drawp for School*
- *Doodle Buddy*

_____If using student workbooks, students can annotate the blank rubric in their workbook (*Assessment 11*) using a tool like iAnnotate or Adobe.
_____For most digital devices, you can supply the template as a PDF to students and they can fill in the blanks using the annotation tool supplied with the digital device.
_____Demonstrate how to complete worksheet:

- *Open drawing program that allows students to write on an imported image.*
- *Demonstrate how to find template on server and bring it into.*
- *Fill in collaboratively on class screen. Use body part words from class. If they say 'jaw' in class, don't put 'mandible', and vice versa.*
- *Show students how to resize font and move text box to align on worksheet.*
- *Decorate with paint bucket, paint brush, and stamps (skills familiar to students).*

_____Now students complete theirs. Display blank sample (*Figures 94a-b*) or completed sample (*Figure 95*) on class screen. Let students know you expect them to come up with as many parts as possible on their own.

Figure 95—Completed human body template

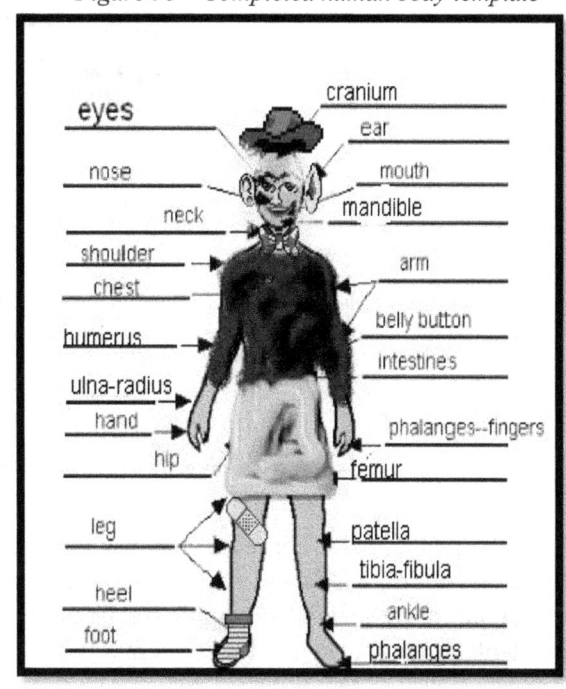

_____Those who finish early can format the picture with stickers, stamps, or other widgets are available on the digital program you select (*Figure 95*).

Label Student Picture

Figure 96a-b—Label student picture

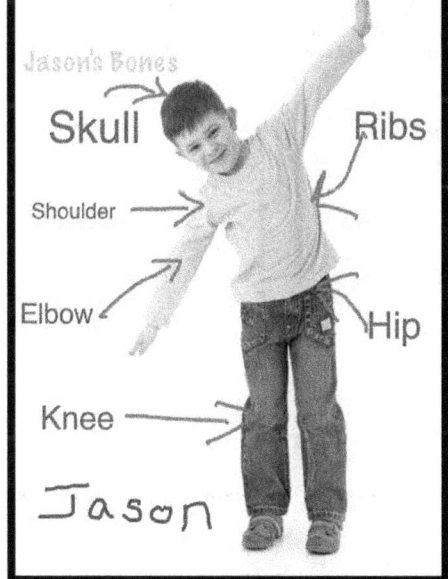
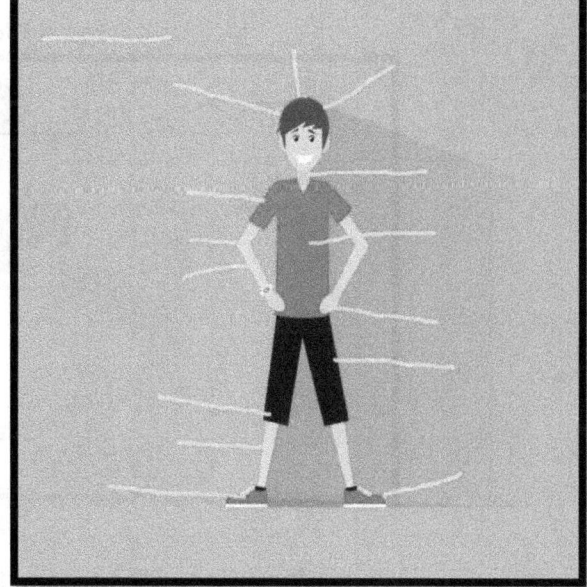

_____Have students help each other take their pictures with the iPad camera. Then, use an iPad app like Doodle Buddy to label parts using a brush and/or text tools. *Figures 96a-b* are examples.
_____You can also open the student picture in Google Draw and annotate via PicMonkey (*Figure 97*):

Figure 97—Mashup of Google Draw and PicMonkey

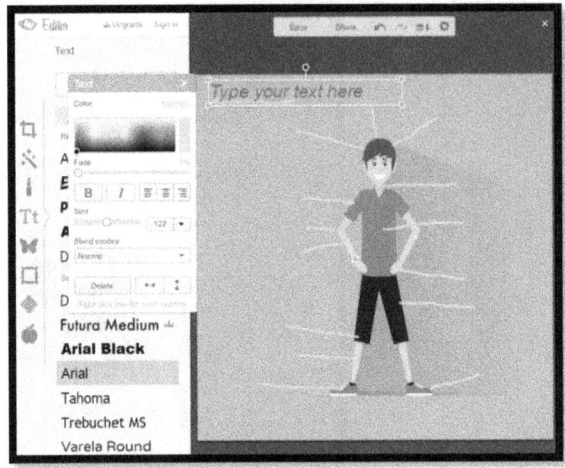

_____If using student workbooks, students open the PDF on their digital device and fill in the blanks with the device's annotation tool (like iAnnotate or Adobe).
_____For most digital devices, you can supply the template as a PDF and students can fill in the blanks using the digital device's annotation tool.

Label an Avatar as Though It is Human

_____This is a great approach to circle back on digital citizenship and the importance of privacy on the internet. Why are avatars a good personal representation rather than a photograph?
_____Students can either draw an avatar or select one they've used before. Load the avatar onto the computer, Chromebook, or iPad. *Figures 98a-b* are examples:

Figure 98a-b—Label avatar bodies

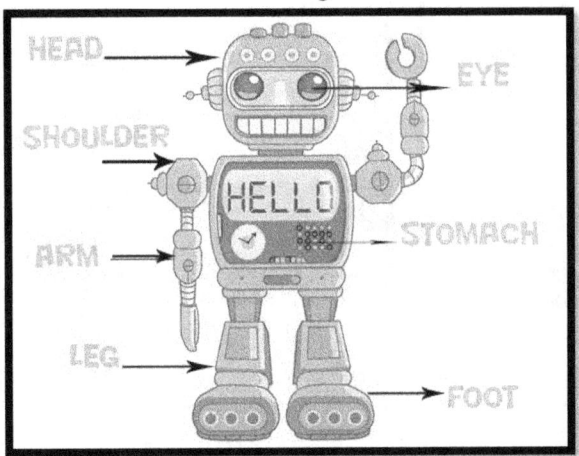
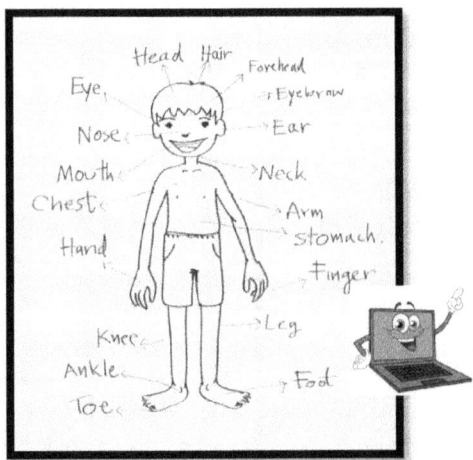

_____Save the drawing as a PDF, use the digital device's annotation tool to fill in the body parts.

_____ If using workbooks, students fill in the blanks with the device's annotation tool (like Adobe).
_____ When done, export/save/publish/share without assistance. Print if desired.
_____ Done? Practice keyboarding on installed software or online website.
_____ Continually throughout class, check for understanding.

Class exit ticket: **None**

Differentiation

- Instead of a template, use the student's picture taken with an iPad.
- If this is NOT a formative/summative assessment, students can work in pairs.
- Done? Visit Human Body websites on the Ask a Tech Teacher resource pages.
- If lesson doesn't work, use one from Inquiry-based Teaching with PBL (from Structured Learning).

Assessment 11—Parts of human body template

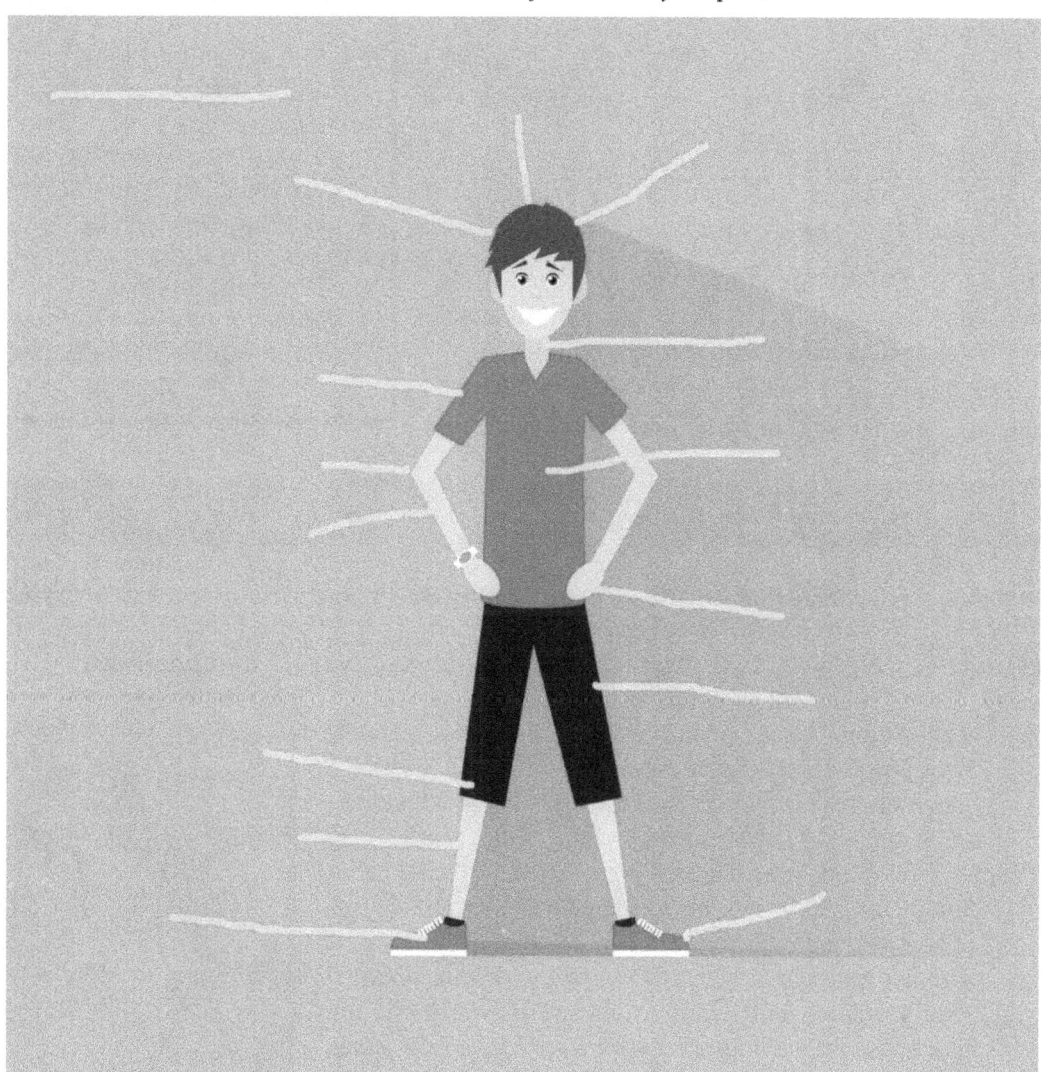

Lesson #23 Stories with Words and Pictures

Vocabulary	Problem solving	Skills
• Cursor • Edit • Export • Font • Format • Plot • Toolbar	• Can't find file folder (check log-in. Are you in correct profile?) • What's the difference between save and save-as? • How do I edit? (backspace/delete) • Why is my last name in file name? • Text covers picture (move text)	**New** **Scaffolded** Storytelling Communicating with images Keyboarding
Academic Applications Digital storytelling	**Materials Required** Drawing program, keyboard program, student workbooks (if using)	**Standards** CCSS.ELA-Literacy.W.2.3 NETS: 4b, 6b-d

Essential Question

Can I use pictures to share details like closure?

Big Idea

Recount a story with words and pictures

Teacher Preparation

- Have digital tools ready to use.
- Talk with grade-level team so you tie into conversations.
- Know which tasks weren't completed last week.
- Integrate domain-specific tech vocabulary into lesson.
- Know if you need extra time to complete this lesson.

Assessment Strategies

- Followed directions
- Completed third image
- Used good keyboarding habits
- Completed warm-up, exit ticket
- Joined class conversations
- Worked well with partner
- [tried to] solve own problems
- Decisions followed class rules
- Left room as s/he found it
- Higher order thinking: analysis, evaluation, synthesis

Steps

Time required: 45 minutes in one sitting or spread throughout the week with 20 minutes set aside for project

Class warm-up: Keyboard all rows. Observe student posture, hand position.

_____This picture is third of four images for the Open House slideshow. This is the story plot. What does that mean?
_____Open drawing program (KidPix, TuxPaint, ABCYaPaint, or another used at your school).
_____If you're a Chromebook school, try ABCYa Paint or SumoPaint. If you're an iPad school, try Drawp for School or Doodle Buddy.
_____Use five different brushes, five colors, to draw a picture.
_____Add sentence, font 48, any font and color. This is the action, the drama, a problem main character solves or a wish s/he has.

165

_____ Use correct grammar and spelling. Remind students to use backspace and delete to edit from where cursor blinks.

_____ Picture may look like *Figures 99a-c*:

Figure 99a-c—Third slide: Plot

_____ Export/save/share/publish to student digital portfolio. Do not print—these are a surprise for parents.

_____ Finished? Practice keyboarding on typing website.

_____ Continually throughout class, check for understanding.

Class exit ticket: **Have neighbor verify that student communicated the same message with text and image.**

Differentiation

- This can be considered a formative assessment as it uses skills already learned.
- Done? Review word study with SpellingCity.com.

```
        Login: yes
Password: I don't have one
   password is incorrect

        Login: yes
    Password: incorrect
   password is incorrect
```

2nd Grade Technology Curriculum: Teacher Manual

Lesson #24 The End (of the Slideshow)

Vocabulary	Problem solving	Skills
• Backspace • Closure • Cursor • Font • Multimedia • Network • Publish • Slideshow	• Volume doesn't work (check control) • Text covers picture (drag and move text box) • I made a mistake (edit) • What's the difference between backspace and delete? • How do I edit where I want to? (with cursor)	**New** **Scaffolded** Digital tools Digital portfolio Digital storytelling Keyboarding
Academic Applications Digital storytelling, writing	**Materials Required** Internet, drawing program, keyboard program, student workbooks (if using)	**Standards** CCSS.ELA-Literacy.W.2.3 NETS: 1d, 4b, 6b-d

Essential Question

Can I use pictures to share details like temporal order?

Big Idea

Recount a story with words and pictures including closure

Teacher Preparation

- Have digital tools ready to use.
- Find out what grammar is being emphasized in class.
- Know which tasks weren't completed last week.
- Integrate domain-specific tech vocabulary into lesson.
- Know if you need extra time to complete this lesson.

Assessment Strategies

- Followed directions
- Completed project
- Image closes series of events
- Completed warm-up, exit ticket
- Joined class conversations
- [tried to] solve own problems
- Decisions followed class rules
- Left room as s/he found it
- Higher order thinking: analysis, evaluation, synthesis
- Habits of mind observed

Steps

Time required: 45 minutes in one sitting or spread throughout the week with 20 minutes set aside for project

Class warm-up: Keyboard all keys with good posture.

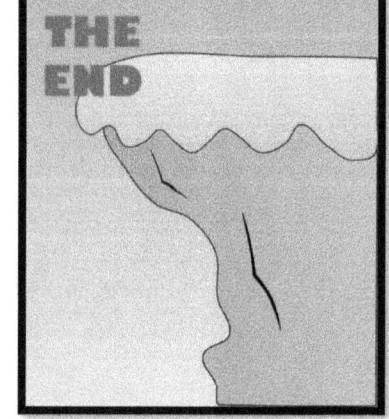

_____This is the fourth and last slide in our story. It resolves the problem, provides the happy ending—includes a sense of closure. What is 'closure'?

_____Prepare students for upcoming slideshow unit by reminding them of Open House. What are slideshows? Remember last year, when students shared their drawings with parents via the native Windows slideshow?

_____Explain that each student will create a slideshow that shares the interdisciplinary array of skills they learned this year.

_____Open drawing program. If you're a Chromebook school, try:

167

- *ABCYa Paint*
- *SumoPaint*

_____If you're an iPad school, try:

- *Drawp*
- *Doodle Buddy*

_____Use five different brushes, five colors, to draw picture.
_____Add sentence, size 48, any font and color. This is the action, the drama, a problem main character solves or a wish s/he has.
_____Use correct grammar and spelling. Remind students to use backspace and delete to edit from where cursor blinks.
_____Check that text doesn't cover picture. If it does, move box.
_____Check that picture and text deliver the same message.
_____Completed project may look like *Figures 100a-c*:

Figure 100a-c—Closure of digital story

_____Export/save to student digital portfolio.
_____Finished? Practice keyboarding on class typing tool. Remember correct posture, correct hand position, and other typing habits.
_____Throughout class, check for understanding.

Class exit ticket: ***Verify that student has all four images for slideshow. If not, arrange a time to make up the missing drawing.***

Differentiation

- *This can be a formative assessment.*

Computer: a device designed to speed and automate errors.

Lesson #25 Internet Pictures

Vocabulary	Problem solving	Skills
• 'scholarly research' • Address bar • Fair use • Images • Internet • Netiquette • Public Domain • Right-click menu • Search • Search bar • Toggle • Watermark	• I can't find the right pictures • I can't find my saved images (where did you save them?) • Picture won't save (is it protected?) • One picture has words on it (it's copyrighted—pick a different one) • My picture came out weird (did you grab the thumbnail?) • Image licensing is difficult to find (adjust Google's search criteria) • How does anyone online know if I'm being polite? It's anonymous.	**New** Save internet images Legality of internet images **Scaffolded** Digital citizenship Digital tools Digital portfolio Keyboarding
Academic Applications Science, history, writing, research	**Materials Required** Internet, safe image websites, topic to use for image research, student workbooks (if using)	**Standards** CCSS.ELA-Literacy.RI.2.7 NETS: 2b-c, 3a

Essential Question

How do I safely collect images from the internet?

Big Idea

I can collect information from online images for research

Teacher Preparation

- Know which tasks weren't completed last week.
- Know if you need extra time to complete this lesson.
- Have kid-safe image websites or set Google to safe mode.
- Talk with grade-level team so student image searches ties into their preparation for the upcoming report.
- Authentically integrate domain-specific tech vocabulary into lesson.

Assessment Strategies

- Used internet safely
- Saved 5 pictures to digital portfolio
- Completed warm-up, exit ticket
- Worked well with partner
- Joined class conversations
- [tried to] solve own problems
- Decisions followed class rules
- Left room as s/he found it
- Habits of mind observed

Steps

Time required: **45 minutes in one sitting or spread throughout the week with 15 minutes set aside to collect pictures and 20 minutes set aside to discuss the safe, legal collection of images from the internet**

Class warm-up: **Keyboard all keys with proper posture and habits. Anecdotally assess student progress with keyboarding.**

_____Today starts the first of three weeks on a report. Students gather information from classroom resources (books, discussion, and internet sites) that answer questions in a specific topic (in this sample, *Life Cycle of an Animal*). Today, we will find web-based pictures to support inquiry.

_____Before beginning, discuss how images contribute to and clarify text.
_____You want students to search:

- safely
- legally
- effectively

Search for Online Images Safely

_____For this project, students will draw on knowledge learned in class about stages in their animal's life cycle, to select the correct internet images. For example, one stage in a butterfly's life cycle is 'caterpillar'. They should know this without prompting.

_____Before starting project, remind students of conversations in prior weeks about the safe use of the internet and online images. Review *Figure 101a* and *Figure 101b* (poster in Appendix):

Figure 101a—Want to use this image? 101b—Using online images legally

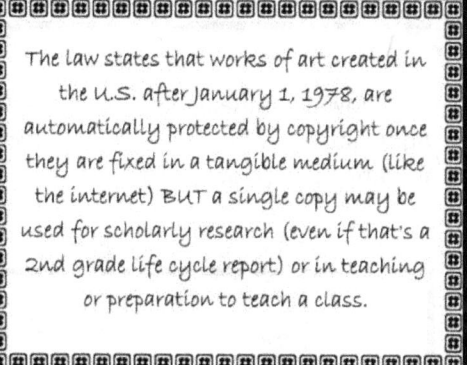

_____Show students how to set up Google 'safe search' for a more positive search experience.

Figure 102—Google safe search

_____You may have this as the default in your school, but students probably don't at home.

Search for Online Images Legally

_____With Safe Search established, demonstrate how to type an animal name into website search bar (for 'chicks', use 'chickens' or 'baby chickens'). Select 'Images' and search. There will be many images (*Figure 103a*). Select one by clicking (*Figure 103b*):

Figure 103a—Google search; 103b—Select one

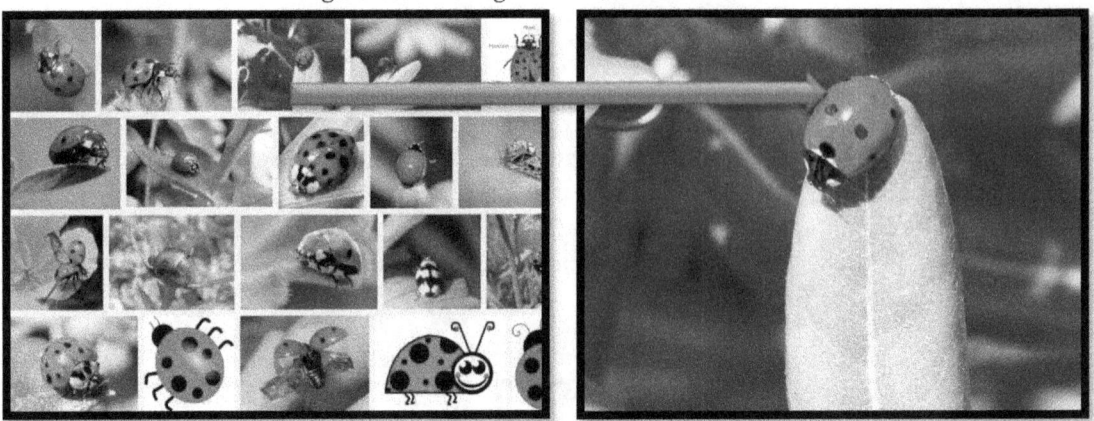

_____But how do students know whether a picture is free or copyrighted—whether it's legal to use? Show students how to narrow search results on Google to only those 'labeled for reuse with modification' (*Figure 104*):

Figure 104—Image use settings on Google

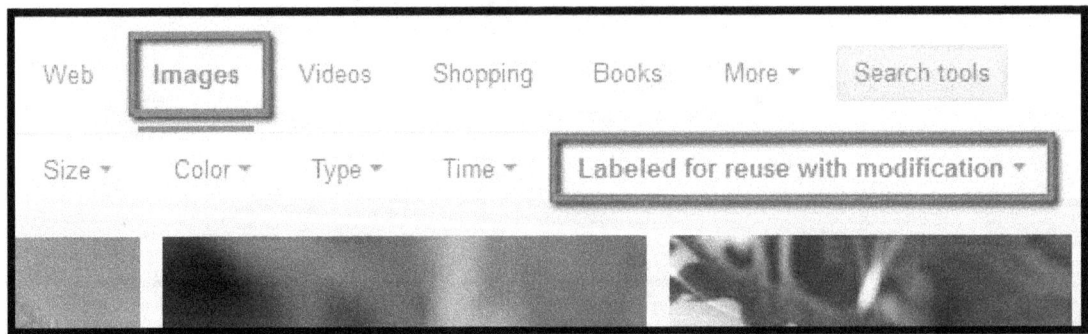

_____Discuss 'public domain'. Why are pictures posted on the internet if they aren't free? This is a subject you cover in much detail by the end of fifth grade.

_____As a student, most pictures are covered under 'fair use' and free to use for 'scholarly purposes', which includes schoolwork. This doesn't mean students can use them for free outside of educational uses.

_____If the Google Images search setting is not available (maybe you're on a website already and want to use a picture found there), show students how to explore the image to find the evidence to make a go-nogo decision. Sometimes, it's a tab on the website. Other times, it pops up when you access the image (for example, if you use an image curator like Flikr)

_____Decide what your second graders are ready for on this topic. Do know: The sooner students learn the legalities built into online media like pictures, the better digital citizens they will be.

_____In *Figure 105,* the top picture is 'Public Domain Dedication'—free to use. Read the fine print to the right of the image and you'll see that no linkback or citation is required. The bottom image requires attribution and a link back (which I've provided):

Figure 105—Image use permissions

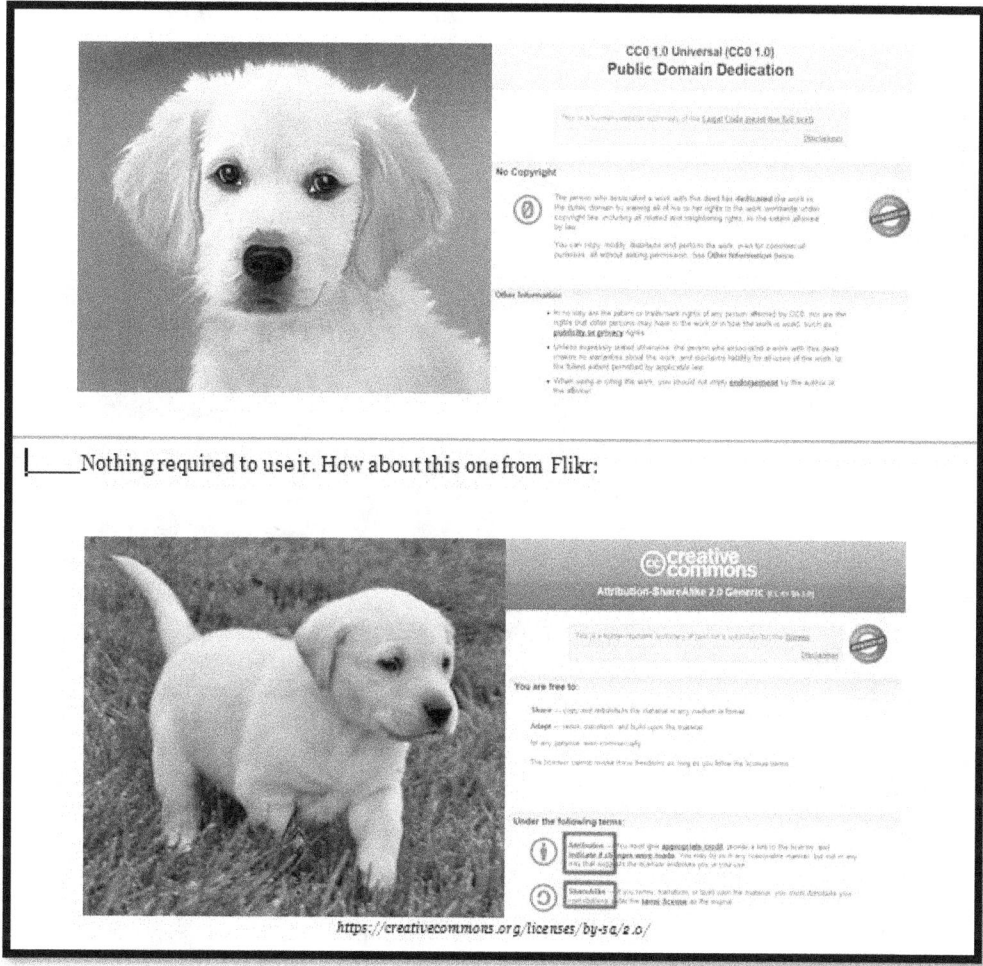

|_____Nothing required to use it. How about this one from Flikr:

Click for permission to use Lisa Wledmeler's Puppy picture

Search for Online Images Effectively

_____Type animal name in website search bar (for 'chicks', use 'chickens' or 'baby chickens' instead). Verify spelling is correct. Select 'Images' and search.
_____Show students how to add quote marks around a phrase if necessary, such as "life cycle of a butterfly", to refine results.
_____Find animal picture (i.e., *lady bug*). Right click on picture; 'save image as' to student digital portfolio. No need to change name.
_____Repeat until student has one picture for each life cycle stage.
_____Done? Select a website from Ask a Tech Teacher's internet safety resources pages or:

- *BrainPop Jr's video on Internet Safety*
- *Clicky's Netsmartz Kids (available on YouTube)*

2nd Grade Technology Curriculum: Teacher Manual

- o   *Garfield's Cyberbullying (on YouTube)*
- o   *My Online Neighborhood (available on YouTube)*

_____Continually throughout class, check for understanding.

Class exit ticket: ***Have neighbor check student digital portfolio to be sure all five pictures are there.***

Differentiation

- Full digital citizenship curriculum for K-8 available from Structured Learning.
- Replace this lesson with one from Inquiry-based Teaching with PBL (from Structured Learning).

_____

_____

_____

_____

_____

_____

_____

_____

_____

2nd Grade Technology Curriculum: Teacher Manual

Lesson #26 Report in Word Processing I

Vocabulary	Problem solving	Skills
• Ctrl+Enter • Export • Footer • Greyed out • Handles • Horizontal • Insert • Pound sign • Tool • Toolbar • Vertical	• How do I start a new page (Ctrl+Enter) • Can't resize a picture (corner handles) • Missed one stage (search for missing picture as done in prior lesson, then copy-paste directly into report. • How do I center cover vertically and horizontally? • I can't see page number in footer (it's the pound sign) • My text is greyed out (did you enter it in the footer?)	**New** Collages (maybe) Word processing report **Scaffolded** Digital citizenship Digital tools Digital portfolio Word processing—editing
Academic Applications Science, history, literacy—anything requiring research	**Materials Required** word processing program, drawing program, student workbooks (if using)	**Standards** CCSS.ELA-Literacy.W.2.5 NETS: 1d, 3c-d, 4a

Essential Question

What elements make up good writing?

Big Idea

Good writing requires editing and revising

Teacher Preparation

- Have digital tools ready to use.
- Talk with grade-level team so you tie into conversations.
- Know which tasks weren't completed last week.
- Integrate domain-specific tech vocabulary into lesson.
- Know if you need extra time to complete this lesson.

Assessment Strategies

- Completed cover page
- Began body of report
- Found pictures in student folder
- Used good keyboarding habits
- Completed exit ticket
- Joined class conversations
- [tried to] solve own problems
- Decisions followed class rules
- Left room as s/he found it
- Higher order thinking: analysis, evaluation, synthesis

Steps

Time required: 45 minutes in one sitting or spread throughout the week with 15 minutes set aside to draw animal picture and 30 minutes set aside for project

Class warm-up: None

_____Open drawing program (i.e., KidPix, TuxPaint, or other).

_____If you're a Chromebook school, try:

- *ABCYa Paint*
- *SumoPaint*

_____If you're an iPad school, try *Doodle Buddy*.

_____Draw a picture of animal being researched. This will be the report cover (see *Figures 107a-b*). Use paint (or pencil) only—no stamps, stickers, backgrounds.

_____Export to digital portfolio and close drawing program. *Figures 106a-c* are examples:

Figure 106a-c—Animals created with drawing tool

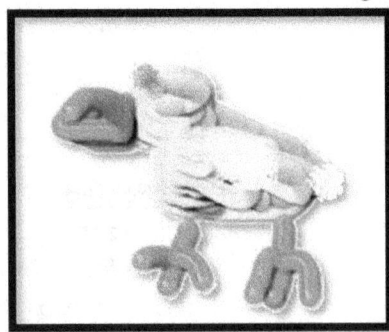  

_____Discuss this personal drawing as it relates to pictures students copied from the internet last week. Now student is the artist. Would they want anyone to steal/borrow/use the picture they drew? What if someone sold it? What if picture was used to support a topic student disagreed with? Tie this into last week's discussions of image copyrights—make those conversations more personal. Take time so students can share their thoughts.

_____Open word processing program that allows for picture insert and formatting. Quickly review start page, tools, toolbars, ribbons, and layout. Remind students of projects they completed using this word processing tool (maybe you have samples in classroom gallery).

_____Create a cover page by centering name of animal, student, teacher, vertically and horizontally. Use font 36, any font. Add picture student drew underneath. See *Figures 107a-b*:

Figure 107a-b—Report cover

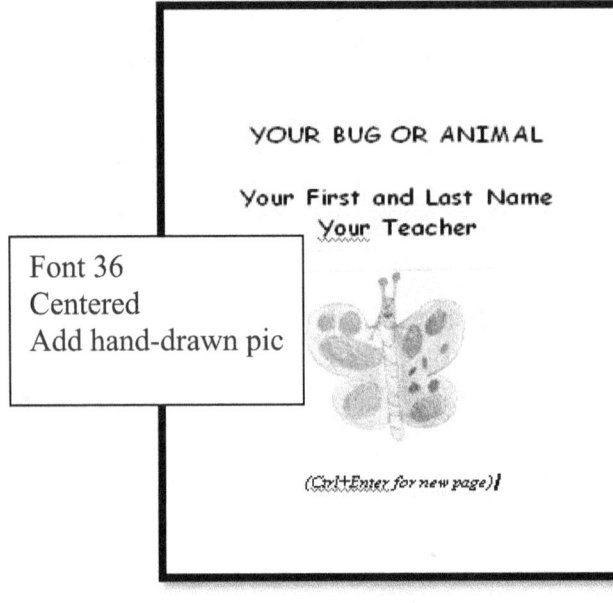 

_____Add footer with student name and page. Explain footer. Close footer.

_____Ctrl+Enter for new page. Begin typing on **Page 2**. Use font size 14, Times New Roman. Center and bold section titles; left-align sections; tab to start each section. When each section is typed, revise and edit, check grammar and spelling, smooth out sentence fluency, add formatting.

Figure 108a-b—Report interior pages

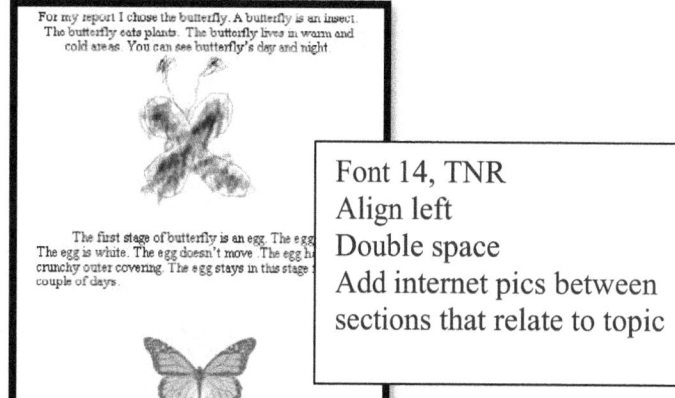

_____ Insert animal picture from internet after each section. Be sure to center and resize to fit.

_____ Continually throughout class, check for understanding.

_____ Instead of word processing, use a desktop publishing app like Canva (*Figures 109a* and *b*), PicMonkey, or a poster app like Pic Collage (*Figure 109c*)—Google for addresses:

Figure 109a-b—Report with Canva; 109c—PicCollage

 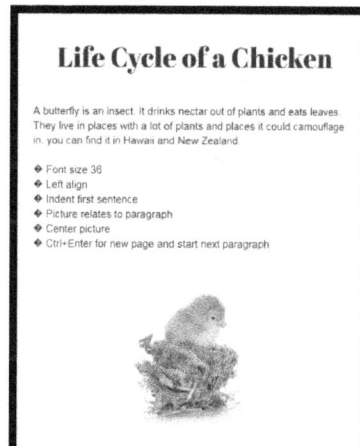 

Class exit ticket: *Have classmate verify that their neighbor saved this week one draft into student digital portfolio.*

Differentiation

- Add a border to title page.
- Create cover in a DTP tool or an online site like Big Huge Labs (Google for address).
- Replace lesson with one from Inquiry-based Teaching with PBL (from Structured Learning)).

Article 19 "Where Can I Find Kid-safe Images?

Where Can I Find Kid-safe Images?

Here's a great question I got from a reader:

> *I am a computer lab teacher and teach grades 1-5. I can really use some advice from others. Do you have a good place for students to go and get images that are appropriate - I teach grades 1-5 and Google even with strict settings as well as MS Office clipart have some inappropriate images that come up from searches*

This is harder than it should be. I use Google as a default because it is the safest of all the majors, not to say it's 100%. I spent quite a few hours one weekend checking out kid-friendly child search engines (KidsClick, KidRex, and more—Google for addresses), but none did a good job filtering images. Content—yes, but images dried up to worthless for the needs of visual children.

So I went back to Google and tried their Safe Search settings. Normal Google search is set to moderate. For school age children, they can easily be set to Strict.

For some, even 'strict settings' isn't enough. Take the opportunity to teach students about internet safety, about what to do if they encounter inappropriate images, about never straying from assigned websites. There's no way to protect children 100% from the world around them. Better we give them the knowledge required to survive and thrive, prepare them for the day we won't be there to protect their back.

Lesson #27 Report in Word Processing II

Vocabulary	Problem solving	Skills
• Alignment • Ctrl+Enter • Ctrl+S • Cursor • Double space • Font • Format • Grammar-check • Indent • Right-click • Spell-check • Tab • Word wrap	• Can't find file (Start-search) • Double-space doesn't work (toolbar) • How do I create a new page (Ctrl+Enter) • Indent doesn't work (use tab) • What's the difference between backspace and delete? • Why can't I double space by pushing enter at end of a line? • Why can't I push spacebar to indent instead of tab? • Picture looks squashed (or skinny)? Resize only with corner handles.	**New** **Scaffolded** Digital tools Digital portfolio Word processing
Academic Applications Writing, any subject that requires a summative report	**Materials Required** word processing program, drawing program, collage apps (if using), student workbooks (if using)	**Standards** CCSS.ELA-Literacy.W.2.5 NETS: 1d, 3c-d, 4a

Essential Question

What elements make up good writing?

Big Idea

Good writing requires editing, revising and guidance

Teacher Preparation

- Know which tasks weren't completed last week.
- Integrate domain-specific tech vocabulary into lesson.
- Know if you need extra time to complete this lesson.

Assessment Strategies

- Followed directions
- Used good keyboarding habits
- Completed project—revised and edited as needed with partner
- Worked well with partner
- Joined class conversations
- [tried to] solve own problems
- Left room as s/he found it
- Habits of mind observed

Steps

Time required: 45 minutes in one sitting
Class warm-up: None

_____Continue classroom report. This is week 3 of 3 on this project.
_____Any problem finding work saved last week? If students have trouble, try one of these:

- Did you save it to the local drive (i.e., '**My Documents**')?
- If you saved with **student name in the file name**, search with **Start>Search**.
- Were you **sitting somewhere else?** Start>Search might not find those files.

_____Start each paragraph with an indent (tab). Font size is 14, Times New Roman. Change line spacing to double space if desired.
_____Begin typing in font size 14, Times New Roman. Center and bold section titles; left-align sections; tab to start each section. Help students with writing conventions where necessary. When completed, revise and edit, check grammar and spelling, smooth sentence fluency, format.
_____When done, review with a neighbor to see if they catch any mistakes.
_____Save/share/publish/print, as expected in your classroom culture.
_____Continually throughout class, check for understanding.

Class exit ticket: None

Differentiation

- *Use an audio (Voki) or video (iPad camera) digital tool to create this report.*

"hAS aNYONE sEEN MY cAPSLOCK kEY?"

_____
_____
_____
_____
_____
_____
_____

2nd Grade Technology Curriculum: Teacher Manual

Lesson #28 Slideshows I

Vocabulary	Problem solving	Skills
• Editors • Multimedia • PowerPoint • Ribbon • Slide • Slideshow • Subtitle • Task pane • Title	• Program disappeared (check taskbar) • Computer broken (Did you push power on CPU or monitor?) • No task pane (check 'view') • Can't find slideshow program on computer (Start>search) • I don't like slideshows (is there another tool you can use to share their work?) • I can't find a tool (check the toolbar)	**New** PowerPoint, Google Slides **Scaffolded** Digital citizenship slideshow
Academic Applications History, science, other, speaking/listening, research	**Materials Required** Slideshow program, compare-contrast tables, storyboard template, student workbooks (if using)	**Standards** CCSS.ELA-Literacy.W.2.6 NETS: 1d, 3c-d, 6a-d

Essential Question

How do I communicate knowledge if I'm not a great writer?

Big Idea

Good writing communicates with all the ways readers read—text, images, color, layout, movement, even sound

Teacher Preparation

- Have slideshows from last year's 2nd graders available.
- Talk with grade-level team so you tie into conversations.
- Integrate domain-specific tech vocabulary into lesson.
- Know if you need extra time to complete this lesson.
- Know which tasks weren't completed last week.

Assessment Strategies

- Completed cover
- Followed instructions
- Used good keyboarding habits
- Completed warm-up, exit ticket
- Joined class conversations
- Worked well with partner
- [tried to] solve own problems
- Decisions followed class rules
- Left room as s/he found it
- Higher order thinking: analysis, evaluation, synthesis
- Habits of mind observed

Steps

Time required: 45 minutes in one sitting or spread throughout the week with 30 minutes set aside for project

Class warm-up: Keyboard on all keys

_____The year's last project is a slideshow summation of technology student learned this year. It collects the projects they completed into one presentation, to share at Open House.

_____Explain slideshows: a story with words, color, movement, dazzling layout, and sound. It allows for differentiation of instruction.

_____Why not use word processing? Or DTP? Compare-contrast these two. As a class, complete the table in *Figure 110* comparing elements of each type of tool. *Figure 110a* leaves blanks students can fill in. *Figure 110b* is the complete table:

Figure 110a-b—Compare-contrast slideshows vs word processing

Element	Slideshow	Word processing
Purpose	Presentation	
Basics		Text-based; words communicate Design is secondary to content Layout may detract from words
Sentences	Bullets, phrases	
Content		Thorough discussion of a topic. Meant to be complete document
Use	Back-up to presentation	Complete resource
Presentation	Speaker presents with their back to slideshow	
Other		

Element	Slideshow	Word processing
Purpose	Presentation	Written text
Basics	Graphics-based Design is important to content Layout communicates info Few words, lots of images	Text-based Design is secondary to content Layout may detract from words Primarily words communicate
Sentences	Bullets, phrases	Full sentences with proper writing conventions
Content	Slides cover basics, to remind presenter what to say	Thorough discussion of a topic. Meant to be complete document
Use	Back-up to presentation	Complete resource
Presentation	Speaker presents with their back to slideshow	Speaker (likely) reads from document
Other		

_____Add more thoughts to 'Other'. These will be ideas specific to your school's use of digital tools. They might include 'ability to use tool at home' or 'allows for student collaboration'. See what students come up with from their experience.

_____Students create slideshows in K-4th grade. If you don't get through all of the skills for this project, make a note to yourself so you can add it to the list of skills for students when they create Government slideshows in 3rd grade and Invention Convention slideshows in 4th grade (or whatever topics the teachers pick in those years).

_____Remind students of last year's slideshow (if you used the SL curriculum), created using the Windows image slideshow or Mac OS X's Quick Look slideshow feature (see *Figure 111*)?

Figure 111—K/1st grade slideshows

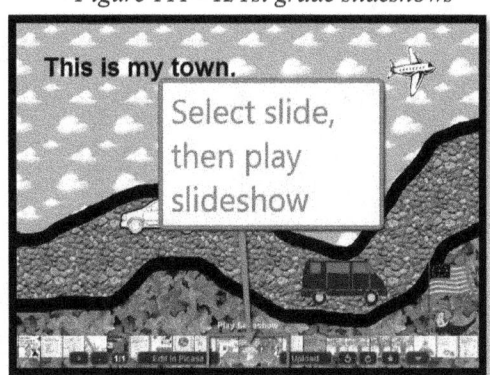

_____Share several slideshows created by last year's 2nd graders, to give an idea of what students will be doing (see *Figures 112a-c*):

Figure 112a—2nd grade slideshow cover; 112b—interior slide; 112c—ending slide

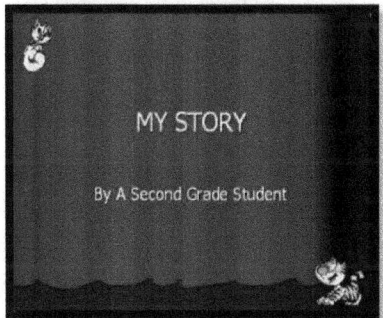  

_____What's included in this slideshow that isn't in last year's?

- *animations*
- *annotations*
- *formatting*
- *movement*
- *plays on iPads (if using one of those options)*
- *transitions*

_____Open the slideshow program used in your school (Google Presentations, Presentation, Zoho, PowerPoint, or an online tool like Haiku Deck.

_____If you have iPads, use one of the amazing iPad apps for digital storytelling such as Adobe Voice, Adobe Slate, or Haiku Deck (Google for websites).

_____If you have Chromebooks, try the PowerPoint or Google Slides app. You can also use an online slideshow creator like PhotoPeach or Kizoa (Google for addresses). Simply adapt the steps in this project to the tools they have available.

_____We use PowerPoint for this lesson. Review screen layout, adapted for your tool (*Figure 113a* is Word; *Figure 113b* is Haiku Deck):

Figure 113a—PowerPoint canvas; 113b—Haiku Deck canvas

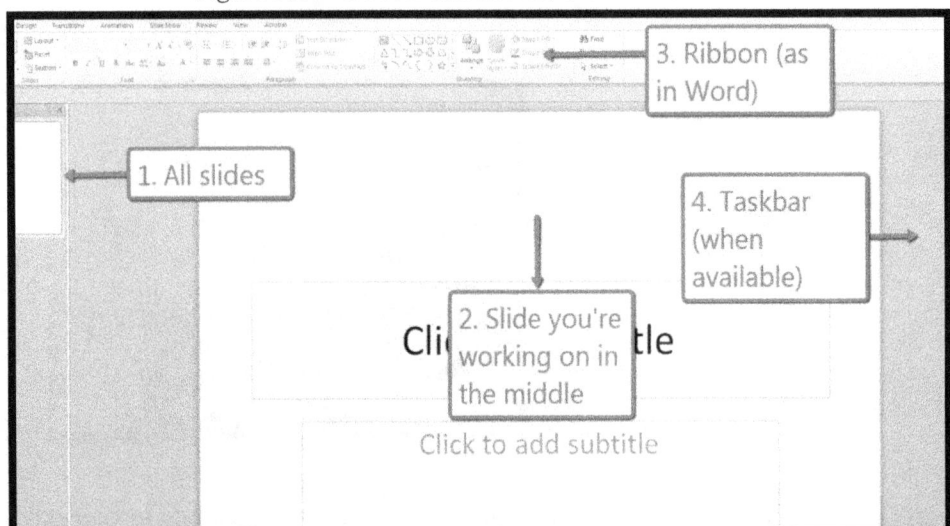

1. slides available (on left)

2. *slide being worked on (in middle)*
3. *ribbon (at top)*
4. *task pane (on right)—when available*

_____Click to add title on the first slide—'My Story'; click to add subtitle—'your name'.
_____Add five slides. That's a total of six slides—one for cover, four for pictures, one for closing.
_____Save to student digital portfolio.
_____Throughout class, check for understanding.

Class exit ticket: **Have neighbor verify that student saved their slideshow to digital portfolio. Student will need this project for multiple weeks.**

Differentiation

- *Instead of a slideshow, consider a tool like Canva, PicCollage or SonicPics that collects pictures into a collage (Google for addresses).*
- *Instead of the native slideshow program in your digital device, use a tool like Little Bird Tales to add images and voice overlay, then turn it into a movie.*
- *Students who finish can make parent invitations for slideshow presentations using DTP tools they explored this year.*
- *If this lesson doesn't work for students, use one from Inquiry-based Teaching with PBL (from Structured Learning).*

2nd Grade Technology Curriculum: Teacher Manual

Lesson #29 Slideshows II

Vocabulary	Problem solving	Skills
• Design • Handles • Minimize • Network • Right-click • Slideshow • Software • Task pane • Toolbar	• More than four pictures (use any four) • I can't find my project (where did you save it?) • Where is period? (by question mark) • How do I capitalize? (Use shift for one letter, caps for all) • Picture got weird (only use corner handles to resize) • Can't find right picture (use any)	**New** PowerPoint or another slideshow program **Scaffolded** Digital tools Digital portfolio Slideshows Keyboarding
Academic Applications Writing, speaking and listening	**Materials Required** Slideshow program, keyboarding tool, student pictures created throughout the school year	**Standards** CCSS.ELA-Literacy.W.2.6 NETS: 1d, 3c-d, 6a-d

Essential Question

I'm not a writer. Can I still communicate my ideas?

Big Idea

Technology provides a variety of methods to communicate ideas

Teacher Preparation

- Have digital tools ready.
- Know which tasks weren't completed last week.
- Integrate domain-specific tech vocabulary into lesson.
- Know if you need extra time to complete this lesson.

Assessment Strategies

- Followed directions
- Saved correctly
- Completed warm-up
- [tried to] solve own problems
- Decisions followed class rules
- Left room as s/he found it
- Higher order thinking: analysis, evaluation, synthesis
- Habits of mind observed

Steps

Time required: 45 minutes in one sitting or spread throughout the week with 30 minutes set aside for project
Class warm-up: Open slideshow begun last week without assistance

_____ Minimize slideshow project (show students how if they aren't familiar with this skill) and practice keyboarding for ten to fifteen minutes. Remind students of good habits—elbows at sides, keyboard in front of body.

_____ Remind students: A slideshow is one of many digital tools they have used this year to advance their education.

_____ Have students open projects saved last week. If they can't find them, remind them of the strategies discussed in earlier lessons.

About the Author

My name is Carminda and I live with my mom, my dad, my brother Felice who is 13 years old, my kittens Cuddles, Cutie, and Caper, and my puppy Casey. My favorite books are animal ark books especially Kittens in the Kitchen. My favorite song God Bless America. My favorite activities are playing with my pets, playing on the computer, and soccer. My dream when I grow up is to be a veterinarian and own a pet hospital. That is all.

_____**Slides 2-5:** Add one picture to each drawn by student during the year. Resize by grabbing corner handles and moving toward center. Then, add a title at the top that summarizes the picture (*Figures 114a-c*).

Figure 114a-c—Slideshow slides

_____**Slides 2-5:** Pick a 'Design' from menu to be used as background on all slides. How this is done will vary depending upon the tool you're using. If this option isn't available, skip this step.

_____Use 'x' in upper right corner to close. Why use 'x' instead of 'save'? It will save project where student opened it. If using an online tool, it may save automatically.

_____Continually throughout class, check for understanding.

Class exit ticket: None

Differentiation

- *Instead of My Story, create a slideshow coupon book for parents with special stuff students will do for them over the summer.*
- *Students who finish can add more pictures to slideshow.*
- *Students who finish can make parent invitations for slideshow presentations using DTP skills learned this year.*

"As a computer, I find your faith in technology amusing."

Lesson #30 Slideshows III

Vocabulary	Problem solving	Skills
• Animation • Author • Flash drive • Handles • Menu bar • Resize • Scheme • Software	• No title box? Picture is probably covering it. Resize. • What's the difference between software and an internet tool? • Can't find project (where did you save it?) • How do I keep 'animation' on slide (once clicked, it's there)	**New** PowerPoint or another slideshow program **Scaffolded** Digital tools Digital portfolio Slideshows
Academic Applications Writing, speaking and listening	**Materials Required** keyboarding program, slideshow tools, student pictures (collected throughout school year)	**Standards** CCSS.ELA-Literacy.W.2.6 NETS: 1d, 3c-d, 6a-d

Essential Question

How can tech communicate ideas better than other ways?

Big Idea

Tech makes it easy to communicate to address varied audiences

Teacher Preparation

- Have digital tools ready to use.
- Integrate domain-specific tech vocabulary into lesson.
- Know whether you need extra time to complete lesson.
- Know which tasks weren't completed last week.
- Talk with grade-level team about slideshow presentations.

Assessment Strategies

- Followed directions
- Used good keyboarding habits
- Completed warm-up, exit ticket
- [tried to] solve own problems
- Decisions followed class rules
- Left room as s/he found it
- Higher order thinking: analysis, evaluation, synthesis
- Habits of mind observed

Steps

Time required: 45 minutes in one sitting or spread throughout the week with 30 minutes set aside for project

Class warm-up: Open slideshow begun last week without assistance

_____Minimize slideshow project (show students how if they aren't familiar with this skill) and practice keyboarding for ten to fifteen minutes. Remind students of good habits—hands curled over home row, elbows at sides, keyboard in front of body.

_____Have student open project saved last week. If s/he can't find it, try strategies discussed in earlier lessons.

- *search* using last name

- remember **what name you saved it under**
- remember **where you saved it**
- recall **where you were sitting** when you saved

_____Finish adding pictures from student folder until four slides are completed. Resize as needed.
_____Click to add title. Create a title that sums up intent of picture.
_____**Slide 6:** Add title, 'The End' (*Figures 115a-b*):

Figure 115a-b—The End slide

_____Instead of 'The End', students can add '*About the Author*' (*Figures 116a-b*) and answer:

- *Where do you live?*
- *Who's in your family?*
- *What's your favorite book?*
- *What's your goal/What do you want to do when you grow up?*

Figure 116a-b—About the Author

_____**Slide #1-6:** Go to 'Animation' (if available). Explain what this means and show examples. Have students animate only title of slide. Animate all slides.

Class exit ticket: *Have students review each other's slideshows and make suggestions.*

Differentiation

- Create a Voki audio to narrate pictures presented in any format (not just a slideshow).
- Students who finish can make parent invitations for slideshow presentations using one of the DTP tools explored this year.

2nd Grade Technology Curriculum: Teacher Manual

Lesson #31 Slideshows IV

Vocabulary	Problem solving	Skills
• Animation • Author • Handles • Menu bar • Resize • Scheme • Software	• What's the difference between software and an internet tool? • I can't find my project (where did you save it?) • Where did I save (use Search) • How do I keep 'animation' on slide (once clicked, it's there)	**New** PowerPoint or another slideshow program **Scaffolded** Slideshows Annotate workbooks
Academic Applications Writing, speaking and listening	**Materials Required** keyboarding program, slideshow tools, student pictures	**Standards** CCSS.ELA-Literacy.W.2.6 NETS: 1d, 3c-d, 6a-d

Essential Question

How can technology communicate better than other ways students are familiar with?

Big Idea

Technology makes it easy to communicate to varied audiences for varied purposes

Teacher Preparation

- Know which tasks weren't completed last week.
- Integrate domain-specific vocabulary into lesson.
- Know if you need extra time to complete lesson.
- Talk with grade-level team about the best time/way to present student slideshows.

Assessment Strategies

- Finished/shared/published slideshow; submitted rubric
- Good keyboarding habits
- Completed warm-up
- Annotate workbook (if using)
- Worked well with a partner
- [tried to] solve own problems
- Decisions followed class rules
- Left room as s/he found it
- Higher order thinking: analysis, evaluation, synthesis
- Habits of mind observed

Steps

Time required: 45 minutes in one sitting or spread throughout the week with 30 minutes set aside for project
Class warm-up: Open slideshow begun last week without assistance

_____Minimize slideshow project (show students how if they aren't familiar with this skill) and practice keyboarding for ten to fifteen minutes. Remind students of good habits—elbows at sides, keyboard in front of body.

_____Have student open project saved last week. If s/he can't find it, 1) check My Documents, 2) search using their last name.

_____Open slideshow tool. Go to 'Transition'. Discuss what it is. Compare it to other words with prefix 'trans-'.

_____**Slides 1-6**: Add three items:

- *transition between slides*
- *speed of transition*
- *auto-advance*

_____**Slides 1-6**: Add two pictures to each slide:

- *non-moving picture with clipart; search for topic that fits slide*
- *moving picture via 'movie' or an organic collection of GIFs*

_____Done with everything? Pair up with a neighbor and fill out rubric checklist (see *Figure 117* and *Assessment 12*) on each other's slideshow. Help with editing, formatting, and all required items. Present slideshow to each other in preparation for class presentation. Try to talk without reading slide and fit all information in time allotted (approx. five seconds per slide).

Figure 117—Slideshow rubric

1. Cover slide _____
2. The end slide with your picture _____
3. Each slide has title _____
4. Each slide has KidPix picture _____
5. Each slide has clip art and GIF _____
6. No spelling/grammar errors _____
7. Animations _____
8. Transitions _____
9. Slides auto-advance _____

_____If you have the student workbooks, remind students how to use their annotation tool to complete rubric (*Assessment 12*) and a screenshot tool to submit.
_____Continually throughout class, check for understanding.

Class exit ticket: **None**

Differentiation

- Done? Make parent invitations for slideshow presentations using DTP tool explored this year.

Assessment 12—Slideshow rubric

SLIDESHOW RUBRIC

Name_____ Teacher_____

Here's a list of required skills in your slideshow project. Check off those you included. Then, add those you missed. When done, turn in the rubric and I'll grade your project.

1. Cover slide _____
2. The end slide with picture _____
3. Each slide has title _____
4. Each slide has student project picture _____
5. Each slide has two additional pics _____
6. No spelling/grammar errors _____
7. Animations _____
8. Transitions _____
9. Slides auto-advance _____

10. Class presentation _____
    a. Face audience _____
    b. Talk to audience _____
    c. Introduce yourself _____
    d. Speak loud enough _____
    e. No 'umms' or stuttering _____

2nd Grade Technology Curriculum: Teacher Manual

Lesson #32 Presentations

Vocabulary	Problem solving	Skills
• Digital tools • Slideshows • Speaking and listening skills	• Parent asked a question I didn't know how to answer (that's OK) • I can't remember what I wanted to say (class screen)	**Scaffolded** Speaking/listening, slideshows
Academic Applications speaking and listening, digital citizenship	**Materials Required** Student slideshows, popcorn?	**Standards** CCSS-Literacy.SL.2.4 NETS: 6d

Essential Question

What have I learned this year?

Big Idea

I know more than I think I do

Teacher Preparation

- Test equipment so everything works for parent show.
- Know which tasks weren't completed last week.
- Integrate domain-specific tech vocabulary into lesson.
- Know if you need extra time to complete this lesson.

Assessment Strategies

- Followed directions
- [tried to] solve own problems
- Left room as s/he found it
- Higher order thinking: analysis, evaluation, synthesis
- Habits of mind observed

Steps

Time required: 45 minutes in one sitting
Class warm-up: None

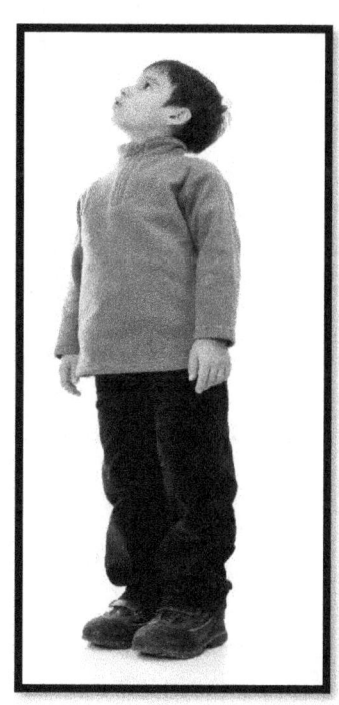

_____Students review their slideshow.

_____Pick a random order for presentation, i.e., alphabetically. If there is a reason a student needs to go early, try to accommodate that. For example, his parents can only be there at a certain time.

_____Student comes to the front of the room, waits until the audience quiets, and then begins his/her presentation.

_____Student tries to present as much as possible without looking at class screen. Each student (*Figure 118*):

- *introduces themselves to the audience*
- *describes drawings as slideshow progresses, including key details they feel important*
- *speaks loud enough everyone can hear*
- *makes eye contact with as many people as possible without rushing between individuals*
- *answer parent questions to clarify*
- *remember to smile*

Figure 118—Presentation rubric

10. Class presentation _____
    a. Face audience _____
    b. Talk to audience _____
    c. Introduce yourself _____
    d. Speak loud enough _____
    e. No 'umms' or stuttering _____

_____When presentations are completed, award certificates (full size at end of text).

Figure 119—Certificate

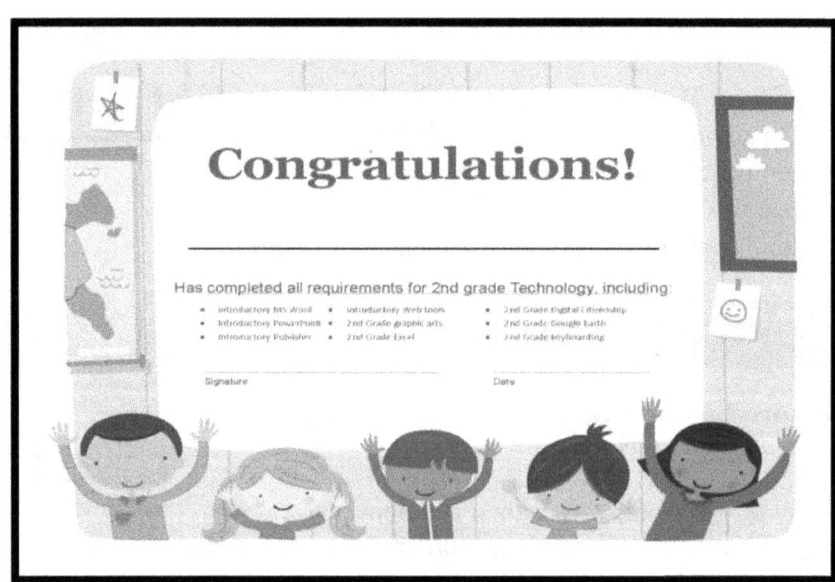

_____Tuck chairs under, headphones over tower; leave station as it was. Have a great summer!

Class exit ticket: None

Differentiation

- Let students draw anything they'd like in the class drawing program, to be printed for parents.

PS

If you teach technology, it's likely you're a geek. Even if you didn't start out that way–say, you used to be a first grade teacher and suddenly your Admin in their infinite wisdom, moved you to the tech lab—you became a geek. You morphed into the go-to person for tech problems, computer quirks, crashes and freezes.

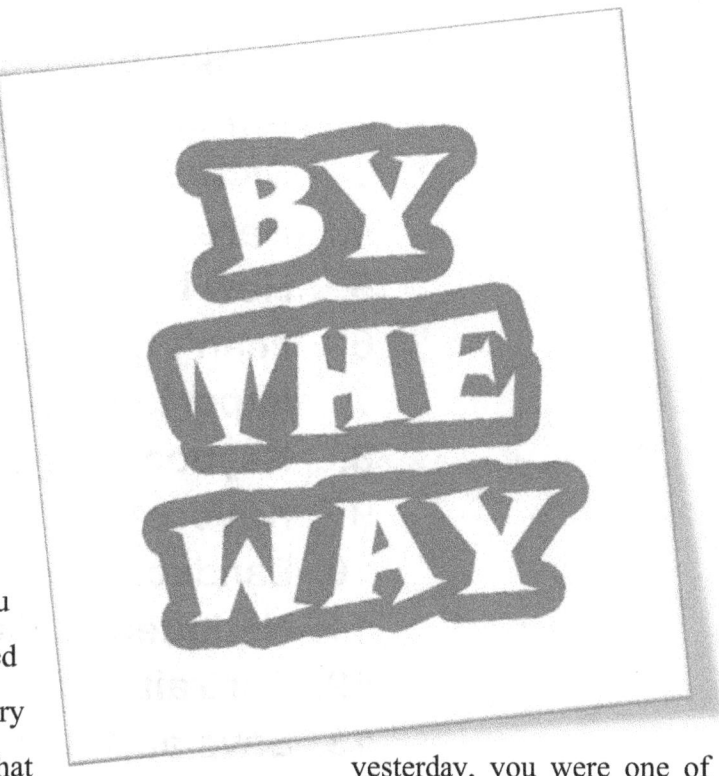

Overnight, your colleagues assumed you received an upload of data that allowed you to Know the answers to their every techie question. It didn't matter that yesterday, you were one of them. Now, you are on a pedestal, their necks craned upward as they ask you: *How do I get the class screen to work?* or *We need the microphones working for a lesson I'm starting in three minutes. Can you please-please-please fix them?*

Celebrate your cheeky geekiness. Flaunt it for students and colleagues. Play Minecraft. That's you now–you are sharp, quick-thinking. You tingle when you see an iPad. You wear a flash drive like jewelry. The first thing you do when you get to school is check your email

It's OK. Here at Structured Learning and Ask a Tech Teacher, we understand. The readers understand. You're at home. To honor you, we've created these two posters (see next pages). They provide more ways to get your geek fully on as you go through your day.

CLASSROOM POSTERS

1. Backspace-Delete
2. Digital neighborhood
3. Digital online image law (reworded)
4. Here's what we've done
5. How to solve a problem
6. I can't find my file
7. Important keys
8. Keyboarding Hints
9. Keyboarding Stages
10. Landscape
11. Netiquette rules
12. Portrait
13. Save and save-as
14. Select-Do
15. Steps for internet research
16. Undo is your friend
17. Use keyboard shortcuts
18. Want to use this image?
19. What's a Mulligan
20. Why learn to keyboard

WHAT'S THE DIFFERENCE BETWEEN SAVE AND SAVE AS?

SAVE
- Save the first time
- Resave changes to the same location

SAVE AS
- Resave under a new name
- Resave to a new location

PORTRAIT

LANDSCAPE

2nd Grade Technology Curriculum: Teacher Manual

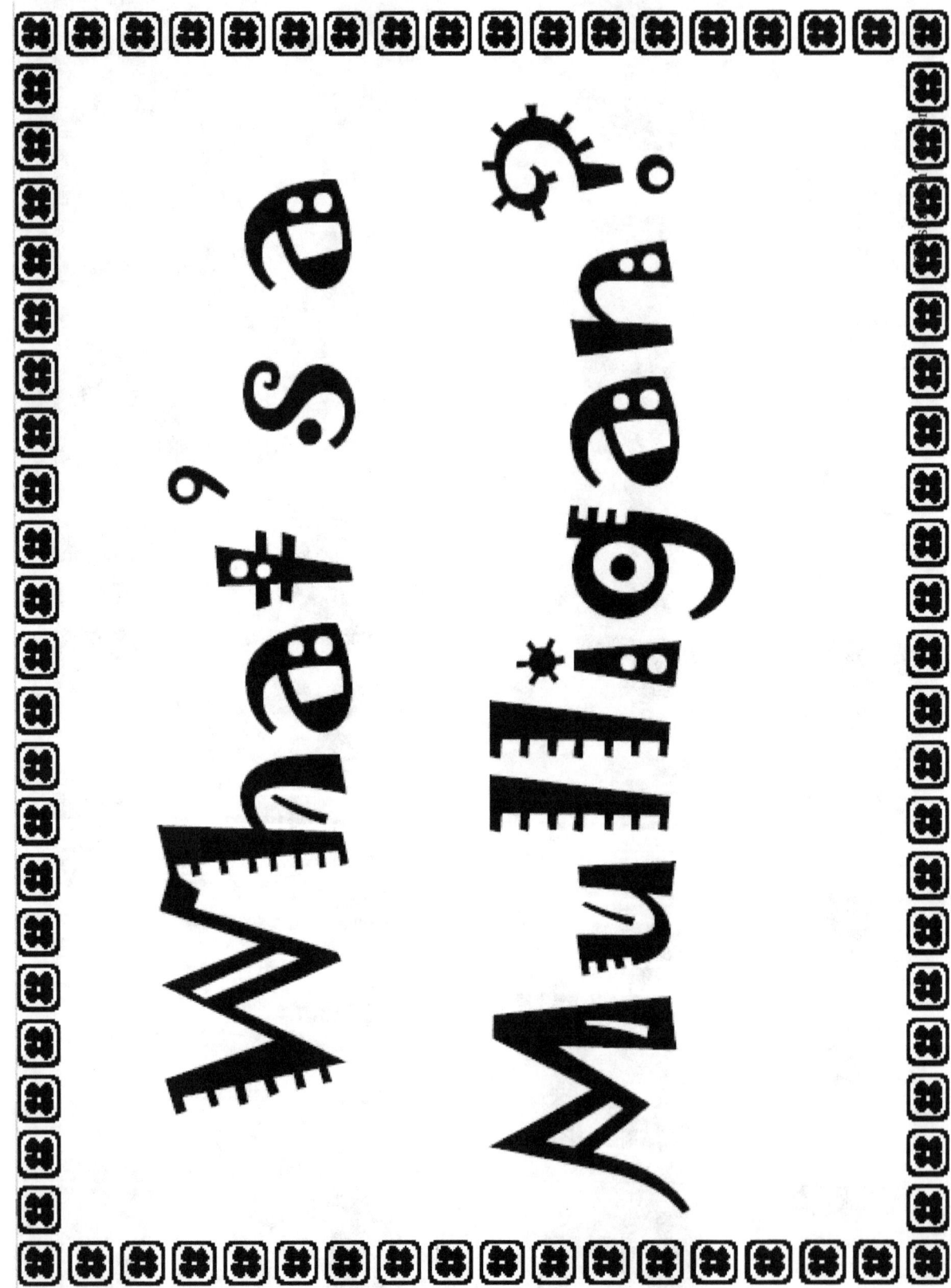

UNDO

is your Friend

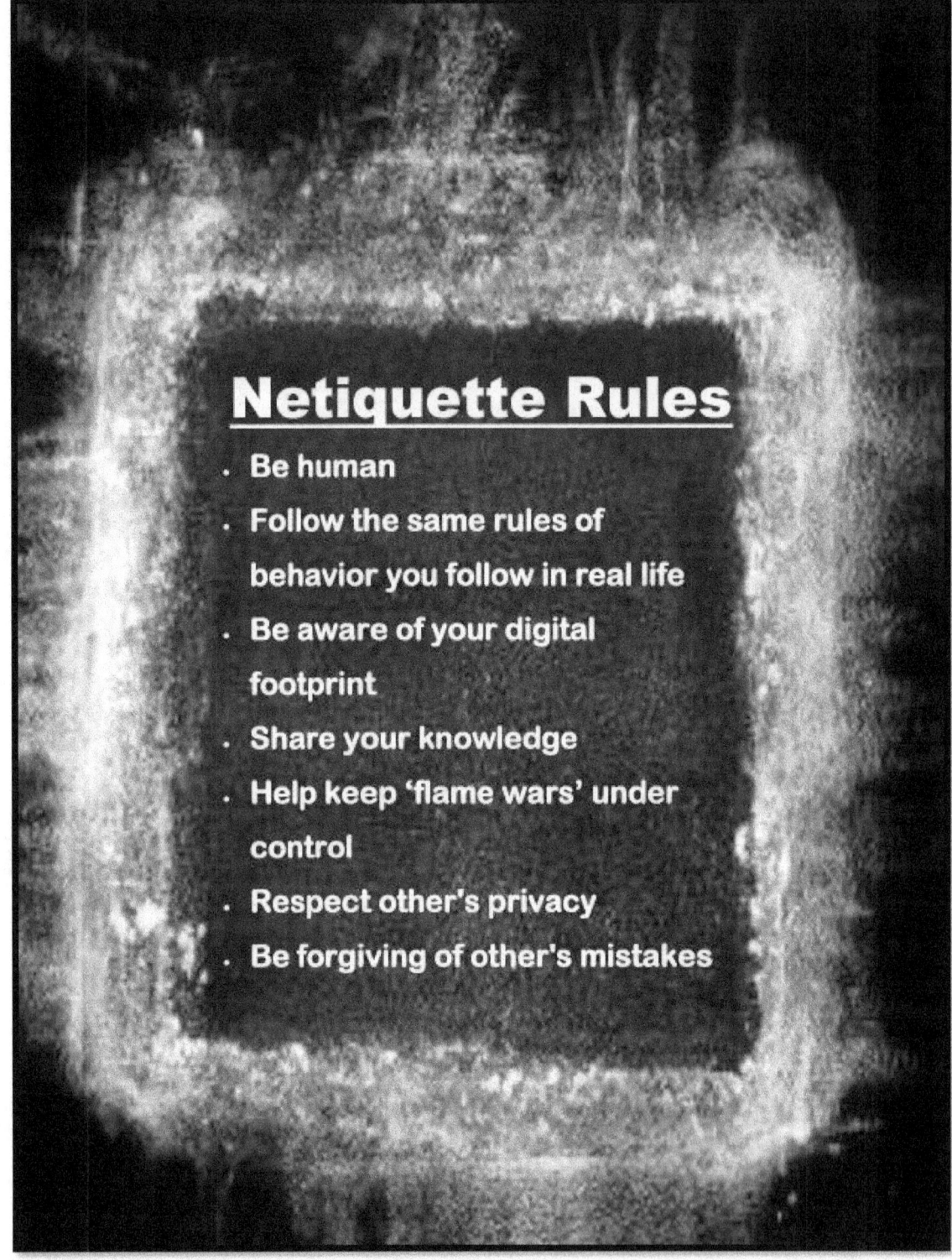

2nd Grade Technology Curriculum: Teacher Manual

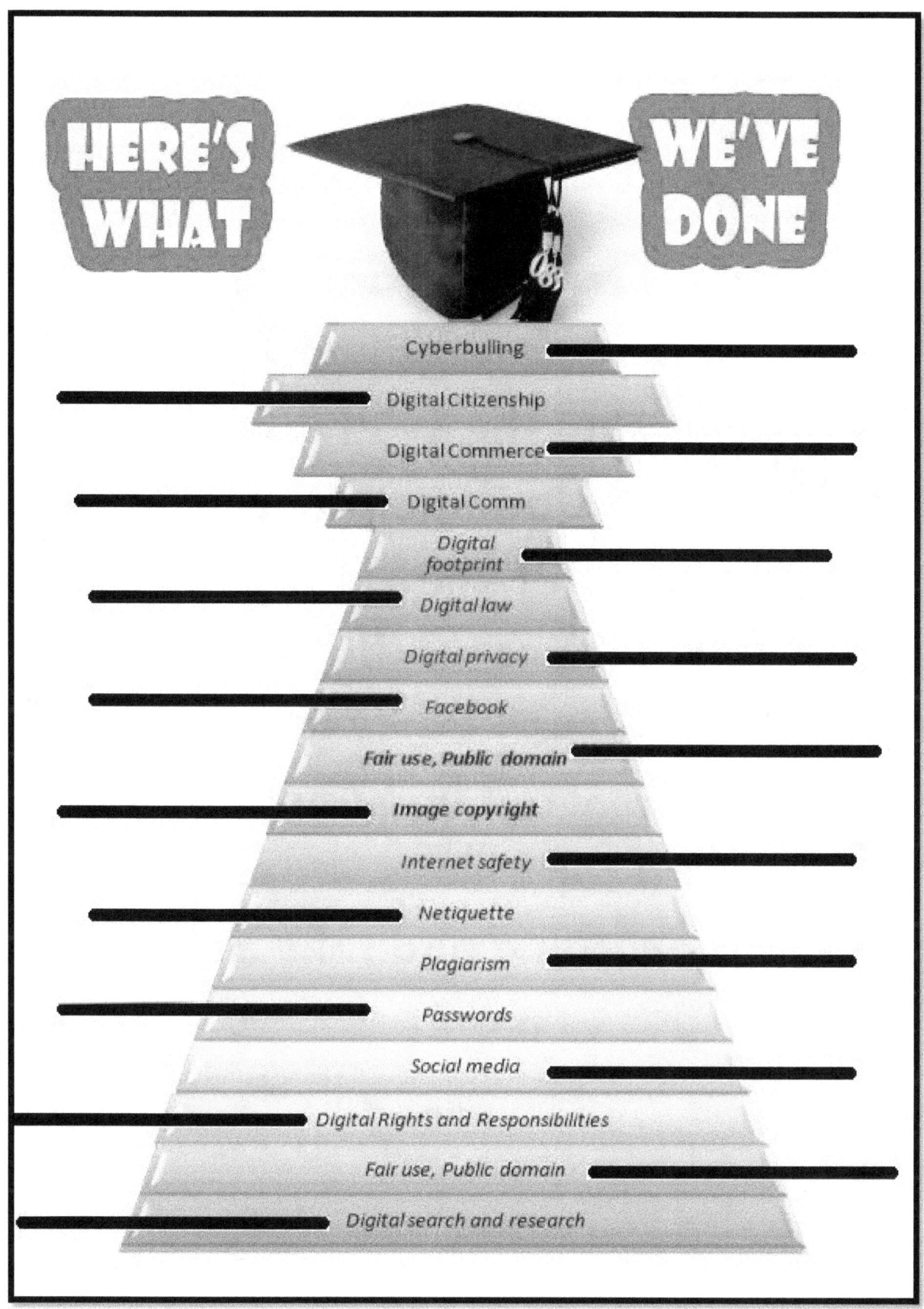

Don't talk to strangers. Look both ways before crossing the (virtual) street. Don't go places you don't know. Play fair. Pick carefully who you trust. Don't get distracted by bling. And sometimes, stop everything and take a nap.

©AskaTechTeacher

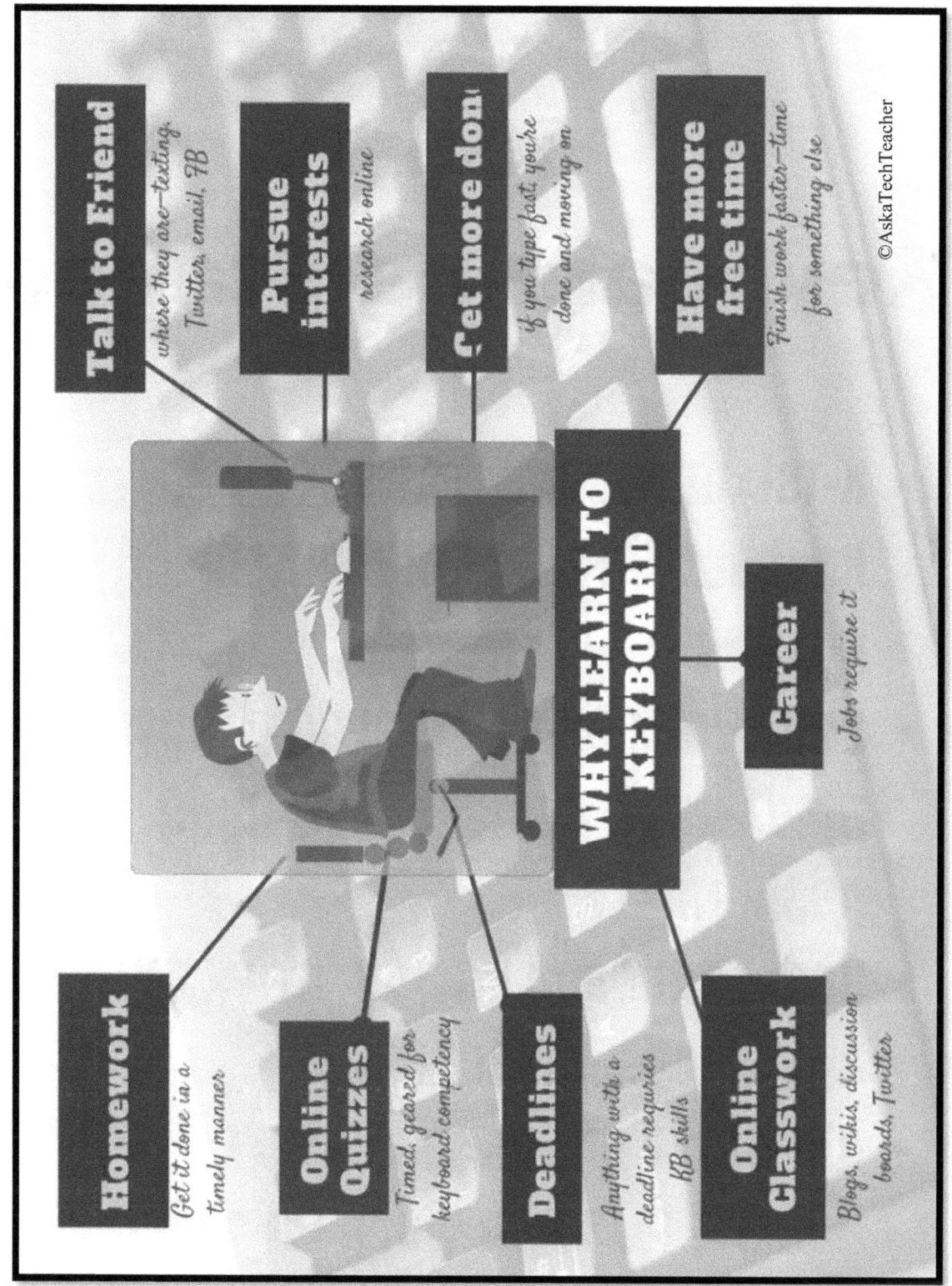

K-5 Keyboarding Stages

- **K-1st:** Introduce mouse skills, keyboarding, key placement, posture
- **2nd:** Work on keyboarding, key placement, posture, two-hand position
- **3rd:** Reinforce basics, work on accuracy and technique
- **4th-5th:** Continue accuracy, technique. Begin work on speed

©AskATechTeacher

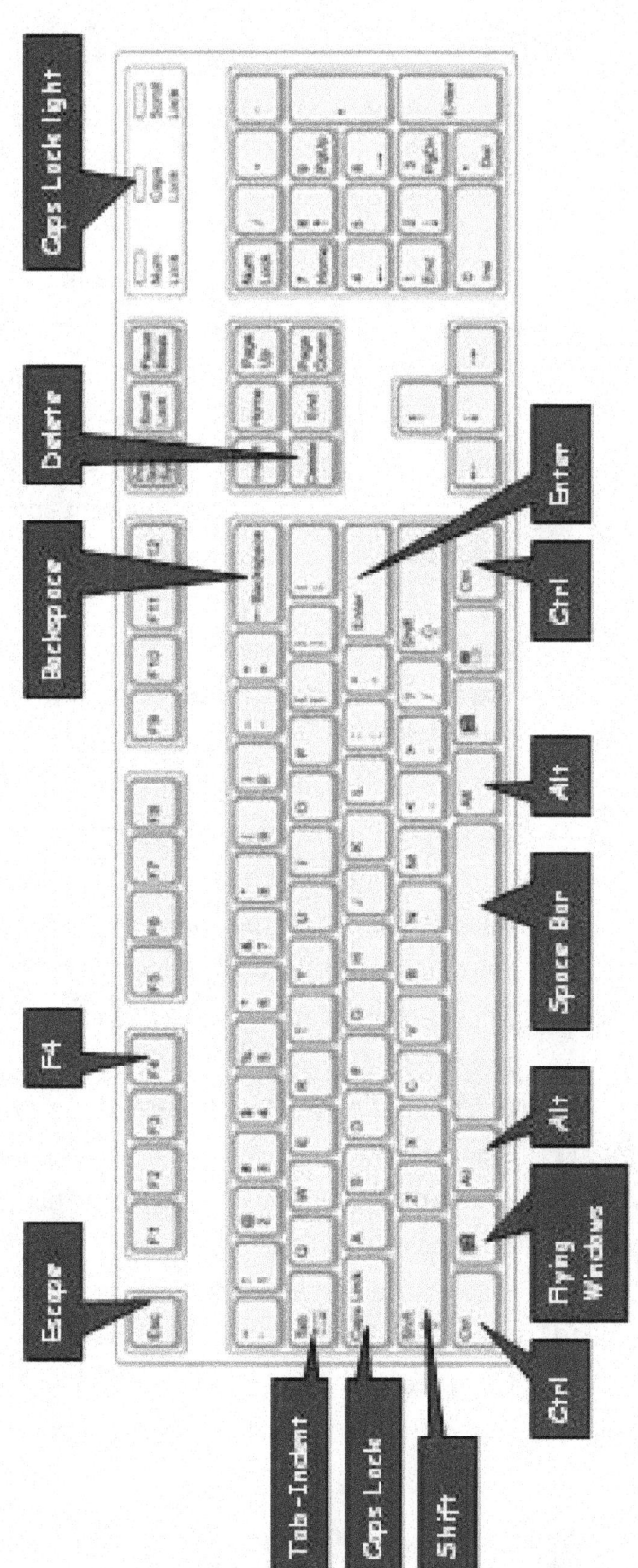

Keyboarding Hints for K-2

1. Make sure the keyboard remains in front of the student and the mouse to the right (or left for lefties). Students want to push the keyboard out of the way so they can concentrate on the mouse. Don't let them. Make it a habit to keep the keyboard centered in front of their body with the mouse comfortably on the side.
2. Have student tuck their elbows against the sides of their bodies. This keeps hands in the right spot—home row.
3. Use thumb for the space bar. That leaves hands on home row.
4. Curl fingers over home row—they're cat paws, not dog paws
5. Use inside fingers for inside keys, outside fingers for outside keys.
6. Use the finger closest to the key you need. Sounds simple, but this isn't what usually happens with beginners.
7. Keep pointers anchored to f and j.
8. Play keyboard like a piano (or violin, or guitar, or recorder). You'd never use the pointer for all keys.
9. Fingers move, not hands. Hands stay anchored to the f and j keys
10. Don't use caps lock for capitals! Use shift.
11. Students must keep hands to themselves. Don't touch others mouse, keyboard, monitor. This gives them a sense of responsibility over their own station, knowing no one can touch it but them.
12. Extra: Add a barrier between the sides of the keyboards. I fashioned one from cover stock. That reminds students to stay on the correct side of the keyboard.

2nd Grade Technology Curriculum: Teacher Manual

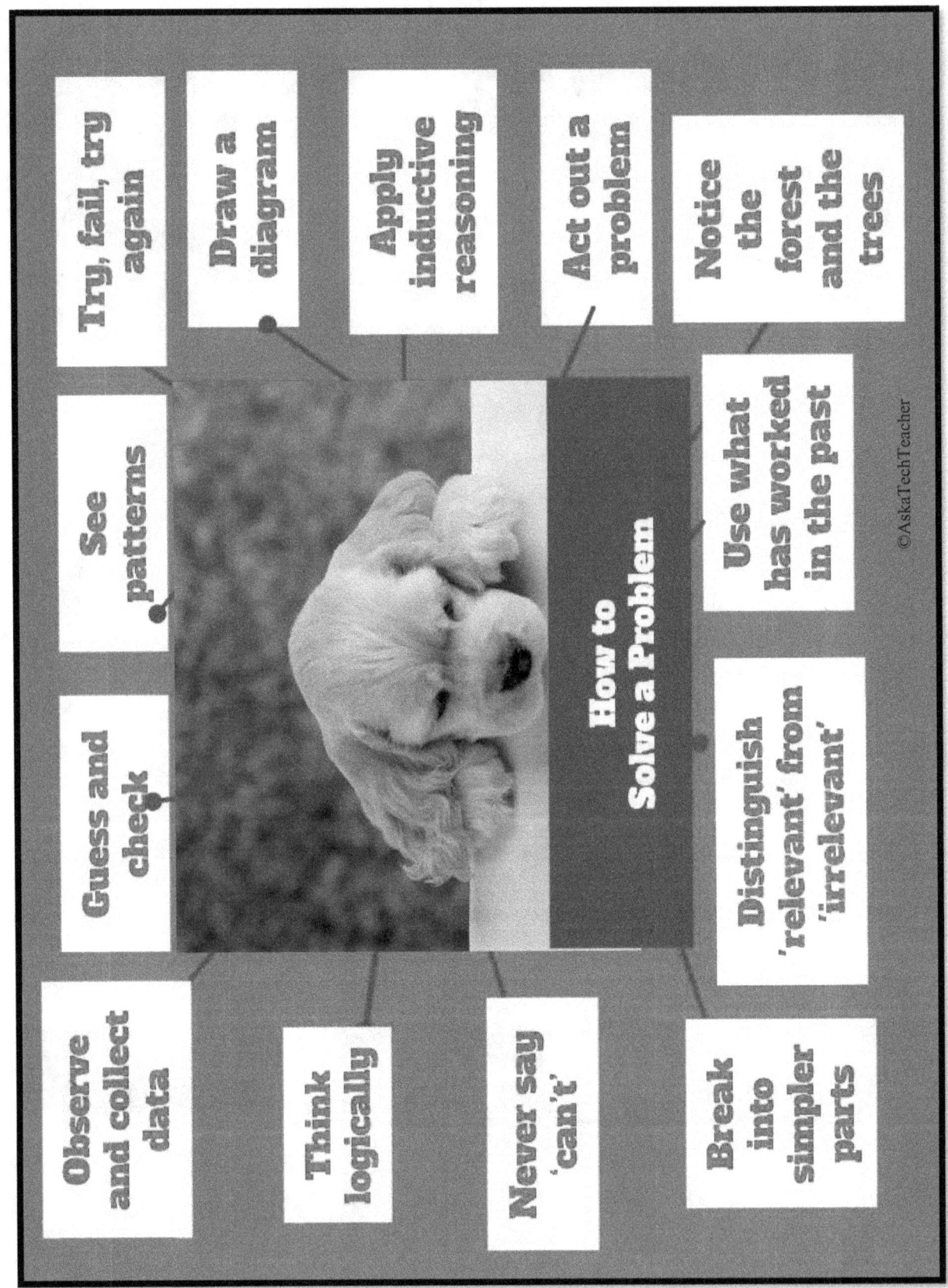

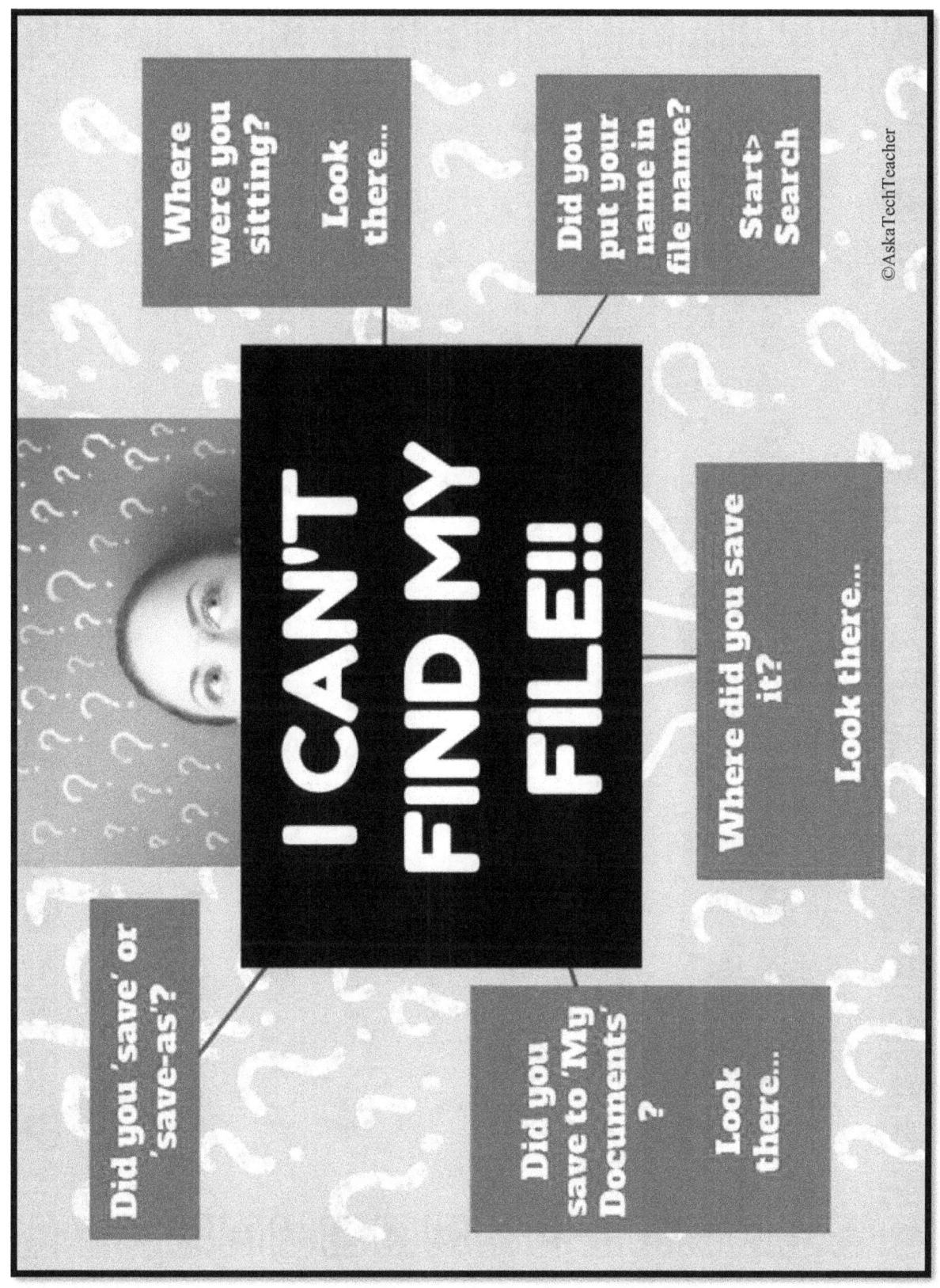

The law states that works of art created in the U.S. after January 1, 1978, are automatically protected by copyright once they are fixed in a tangible medium (like the internet) BUT a single copy may be used for scholarly research (even if that's a 2nd grade life cycle report) or in teaching or preparation to teach a class.

STEPS FOR INTERNET RESEARCH

Know Key Words — **General understanding of topic** — **Reliable site extensions** — **Read sidebars, headings, hyperlinks** — **Read pictures, insets, maps**

GET YOUR DUCKS IN A ROW

©AskaTechTeacher

Index

21st Century Lesson Plan 34
ABCYa Paint 148
Adobe Slate 182
Adobe Voice 182
Animation 91, 94, 186, 188
annotation tool ... 11, 44, 49, 70, 105, 144, 160, 162, 163, 189
ASCII Art 76
Ask a Tech Teacher 16
Assessment 7, 35, 45, 52, 53, 54, 69, 70, 105, 107, 112, 113, 119, 120, 122, 124, 138, 140, 141, 144, 145, 160, 163, 189, 190
Avatar 51, 162
Avery 132
Back button 57
big idea 5, 35
Blogs 9
Board 15
calendar 49, 50
Canva 98, 175
Certificate of Completion 5
certificates 192
Chromebook ... 14, 40, 46, 47, 48, 94, 103, 148, 149, 157, 160, 162, 164, 166, 173
Class Calendar 49
Class internet start page 15, 16, 38, 50
Class warm-up... 30, 44, 57, 67, 77, 87, 91, 101, 104, 108, 114, 117, 121, 126, 130, 136, 139, 142, 146, 152, 156, 159, 164, 166, 168, 173, 177, 179, 184, 186, 188, 191
Class website 44, 50
Class Webtools 50
Close Reading 123, 124
Cloud 49
Code 6, 9, 11, 91-93, 96, 97, 131
Collaboration 6, 34, 108
Common Core 4, 6, 7, 16, 36, 37, 92
Common Core State Standards 7
companion wikis 4
Compare-contrast.. 50, 87, 108, 109, 130, 131, 132, 179, 180
Computer etiquette 9
copyrights 57, 61
coupon code 10
cover page 174
Critical thinking 9
Ctr+S 134
curriculum map 5, 8, 9
Cyberbullying 60, 63, 172
Dance Mat Typing 67, 68, 77, 87, 101
Desktop 5, 44, 47, 48, 83, 121, 130
detail 60, 64, 152, 153, 154, 156, 157, 170
Differentiation 6, 35
Digital citizenship 5, 6, 30, 33, 35, 44, 57, 60, 63, 77, 91, 93, 101, 108, 121, 126, 142, 156, 159, 168, 173, 179

Digital Citizenship 9, 15, 17, 33, 40, 57, 60, 63, 64
Digital commerce 60, 63
Digital communications 60
digital devices. 6, 14, 31, 40, 44, 46, 51, 87, 89, 160, 162
Digital footprint 57, 60, 63
Digital law 60, 63
digital lockers 49
Digital neighborhood 35, 57, 59, 194
Digital Portfolios 49
Digital privacy 60, 61, 63
Digital rights 60
Digital rights/ responsibilities 61, 63
Digital search and research 60
Digital student 32
Digital Tools 17, 44, 48, 123, 124
Drawing program 5
Drawp 157, 160, 167
Dropbox 49
DTP 5, 9
Email 5
essential question 5, 35
exit ticket ... 5, 6, 8, 11, 15, 33, 51, 62, 71, 81, 89, 95, 103, 106, 112, 116, 119, 123, 129, 135, 137, 140, 144, 149, 155, 158, 163, 165, 167, 172, 175, 178, 183, 185, 187, 189, 192
Failure 35
Fair use 57, 60, 63, 168
find my file 194
Games 9, 76
Goodreader 123
Google 'safe search' 169
Google Apps 50
Google Calendar 50
Google Docs 50, 58, 109, 110, 115, 127, 143, 160
Google Draw 128, 137, 160, 162
Google Drive 115, 125, 143
Google Earth 5, 9, 10, 101
Google Presentations 181
Google Slides 94, 179, 182
Graphic organizer 126, 127, 128
Graphics 9, 10
Greeting Card 131, 132
Habits of Mind 6, 13, 36
Haiku Deck 98, 181, 182
handles 111
Hardware 9, 10, 30, 52, 79, 87
higher order thinking 6
homework 5
Hopscotch 93, 97
Hour of Code 92, 93
iAnnotate 11, 45, 48, 49, 70, 112, 119, 125, 140, 160, 162
Image copyright 60, 63
Image editor 5
Important keyboard keys 71

217

inquiry..... 7, 11, 14, 15, 42, 43, 57, 59, 76, 84, 88, 94, 101, 139, 159, 160, 168
Inquiry-based Teacher 42
Internet basics 58
internet neighborhood 121
Internet Pictures 17, 168
Internet privacy 10
internet research 194
Internet safety 59, 60, 63
iPad 14, 46, 53, 67, 70, 93, 95, 103, 133, 149
ISTE Standards 5
Keyboard posture 32, 69
keyboard shortcuts 69
Keyboarding.. 5, 6, 10, 15, 17, 35, 40, 67, 68, 69, 70, 71, 73, 75, 77, 87, 91, 104, 108, 114, 117, 121, 126, 130, 136, 139, 142, 146, 152, 156, 159, 164, 166, 168, 177, 179, 209
keyboarding hints 69
KidPix 89, 131, 148, 157, 160, 164, 173
Kid-safe Images 176
Kodable 93, 97
laptop 14
Lesson 14
Letter writing 114, 117, 120, 143, 145
library 135
links 59
literacy 4
LiveBinders 16
Logins 44, 46
Macs 14, 40, 69, 80, 94, 103, 149
Mashup 101, 102, 156, 162
mindmapping 11
Minecraft 91, 93
Mouse Skills 9
MS Word 58, 73, 109, 127, 128, 132, 160
Mulligan 194
National Educational Technology Standards 4
Netiquette 59-63, 168, 194
Notable 11, 45, 48
Notes 115, 143
Number Square 104, 105, 106, 107, 108, 118
Office 365 .... 50, 115, 143
Online Images 169, 170, 171
Online presence 60
online tools 34, 75, 129, 130
Open House 140, 146, 155, 156, 164, 166, 179
Open Office 109, 115, 132, 133, 143
Padlet 38, 39, 50
Pages 143
Paint 131, 132, 139, 148, 157, 160, 164, 167, 173
Passwords 60, 63
PCs 14, 40, 69, 80
Pic Collage 175
PicMonkey 162, 175
Pixie 131, 148
Plagiarism 57, 60, 61, 63
Popcorn Typer 67, 68, 77, 87, 101, 104, 108, 114, 117, 121, 126, 130
posters 5, 12, 31, 194
PowerPoint 64, 94, 179, 181, 182, 184, 186, 188

Presentation tools 5
Problem solving. 7, 10, 30, 35, 44, 57, 67, 77, 87, 91, 101, 104, 108, 114, 117, 121, 126, 130, 136, 139, 142, 146, 152, 156, 159, 164, 166, 168, 173, 177, 179, 184, 186, 188, 191
Problem-solving Challenge 81
Programming 9, 91-93
Protopage 16, 39
Public domain 57, 60, 61, 63, 170
Publisher 50, 132
QR codes 130, 135
Reading 17, 121, 124, 125
reflect 135
Research 10
risk takers 12
rules 31, 61
Safe Search 170, 176
Scan 135
Scope and Sequence 5
Scratch 35, 93
screenshot ... 70, 91, 94, 95, 103, 106, 112, 119, 144, 149, 189
Select-Do 31, 194
Sequencing 94
sharing 6
shortkeys 67, 69, 72, 76, 80, 81, 87, 88, 98
Sixth Edition 6
Skills. 7, 30, 44, 57, 67, 77, 87, 91, 101, 104, 108, 114, 117, 121, 126, 130, 136, 139, 142, 146, 152, 156, 159, 164, 166, 168, 173, 177, 179, 184, 186, 188, 191
slideshow ... 34, 69, 94, 140, 146, 148, 155, 164, 166, 167, 179, 180, 181, 182, 183, 184, 186, 188, 189, 190, 191
smartphone 12, 54
Snap! Learning 125
Social media 60, 63
software 6, 14, 34, 40, 44, 73, 112, 129, 130, 131, 136, 157, 163, 186, 188
Speaking and Listening 10
Spreadsheets 10, 34, 104
Standards for Mathematical Practice 92
Stranger Danger 60, 63
Student digital portfolios 49
student workbooks.. 6, 10, 13, 44, 45, 48, 57, 67, 77, 87, 101, 104, 108, 112, 114, 117, 119, 121, 130, 136, 137, 139, 140, 142, 144, 146, 152, 156, 159, 160, 162, 163, 164, 166, 168, 173, 177, 179, 189
Subtext 121, 123
Surface tablet 95, 103, 149
Symbaloo 16, 38, 39
symbols 65, 87, 88, 89, 90, 96, 97, 98, 101
tabbed browsing 58
Tagxedo 50
Teacher manual 15
tech lab 14, 35, 40, 56, 193
Technology Curriculum 4, 5
Template 126, 130, 136, 138, 139, 159, 160
Tomorrow's student 7
Tools and Toolbars 17, 87, 89

TuxPaint 89, 131, 148, 157, 164, 173
Twitter 60, 63, 65, 66, 150
Tynker 93, 97
Typing 67, 146
USB 45, 52
Visual learning 10
Vocabulary 7, 9, 10, 30, 35, 41, 44, 51, 57, 67, 77, 87, 91, 101, 104, 108, 114, 117, 121, 126, 130, 136, 139, 142, 146, 152, 156, 159, 164, 166, 168, 173, 177, 179, 184, 186, 188, 191
Voki 187
warm-up 6, 11, 15
Weebly 50
who, what, when, where, why, how 134
Windows 6, 47, 48, 52, 72, 82, 94, 95, 103, 149, 166, 181
Wix 50
Word 5
word processing 34, 69, 76, 102, 104, 105, 108, 109, 110, 111, 114, 115, 117, 118, 126, 127, 128, 132, 137, 142, 143, 144, 146, 152, 154, 156, 160, 173, 174, 175, 177, 180
Wordle 50
Wordpress 50
Zoho 181

Which book	Price (print/digital/Combo)
K-8th Tech Textbook (each)	$25.99 p&h (print delivery by Amazon)
K-8 Combo (all 9 textbooks)	$248-450 + p&h
K-8 Student workbooks (per grade—tech/kb)	$199/550/1500 (room/school/district)
35 K-6 Inquiry-based Projects	$31.99/25.99/52.18 + p&h
55 Tech Projects—Vol I,II, Combo	$18.99 /$35.38–digital
K-8 Keyboard Curriculum—3 options	$20 and up + p&h
K-8 Digital Citizenship Curriculum	$29.95/25.99/50.38 + p&h
CCSS—Math, Language, Reading, Writing	$26.99 ea/80 for 4–digital only
K-5 Common Core Projects	$29.95/23.99/48.55 + p&h
Themed webinars	$8-30
Weekly tech webinars	Free or $99 per year for 180+ per year
Summer PD classes (online—for groups)	$795
Summer tech camp for kids	$179 + p&h
College credit classes (online)	$497 and up
Digital Citizenship certificate class	Starts at $29.99
Classroom tech poster bundles	Start at $9.99
PBL lessons--singles	$1.99 and up
Bundles of lesson plans	$4.99 and up (digital only)
Tech Ed Scope and Sequence (K-6 and 6-8)	$9.99 and up (digital only)
New Teacher Survival Kit	$285-620+ p&h
Homeschool Tech Survival Kit	$99 + p&h
Mentoring (30 min. at a time)	$50/session
169 Tech Tips From Classroom	$9.99 (digital only)
Consulting/seminars/webinars	Call or email for prices

**Free sample? Visit Structured Learning LLC.
Prices subject to change
Email Zeke.rowe@structuredlearning.net**

Pay via PayPal, Credit Card, Amazon, TPT, pre-approved school district PO

Structured Learning
Premiere Provider of Technology Teaching Books to the Education Community

www.ingramcontent.com/pod-product-compliance
Lightning Source LLC
Chambersburg PA
CBHW080224170426
43192CB00015B/2743